Getting the Most Out of
RootsMagic

Fifth Edition

W9-ART-418

Bruce Buzbee

RootsMagic, Inc.
PO Box 495
Springville, Utah 84663
USA

About the Author

Bruce Buzbee is the founder and president of RootsMagic, Inc., and the author of the RootsMagic genealogy software. He has been writing genealogy software for over 20 years, having previously written the popular Family Origins software. Bruce is happily married with 5 children and 3 grandchildren.

Conventions

☺ **Tip**	Advice on easier ways to accomplish a task.
☀ **Warning**	Warns you about things you might not want to do.
✎ **Note**	Additional information about the current topic.
"File > New"	For example, **"File > New"** means to select **"File"** from the main menu, then select **"New"** from the **"File"** menu.
Ctrl+Tab	A key sequence where the first key (in this case **Ctrl**) is held down while the next key (in this case **Tab**) is pressed and released.

Table of Contents

Introduction

What is RootsMagic?

RootsMagic is a genealogy database program, meaning that its main function is to provide a place to enter information about your family. But while RootsMagic is an easy program to learn to use, it is also one of the most powerful genealogy programs on the market.

Unfortunately, many people will barely touch the tip of the iceberg of RootsMagic's features. Hopefully this book will help you get the most out of your copy of RootsMagic.

How This Book is Organized

This book is not intended to be a software manual. I have tried to make it as informative as possible, while lacing it with insights about how to get the most out of the program.

In the first chapter we will create a sample database with a few individuals to get you up and running using RootsMagic. Subsequent chapters go into detail on various aspects of RootsMagic and your family history. A Quick Summary at the end of the book provides a brief summary of the RootsMagic menu commands, toolbar buttons, and other information.

And finally, while this book will cover RootsMagic from the ground up, it assumes that you have a working knowledge of Windows, such as how to start a program, how menus work, what a dialog box is, etc.

Getting Started

The beginning is the most important part of the work. - Plato

RootsMagic is a very easy program to learn, so we can just jump in and start entering your family. We will be skipping over some details, but don't worry, we will cover them all in later chapters.

Creating a Database

Each time you run RootsMagic you will see the "RootsMagic News".

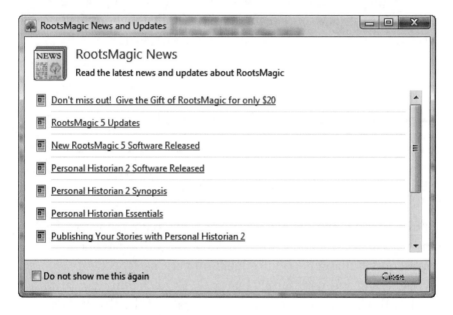

You can read the latest news and updates about RootsMagic, and if there is an update available you will be able to update directly from this screen. When you are ready to continue, just click the "Close" button.

A Welcome screen will appear with several options. You can create, open, import or search for files directly from the Welcome screen. If you have previously opened files in RootsMagic, those file names will also be selectable.

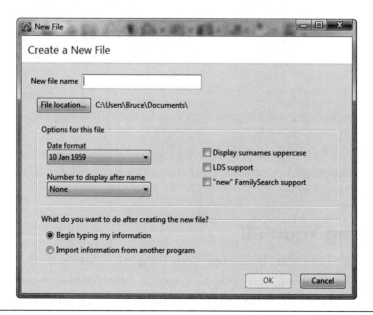

The first thing we will do is create a new database. There are several ways to do this; select **"Create a new file"** from the Welcome screen, or select **"File > New"** from the main menu, or click the "New" button on the toolbar (it looks like the button at the start of this paragraph). RootsMagic will display the following dialog box.

Enter a file name for the database you want to create. It can be something simple like your last name, or longer like "The Smith Family Tree". If you want to create the new database somewhere other than the default folder, you can click the "File location" button and select a different folder.

You can also select several default options for your new database (which we'll cover a little later). Don't worry if you aren't sure which settings you want to use. You can always change them later. After you have made your choices, simply click the OK button, and you have just created a new database to hold your information.

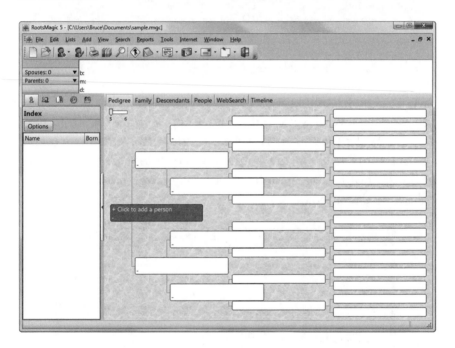

The main RootsMagic screen looks like a five generation family tree. As you add people to your database, RootsMagic adds their names to the tree.

Adding Yourself

 Let's start by adding your own information to the database that you just created. Select **"Add > Individual"** from the main menu, or click the "Add" button on the toolbar (it looks like the button at the beginning of this paragraph) and then select "Individual". Or you can just do it the easy way and click the starting position on the screen where it says "+Click to add a person". This will bring up a screen where you can add your basic information.

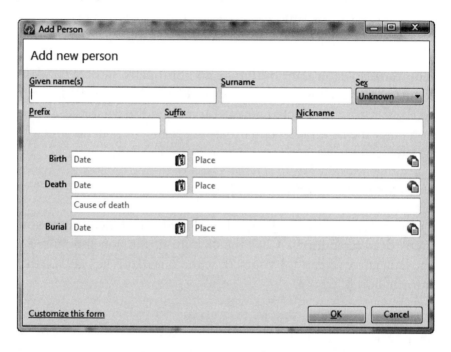

Simply fill in the blanks, using the Tab or Enter key to move on to the next field. If you don't know some of the information, just leave the field empty. If you make a mistake, you can move back to the previous field by pressing Shift+Tab or by clicking the mouse on the field you want to move to.

Enter your given names (first, middle, etc) in the Given name(s) field. Separate each name with a space, like: John Michael.

The Surname field is where you will enter your last name. If you are female, you should enter your maiden (birth) name here.

Enter your sex in the Sex field by typing **M** or **F** as appropriate. RootsMagic also supports Unknown as an option, but hopefully you won't need to make that selection here.

You can also enter any prefix that should come before your name (like "Dr."), any suffix that would come after your name (like "Jr."), and any nickname you are known by (we won't even go there).

You can also enter your birth date and birthplace. Enter the date in just about any format you want, and RootsMagic will convert it to the format you selected when you created the database. When you enter the birthplace, enter it from specific to general with a comma to separate each part of the place, like this:

Albuquerque, Bernalillo, New Mexico, United States

Feel free to leave the death and burial fields blank here, since you aren't dead (or buried). Click the **OK** button, and you should see the data entry screen for yourself, with your name, sex and birth information filled out.

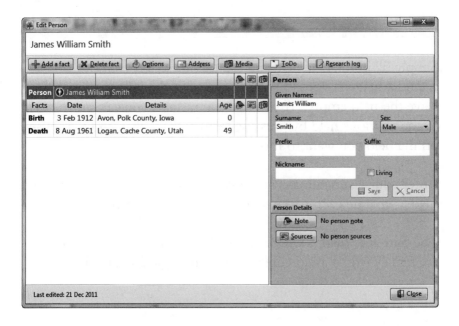

From this screen you can edit the information you just entered, or add other facts (like graduation, occupation, etc), notes, sources (documentation), to do items, multimedia items, and your current address. Add as much information as you want, and if you forget anything you can always come back later to add or change the information. For now, just click Close to finish adding yourself.

Adding Other People

One of the nice things about RootsMagic is that when you add a person to your database, it links the people together at the same time. Notice that when you press the arrow keys on the keyboard, or click on a person's name on the main pedigree view, the highlight bar moves to that person.

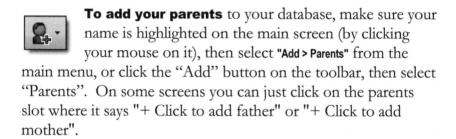 **To add your parents** to your database, make sure your name is highlighted on the main screen (by clicking your mouse on it), then select **"Add > Parents"** from the main menu, or click the "Add" button on the toolbar, then select "Parents". On some screens you can just click on the parents slot where it says "+ Click to add father" or "+ Click to add mother".

The following dialog box will appear to let you select how you want to add the father.

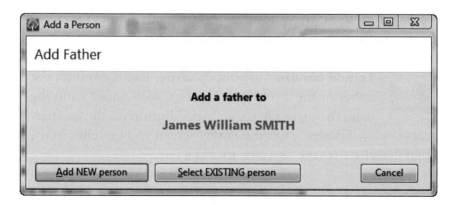

Since your father's information is not already in the database click on the **"Add new person"** button and add your father the same way you added yourself. After you have added your father, you will go through the exact same steps to add your mother.

Once you have entered your parents, RootsMagic will ask if you want to add a marriage event for them. If your parents were married, select **"Yes"** (even if you don't know the date, place, or anything else about the marriage). RootsMagic will never assume a couple is married unless you add a marriage event. If you don't add the marriage event here, you can always add it later.

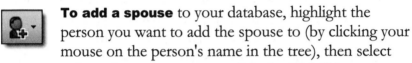 **To add a spouse** to your database, highlight the person you want to add the spouse to (by clicking your mouse on the person's name in the tree), then select **"Add > Spouse"** from the main menu, or click the "Add" button on the toolbar and select "Spouse". On some screens you can also click on the slot where it says "+ Click to add spouse".

Adding a spouse is exactly the same as adding your parents. You will get to choose between adding a new person or linking to an existing person. You will also be asked if you want to add a marriage event for this couple.

If you want to add additional spouses to a person, just repeat these steps for each spouse.

To enter an unmarried couple, you will still use the **"Add > Spouse"** command but just won't add a marriage event.

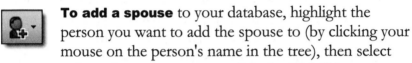 **To add children** to your database, highlight either the father or the mother, then select **"Add > Children"** from the main menu, or click the "Add" button on the toolbar and select "Children". On the family screen you can click in the child list where it says "+ Click to add a child".

Once again, you will get the option to add a new person, or link to an existing person. This time the dialog will look a little bit different.

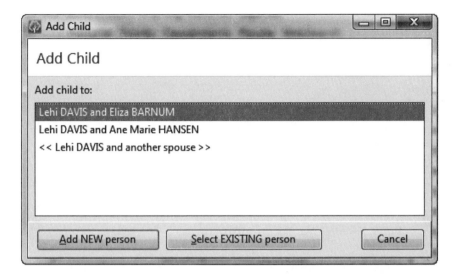

Since the person may have more than one spouse, the add child dialog will also ask which family to add the child to, and will also provide an option to add the child to the person and a new spouse. Highlight the family you want to add the child to then choose whether to add a new child or select an existing child.

When you finish adding a child, RootsMagic will display the family members and ask if you want to add another child to the same family. If you select **"Yes"**, you can simply repeat these steps to add more children.

When you have finished adding children, RootsMagic will bring up a list of the children in the family, and will ask you to arrange them in the proper birth order. Just use your mouse to drag and drop the children into the proper order, then click the **OK** button.

This child order is used when RootsMagic prints family group sheets, books, and other printouts where the children in a family are included.

That's all there is to it. Just highlight a person on the main screen and add a spouse, parents, or child to the person.

And now, on with the show...

The Main Screen

The views are wonderful from here.

One of the first things you may notice about RootsMagic is that it offers six different views: the **Pedigree View**, the **Family View**, the **Descendants View**, the **People View**, the **WebSearch View** and the **Timeline View**. To select one of the views, simply click on the tabs at the top of the views, or press the Tab key to switch between the views.

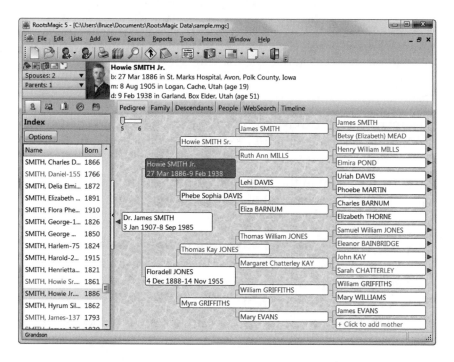

Above the tabs is an information area where RootsMagic displays information about the currently highlighted person. When you highlight a new person in any view, RootsMagic will update this area with the person's picture, name, birth, marriage, and death information.

A four line status area lies to the left of the information area.

The top row of the status area will display small icons if the highlighted person has notes, sources, multimedia items, addresses, or to-do items. If you click on the camera, envelope or todo note, RootsMagic will allow you to edit that item for the person. If you click on the note or source icon, a list of all notes (or sources) for the person will appear and you can select one to edit.

The second row of the status area shows how many spouses the current person has. You can click on this area to bring up a list of the spouses and children with each spouse. You can select any person from this list to make them the current person in the view. You can also add a new spouse or child, or even rearrange the existing spouses or children.

The third row of the status area shows how many sets of parents the current person has. You can click on this area to bring up a list of the parents and siblings of the person. You can select any person from this list to make them the current person in the view. You can also add a new set of parents, or rearrange the siblings in the family.

If you have LDS options turned on, the fourth row of the status area will show which ordinances have been completed for the highlighted person (B = baptized, E = endowed, P = sealed to parents, S = sealed to spouse). You can click on this area to edit the LDS ordinances for the person.

The Pedigree View

The "Pedigree View" displays a five generation ancestor tree of your family.

As you add individuals to your database, RootsMagic fills out the tree for you. You can move from person to person using the arrow keys on your keyboard, or by clicking on a person's name with the mouse.

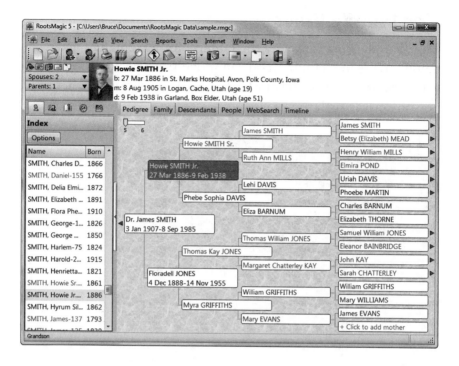

Once you have entered more generations than will fit on screen, RootsMagic will add small arrow buttons next to names to show that there are more individuals you can move to. Just click your mouse on one of these arrows and RootsMagic will scroll the next generation onto the screen. You can also just press an arrow key in the appropriate direction to scroll to another generation.

In the upper left corner of the pedigree view you will see a "slider control". You can click this area to switch between displaying 5 and 6 generations on the screen at once.

You can edit any person in the Pedigree View by double clicking your mouse on the person's name, or you can simply highlight a person and press the Enter key.

The Family View

The "Family View" displays the father, mother, children and grandparents in a family. You can move from person to person using the arrow keys on your keyboard, or by clicking on a person's name with the mouse.

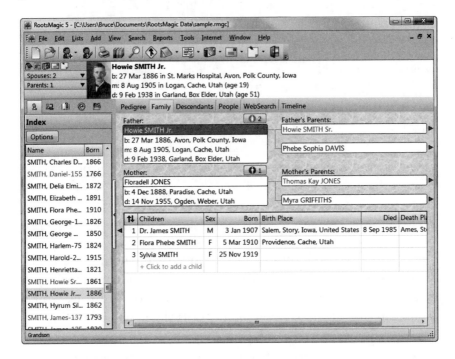

If grandparents are entered, a small arrow will appear to the right of the grandparent's name. Clicking your mouse on one of these arrows will move the grandparents into the parent position in the view.

RootsMagic will also add an arrow to the left of any child in the Family View who is married (or has a partner). Clicking your mouse on one of these arrows will change the view to the family where the child is an adult.

A button will appear above the name of each parent showing how many spouses (or partners) the person has. You can click this button to display a list of the person's spouses, and you can change to a different spouse from the list.

Like the Pedigree View, you can edit any person by double clicking your mouse on the person's name, or you can simply highlight a person and press the Enter key.

If you want to rearrange the children in the family, just click the up/down arrows in the upper left corner of the child list.

The Descendants View

The "Descendants View" displays a five generation indented descendant list of your family. The children of each person in the list are displayed under the parents, and are indented a small amount.

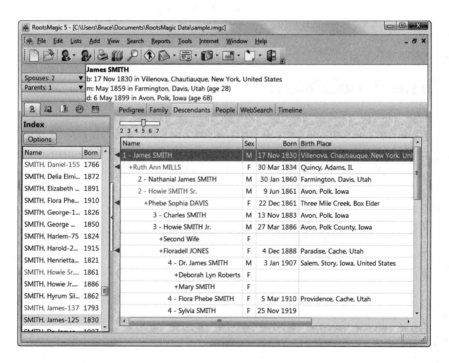

If the first person in the Descendants View has parents entered, an arrow will appear to the left of their name. You can click on this arrow (or press the left arrow key when the person is highlighted) to move one generation back in time.

In addition, RootsMagic will put an arrow to the left of any spouse who has parents entered as well, so that you can navigate to that part of the family. And before you ask why some people in the list **don't** have left arrows next to their names, it is because their parents are already displayed in the list (and pressing the left arrow key while they are highlighted will move to their parents).

If any person in the fifth generation has children, an arrow will be displayed to the right of their information. Clicking that arrow (or pressing the right arrow on the keyboard while they are highlighted) will scroll forward one generation in time to display that person's children.

In the upper left corner of the descendants view you will see "slider control". You can click this area and choose to display 2 through 7 generations on the screen at once.

The People View

The "People View" is a list of people in your database. By default it is an alphabetical list of the entire file with columns for sex, record number, birth date and place, and death date and place. But you can customize which columns to include, which people to include, and what order to sort those people.

> ☺ **Tip**
>
> You can choose whether to show just the primary name for each person, or you can mark the "Show alternate names" checkbox to display people under any alternate names that have been entered for them. If a row is an alternate name RootsMagic will display a little blue plus sign.

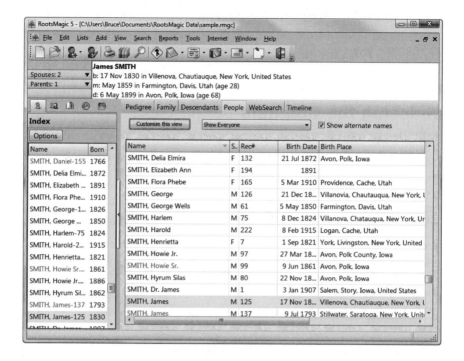

Sorting the Columns

Even though the list is sorted by name, you can click the header on any column to sort by that column. So, for example, if you wanted to sort your file by birth date, just click the words "Birth Date" at the top of that column. If you click it a second time it will sort by that column in the other direction. You can do this for any column in the list.

You will usually have columns that go beyond the screen on the right. If you want to see those columns, use the scroll bar at the bottom of the list. RootsMagic will scroll the columns onto the screen, but will keep the name column on the screen so you don't lose track of which person the data belongs to.

Choosing the People

The People View will normally display everyone in your database, but you can filter the list to only include the people you want.

Click the drop list that says "Show Everyone" above the list of people, and you can create or select a "named group" of people to display. For complete details on how to create, edit and use these named groups, see Named Groups on page 256.

Choosing the Columns

But let's say you want different columns for each person. You can click the "Customize this view" button to choose which columns you really want to display.

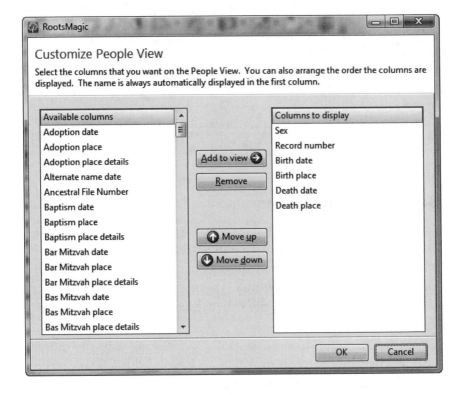

To add a column to the People view, select from the "Available columns" and click "Add to view".

To remove a column from the People view, select the column in "Columns to display" and click "Remove".

To rearrange columns in the People view, select a column in "Columns to display" and click "Move up" or "Move down".

The WebSearch View

The WebSearch view is a bit different from the other views. Instead of being a way to navigate through the people in your database, it helps you find more information about your family on the internet. It works a lot like your regular web browser, except that it is able to automatically search various websites for your family members. Keep in mind that some of these search engines require subscriptions.

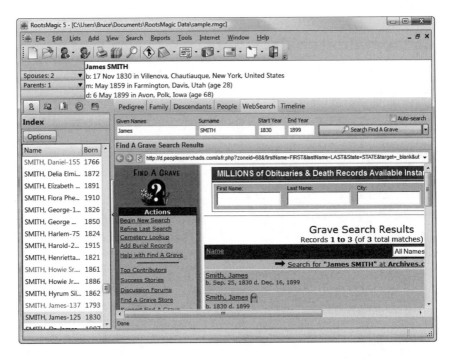

The first thing you need to do is choose the website you want RootsMagic to search. Click the button that says "Pick a Search Provider" and select one from the list. Once you have chosen a search engine, you can select a person from the list on the left side of the screen and then click the search button to actually do the search. The search button is the same one you originally used to select the search engine. It has a little drop arrow on the right side that you can use to switch search engines at any time.

But if you're lazy like me, you may want to just check the "Auto-search" checkbox so that RootsMagic won't make you click that button every time you select a new person.

Standard Search Providers

When you were selecting a search engine, you may have noticed an option to "Manage Search Providers". There are 2 tabs, the first of which is just a list of checkboxes to tell RootsMagic which of the built-in search engines you want to show in the menu.

Custom Search Providers

The second tab ("Custom Search Providers") lets you add other search engines to the WebSearch list.

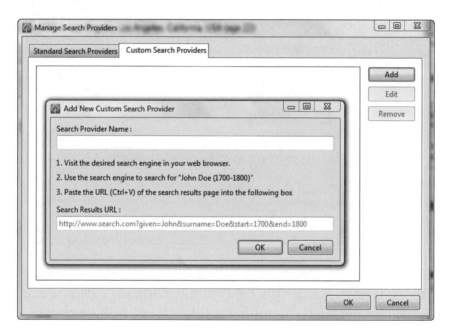

Click the "Add" button to add a new search engine to the list. Just follow the instructions on screen to add a new search engine to the list. The "Search Provider Name" field is what you want RootsMagic to display in the list of search engines. The "Search Results URL" is where you tell RootsMagic how it should search for a person.

The Timeline View

The "Timeline View" offers an overview of a person's life by displaying a list of the events in the person's life, as well as the birth, marriage, and death events for their immediate family members. You can double click on any fact in the Timeline view to edit that fact.

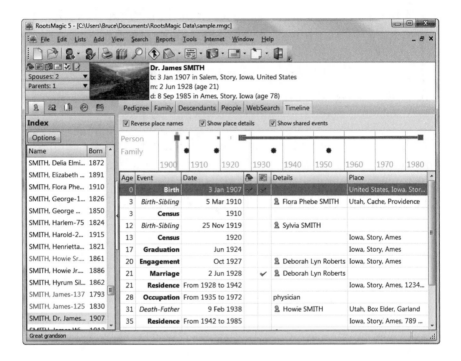

RootsMagic displays a graphical timeline of the person's events (in red) and their family members events (in blue). The graphical timeline is simply a display and is not a "clickable" view.

Event names in the person's life are displayed in a bold font, while events in family members lives are displayed in italics. The Timeline view also displays the date, place, and person's age for each event. You can choose whether to include the place details, and reversing the place will give a better view of how a person may have moved during their life.

Some events in the list involve other people (whether a family event, or a birth, marriage, or death of a family member). Those events will display that other person's name, and will include an icon that looks like a person's head. You can click on that icon to switch the Timeline view to that other person.

☺ **Tip**

When you click one of these icons you may find yourself wanting to return back to the original person. You can press Ctrl+Left to move back to the previous person. You can also customize the toolbar to add a Back button which will do the same thing.

The Timeline view will also display a checkmark for any events that have a note or source. If you hover your mouse pointer over a checkbox it will display the note or list of sources for that fact. Clicking on the checkmark will let you edit that note or source.

The Side Bar

The side bar is the panel on the left side of the screen that contains a list of the people in your database. But it is much more than just that. It is actually five different panels, index, family, bookmarks, history, and groups, each selectable by clicking on its tab.

The Index Panel

 The index panel is simply a list of every person in your database. When you select a person in the index list, RootsMagic will change to that person in whatever main view (pedigree, family, etc) you currently have selected.

Clicking the "Options" button will let you display alternate names in the index, show the birth year for each person, or display the person's record number next to their name.

You can quickly search through the index by clicking on a name in the list and begin typing the name (last name, then comma, then first names).

Index

Options

Name	Born
ALDERDICE, Mary	
ALLEN, Marcia Ann	1872
ANDERSEN, Hannah ...	1877
ANDERSON, Andrew ...	1852
BAINBRIDGE, Eleanor	1832
BAINBRIDGE, Joseph	
BANKHEAD, Erastus ...	1854
BARNUM, Charles	
BARNUM, Charles	
BARNUM, Eliza	1837
BARNUM, Eliza	1837
BELNAP, Gilbert	1821
BENSON, David	1821
BLANCHARD, Helen ...	1878
BRADLEY, Jane	

The Family Panel

 The family panel displays the family members of the person currently highlighted in the main view. As you move around on the main screen RootsMagic will display the spouses, children, parents and siblings of the highlighted person.

You can highlight any family member in the list and click the "Go" button and RootsMagic will jump to that person on the main screen.

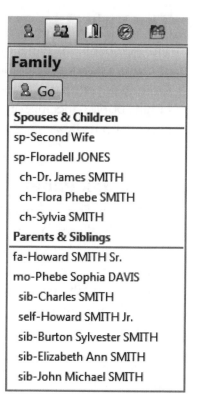

The Bookmark Panel

Often it is necessary to work with one person (or a small group of people) on a regular basis. RootsMagic makes it easy to bookmark and return to a person. Just highlight the person on the main screen, and do "Search > Bookmarks > Manage bookmarks". The Bookmarks panel will open.

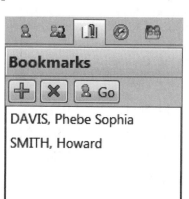

If you want to add the person to the Bookmark list, press Ctrl+B or click the green plus button on the panel.

Later, when you want to return to a bookmarked person, open the Bookmark panel the same way, highlight the person in the Bookmark list, and click the "Go" button. You can also remove a bookmarked person by clicking the red X button on this same panel.

The History Panel

 As you move through your database, RootsMagic keeps a list of the people you have visited during that session. That list is displayed in the History panel of the side list. You can click on any name in that history list to immediately jump to that person on the main screen. You can even add arrow buttons to your toolbar which will go back and forth through the history list.

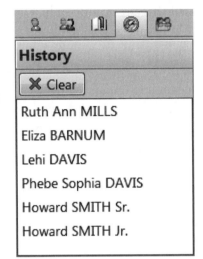

History

✗ Clear

Ruth Ann MILLS

Eliza BARNUM

Lehi DAVIS

Phebe Sophia DAVIS

Howard SMITH Sr.

Howard SMITH Jr.

To add those arrow buttons, just follow the steps in the next section (Toolbars and Menus).

You can highlight any person in the history list and click the "Go to" button to return to that person on the main screen. RootsMagic also offers two commands to help navigate through the history list without actually bringing the list itself up.

➤ **Back** – "Search, Back" from the menu, or Ctrl + Left arrow will move back to the previously visited person on the main screen.

➤ **Forward** – If you have used the Back command, "Search, Forward" from the menu, or Ctrl + Right arrow will move forward again to the next visited person on the main screen.

The Groups Panel

RootsMagic makes it possible to select a group of people in your database and give each of those groups a name.

For example, you can select everyone born in California and call that group "Born in California". You can then select that group by name to use in reports, exporting, etc. For complete details on how to create, edit and use these named groups, see Named Groups on page 256.

Toolbars and Menus

The main RootsMagic screen also includes the main menu, a toolbar, and a status bar.

The main menu is where you will select most of the commands used by RootsMagic. The commands in the main menu are described in more detail in the chapter titled Quick Summary (page 316).

The toolbar is the row of buttons directly under the main menu.

These buttons are shortcuts for some of the commands in the main menu. If you move your mouse pointer over any of the buttons without clicking the mouse, a small yellow box (called a tool tip) will pop up and tell you what that button does.

You can customize the toolbar, by adding or deleting buttons, or rearranging the order of the buttons. Right click your mouse button on the toolbar, and then click on the "Customize" menu, and the following dialog will appear.

Select the Commands tab to bring up a page of available toolbar buttons. The buttons are grouped in categories similar to where they are found in the main menu. Choose a category to see the available buttons. Any time the Customize form is open and the Commands tab is selected you can click and drag toolbar buttons from the form up onto the toolbar, click and drag buttons off the toolbar, or click and drag buttons on the toolbar into a different position. And finally, if you totally mess things up, you can click the Toolbars tab on the Customize form, select the toolbar from the list and click the "Reset" button to restore the toolbar back to its default state.

The status bar is a bar across the bottom of the RootsMagic screen which displays various pieces of information.

The status bar can display the relationship of the highlighted person to any selected person in your database. This feature is described on page 264.

Using Databases

It is a capital mistake to theorize before one has data.
- Sir Arthur Conan Doyle

The heart of any genealogy software is the database engine, and RootsMagic is no exception. A RootsMagic database can hold up to 2 billion individuals, so a single database can easily hold all the family members you can enter.

If you *do* want to separate your information into different databases, RootsMagic will allow you to have as many databases as will fit on your hard disk.

Creating a New Database

Before you can do anything in RootsMagic, you must tell it to create a new database to store your information in.

 To create a new database select "File > New" from the main menu or click the "New" button on the toolbar.

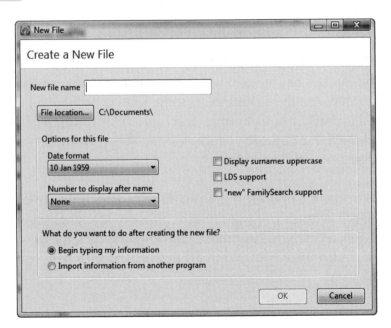

Enter a file name for the database you want to create. It can be something simple like your last name, or longer like "The Smith Family Tree". If you want to create the new database somewhere other than the default folder, you can click the "File location" button and select a different folder. You can also select several default options for your new database.

Date format determines how RootsMagic will display dates you enter. You can actually enter dates in just about any format and RootsMagic will automatically convert them to the format you select here.

Number to display after name lets you choose whether RootsMagic displays the program assigned record number after a person's name, or a user entered reference number, or no number at all.

Display surnames uppercase lets you tell RootsMagic whether you want it to display and print surnames (last names) in all uppercase.

LDS support enables or disables the printing of LDS (Mormon) information on printouts and certain other LDS features.

"new" FamilySearch support enables support for new FamilySearch, a new system which is being released in a phased rollout. It currently is available to some LDS church members, but will eventually be opened to everyone. This is different from the "classic" FamilySearch which you can access from the WebSearch tab in RootsMagic.

Simply select the options you want. Don't worry if you aren't sure which settings you want to use. You can always change them later. After you have made your choices, click the OK button, and you have just created a new database to hold your information.

Opening an Existing Database

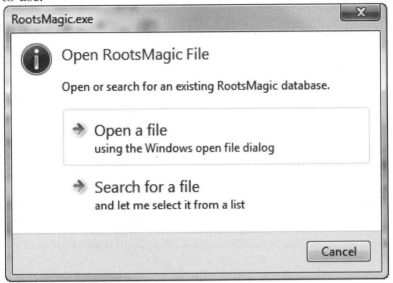 If you have created more than one database, you will need to be able to access the different databases. Clicking the "Open" button on the toolbar, or selecting **"File > Open"** from the main menu will let you select which database you want to use.

RootsMagic.exe ⓧ

ⓘ Open RootsMagic File

Open or search for an existing RootsMagic database.

➜ **Open a file**
using the Windows open file dialog

➜ **Search for a file**
and let me select it from a list

[Cancel]

You can choose to open a file using the standard Windows file open screen, or you can have RootsMagic search your computer for your RootsMagic files.

RootsMagic will also keep track of the most recently used databases, so that you can select one without searching for it. Just select **"File > Recent files"** from the main menu, and select one of the files listed.

If you want to close a database, just select **"File > Close"** from the main menu. If you have more than one database open (we'll talk about that in the next section), make sure you have selected the database you want to close so RootsMagic knows which one you want closed. The selected database is simply the last one you clicked on or were moving around in.

Searching For Files

If you aren't sure where a particular file is on your computer, select "File, Search for Files" from the main menu.

Just tell RootsMagic what type of file to search for and click the "Search for files" button.

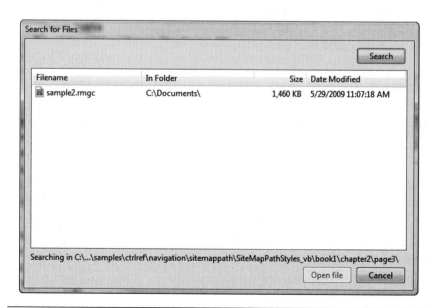

RootsMagic will search your hard drive and will list all the files it finds. You can then highlight any of the files in the list and click the "Open file" button to open or import that file.

Using Multiple Databases

RootsMagic allows you to have more than one database open on screen at the same time. These can be totally different databases, or multiple copies of the same database. Just open (or create) the additional databases exactly the same way you did the first, and RootsMagic will automatically place the two databases side by side on the screen.

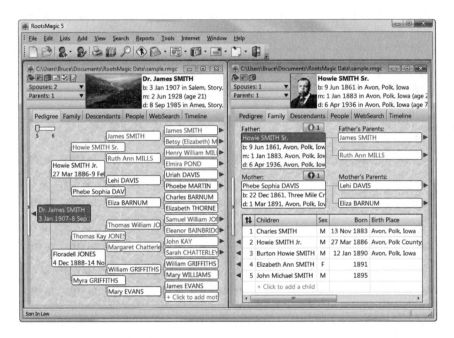

You may have up to 9 databases open at once (although the screen gets really crowded if you do). Each database window acts independently from the others, so you can even view different parts of the same database using two different views at the same time.

Dragging and Dropping People

If you have two different databases open at the same time, RootsMagic will let you drag and drop people from one database to the other. Dragging and dropping a person copies them to the new database, and does not remove them from the original database.

Simply click your mouse on a person in one database (in any of the main views), and while holding the mouse button down, drag the person to the other database. RootsMagic will bring up the following screen in case you want to copy more than just that one person.

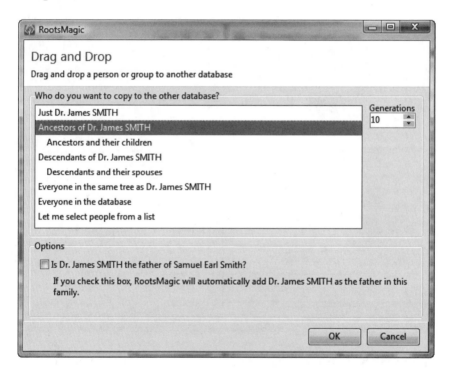

You can select which people you want to drag from one database to the other. Your options are:

> **Just the person** you dragged.
> **Ancestors of the person** copies the direct ancestors (parents, grandparents, etc) of the person you dragged. You

can enter the number of generations to copy. You can also select to have the children of the ancestors copied as well.

➢ **Descendants of the person** copies the direct descendants (children, grandchildren, etc) of the person you dragged. You can enter the number of generations to copy. You can also select to have the spouses of descendants copied as well.

➢ **Everyone in the same tree as the person** copies everyone related to the person you dragged.

➢ **Everyone in the database** copies the entire database.

➢ **Let me select people from a list** brings up the selection screen (page 210) where you can select any group of people to copy.

If you drop a person on top of the same person in the other database, or if you drop the person in an empty parent or child slot in the other database, RootsMagic will offer you the chance to link the dragged person into the new database.

Backing Up Your Database

If you only learn one thing from this book, this should be it. **Always keep a set of current backups of your data.** Nothing is more disheartening than losing everything you've entered into a program, and knowing that you don't have a backup copy of your data.

RootsMagic makes it easy to back up your data. It will even ask you if you want to back up your data whenever you exit the program. If you don't want RootsMagic to ask you to backup each time you exit, do "Tools, Options" from the main menu and uncheck that option. To back up your data at any other time, do "File, Backup" from the main menu. RootsMagic will back up the currently selected database.

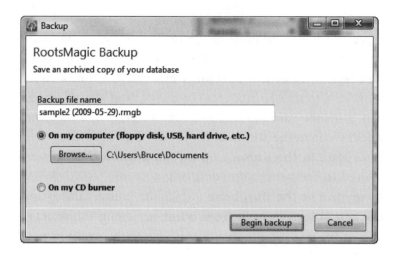

RootsMagic will display a default backup file name which includes the current day's date so you can easily keep multiple backups. The backup is a compressed version of your database and has a .rmgb extension.

You can save your backup to a floppy or hard drive, or to a CD-ROM drive (if it is a writeable drive). If you back up to a floppy or the hard drive, you can enter the drive letter and full path name where you want the backup to be written. If you save the backup to a CD-ROM, you will need to use a blank CD since RootsMagic won't write to a previously written CD.

To restore a backed up database, select "File > Restore" from the main menu.

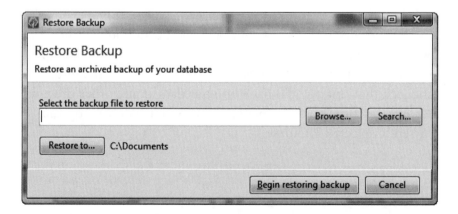

Enter the name of the backup to restore (it will have a .rmgb extension), or click the "Browse" button to select from the file dialog.

RootsMagic will restore the database into your documents folder by default, but you can change the folder you want RootsMagic to restore into by clicking the "Restore to" button. The restored database will have the same name as it had originally. If there is already a database with that name in the directory you choose, RootsMagic will ask if you want to overwrite the existing database. After RootsMagic restores the backup it will open the newly restored database.

✎ Note

While RootsMagic's backup feature will back up links to multimedia items, it does not back up any of the multimedia items themselves (photos, sound or video clips). Those items are often in other directories, or even scattered around in multiple directories. You will want to back those multimedia items up separately.

☺ Tip

While a single backup copy of each database is better than no backup, some backup techniques can provide even more protection.

When creating a backup, try not to always overwrite your previous backup. It is sometimes possible to have corruption in your database without knowing it and your backup could contain a corrupted database. By having multiple backups you can go back to earlier backups that may have been created before the corruption occurred.

Renaming Your Database

The **"File, Rename"** command lets you rename or move your database. RootsMagic will ask you to enter a new file name. If you simply enter a new file name then the file will simply be given the new name. If you also change the folder on the rename screen, the file will be renamed *and* moved to the new folder.

Database Tools

The **"File, Database tools"** command provides 3 simple tools for cleaning up and testing the integrity of your database: 1) Test database integrity, 2) Rebuild indexes, and 3) Compact database. The first command will let you know if the database structure of your database has become corrupted, hopefully before it gets too bad. The other two commands do basic cleanup on the database.

Deleting Your Database

Here is a command you should never use on your database, unless you are absolutely sure you don't need it anymore. The **"File > Delete"** command will completely remove the current database from your hard disk. You must mark the verification checkbox and then click the "Delete this database" button.

Copying Your Database

The **"File, Copy"** command lets you create an exact copy of your database. You can choose what folder and filename you want for the copy. This command can be useful if you want to make a copy of your database that you can make temporary changes to without affecting your main database.

Getting Database Information

The **"File > Properties"** command displays information about the current database, including the full path name, and the number of records (people, families, sources, places, etc) in the database.

Building the Family Tree

Every time I find an ancestor, I need to find two more.

Adding People to Your Database

As with most database programs, RootsMagic allows you to enter new information from the keyboard or by importing data from existing files.

> **Note**
>
> If you are lucky enough to already have data in a GEDCOM, Family Tree Maker, PAF, Legacy or Family Origins file, then you will want to read the chapter titled "Sharing Data with Others" (page 219).

 To add individuals to your RootsMagic database, use one of the four **"Add"** commands from the main menu, or click the "Add" toolbar button.

The "Add > Individual" command simply lets you add an unlinked person to your database. The first person you add to a database must be added this way, since there is nobody to add parents, spouses, or children to yet.

The "Add > Parents" command adds parents to the person who is highlighted on the main screen. You can add more than one set of parents to each person.

The "Add > Spouse" command adds a spouse (or unmarried partner) to the person who is highlighted on the main screen. You can add multiple spouses to each person.

The "Add > Child" command adds a child to the person who is highlighted on the main screen. When adding children to a family, you may want to switch to the Family View to get a clearer picture of the family unit.

As you add a person to your database, RootsMagic will automatically link the person and add their name to the main views.

Adding an Unlinked Individual

 To add an unlinked individual, click the **"Add"** button on the toolbar (it looks like the button to the left) and then select "Individual", or do **"Add, Individual"** from the main menu. You can also just press the letter "I" on the keyboard as a shortcut. This will bring up a screen where you can add the basic information for the person.

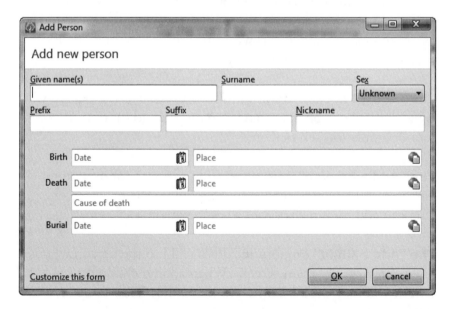

Simply fill in the blanks, using the Tab or Enter key to move on to the next field. If you don't know some of the information, just leave the field empty. If you make a mistake, you can move back to the previous field by pressing Shift+Tab or by clicking the mouse on the field you want to move to.

Enter the given names (first, middle, etc) in the Given name(s) field. Separate each name with a space, like: John Michael.

The Surname field is where you will enter the last name. If you are entering a female, you should enter their maiden (birth) name here.

Enter the person's sex in the Sex field by typing M or F as appropriate. RootsMagic also supports Unknown as an option.

You can also enter any prefix that should come before the name (like "Dr."), any suffix that would come after your name (like "Jr."), and any nickname you are known by (we won't even go there).

You can also enter the birth date and birthplace. Enter the date in just about any format you want, and RootsMagic will convert it to the format you selected when you created the database. When you enter the birthplace, enter it from specific to general with a comma to separate each part of the place, like this:

Albuquerque, Bernalillo, New Mexico, United States

The death and burial fields work exactly the same way as the birth fields.

Although the "Add Person" screen only allows birth, death, and burial by default, you can click the "Customize this form" link to have RootsMagic include other fields as well.

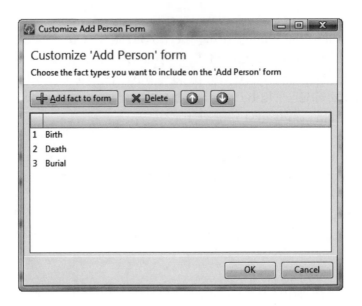

You can add other fact types to the "Add Person" screen, and rearrange the order those facts appear on the form. Select the fact types you want then click OK to return to the "Add Person" form. Any changes made will affect the "Add Person" screen from that point on (until you customize them again).

When you are ready to add the person, click the **OK** button. If RootsMagic thinks you may have already entered this person, it will display the following dialog, where you can continue adding the person, cancel, or link to the existing copy of the person (in cases where you are adding a spouse, parents, or child).

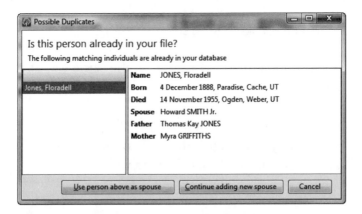

RootsMagic will then bring up the data entry screen for the new person, with the name, sex and birth, death and burial information filled out (if you entered them).

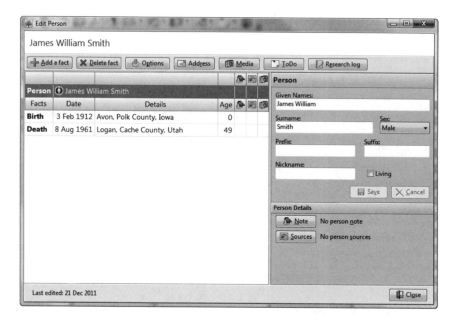

From this screen you can edit existing information, add other facts (like graduation, occupation, etc), notes, sources (documentation), to do items, scrapbook items, and a current address. Add as many items as you want, and if you forget anything, you can always come back later to add or change the information. This edit screen is described in more detail in the next chapter titled "Editing People" (page 51).

When you are satisfied with your entries, click Close to finish adding the unlinked individual.

Adding Parents, Spouses, and Children

One of the nice things about RootsMagic is that when you add a person to your database, it links the people together at the same time. Notice that when you press the arrow keys on the keyboard, or click on a person's name on the main pedigree chart, the highlight bar moves to that person.

To add parents to someone in your database, highlight the name of the person on the main screen (by clicking your mouse on it), then press "P" on the keyboard, or click the **"Add"** button on the toolbar and select "Parents".

The following dialog box will appear to let you select how you want to add the father.

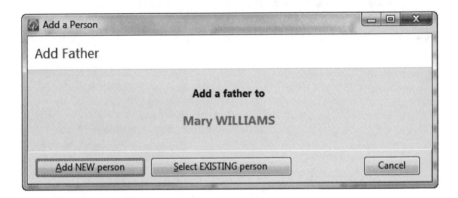

> ➤ **Add NEW person** allows you to add the father's record to the database from scratch. If you click this button, you will add the father exactly the same way you add an unlinked individual.
> ➤ **Select EXISTING person** is available in case the father's information is already in the database. If you click this button, a list of everybody in the database will appear, and you can select the father from the list.
> ➤ **Cancel** lets you cancel adding the father. This is useful if you don't want to add parents after all, or if you don't know the father but still want to add a mother.

After you have added the father, you will go through the exact same steps to add the mother.

Once you have entered the parents, RootsMagic will ask if you want to add a marriage event for them. If the parents were married, select **"Yes"** (even if you don't know the date, place, or anything else about the marriage). RootsMagic will never assume a couple is married unless you add a marriage event. If you don't add the marriage event here, you can always add it later.

You can add additional sets of parents to a person by repeating these steps. This allows you to track natural, adopted, foster, or any other types of relationships.

To add a spouse (or unmarried partner) to someone in your database, highlight the person you want to add the spouse to (by clicking your mouse on the person's name in the tree), then press "S" on the keyboard, or click the **"Add"** button on the toolbar and select Spouse.

Adding a spouse is exactly the same as adding parents. You will get to choose between adding a new person or selecting an existing person. You will also be asked if you want to add a marriage event for this couple.

If you want to add multiple spouses to a person, just repeat these steps for each spouse.

When you encounter a situation where a couple has children but are not married, you will still use the **"Add > Spouse"** command but just won't add a marriage event.

To add a child to someone in your database, highlight either the father or the mother, then press "C" on the keyboard, or click the **"Add"** button on the toolbar and select "Child".

Once again, you will get the option to add a new person, or select an existing person. This time the dialog will look a little bit different.

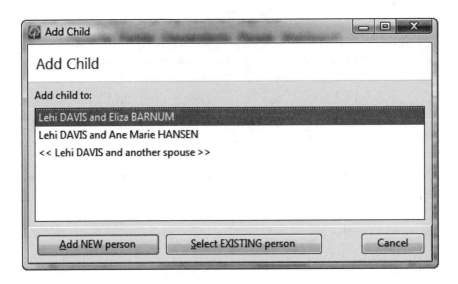

Since the person may have more than one spouse, the add child dialog will also ask which family to add the child to, and will also provide an option to add the child to the person and a new spouse. Choose which family to add the child to and then add the new child or select an existing child.

When you finish adding a child, RootsMagic will display the family and ask if you want to add another child to the family. If you select **"Yes"**, you can simply repeat these steps to add more children.

Once you have finished adding children to the family, RootsMagic will bring up a list of the children in the family, and will ask you to arrange them in the proper birth order. Just use your mouse to drag and drop the children into the proper order, then click the **OK** button.

This child order is used when RootsMagic prints family group sheets, books, and other printouts where the children in a family are included.

Deleting People and Families

If you ever add someone to your database that you really didn't mean to, RootsMagic provides two commands to help you remove them.

To delete a person, highlight the person's name on the main screen, then do "Edit > Delete > Person" from the main menu. RootsMagic will ask if you want to delete the person.

When you delete a person, RootsMagic will unlink the person from all families and will remove the person's record, including facts, notes, source citations, multimedia links, and to do items.

To delete a family, highlight either the father or the mother on the main screen, then do "Edit > Delete > Family" from the main menu. RootsMagic will display the family in the following dialog. RootsMagic offers two methods of deleting a family.

➤ **Unlink the family members from each other.** No other links will be broken, and the people will not be removed from the database. For example, the parents will still be linked to their parents and other spouses, and children will still be linked to their spouses and children. RootsMagic will also delete any marriage facts or notes associated with the family.

➤ **Delete all of the family members from the database.** RootsMagic will delete both parents and each child from the database.

☺ **Tip**

If you ever encounter a situation in your database where a person has an "Unknown" spouse that you can't seem to get rid of, bring up the family with the unknown spouse in the Family View on the main screen, highlight the parent that isn't "Unknown" and do the **"Edit, Delete, Family"** command. Select the option to "Unlink the people as a family" and RootsMagic will remove the "Unknown" spouse.

Unlinking People from Each Other

There will come a time when you will link a person into your family the wrong way. It is not uncommon to accidentally link a person as his own grandfather.

Unlinking a person from their spouse unlinks them as a parent in the currently displayed family. Highlight the person you want to unlink, making sure that the spouse you want to unlink from is also displayed on the screen. Then select **"Edit, Unlink, from Spouse"** from the main menu. Only the link to the currently displayed spouse and children will be broken. All other links will remain intact, including links to parents and other spouses.

Unlinking a person from their parents unlinks them as a child in the currently displayed family. Highlight the person you want to unlink, making sure that the parents you want to unlink from are also displayed on the screen. Then select **"Edit, Unlink, from Parents"** from the main menu. Only the link to the currently displayed parents will be broken. All other links will remain intact, including links to spouses and other sets of parents (if any).

Swapping Husbands and Wives

This isn't what it sounds like. There are times when you may enter a husband and wife backwards. This may be a situation where you couldn't tell the sex based on the name (Kim and Francis Smith), or it may just be accidental. RootsMagic has a command which will let you switch the husband and the wife in a family without having to unlink them first. Just highlight either the husband or wife, and select **"Edit, Swap husband and wife"** from the main menu.

Rearranging Children

To rearrange the children in the family, highlight either parent and select **"Edit > Rearrange > Children"** from the menu, and the following dialog will appear.

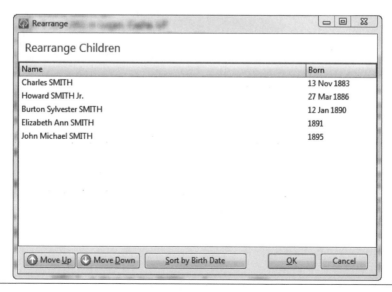

The children in the list can be rearranged by clicking your mouse on a child's name, and while holding the mouse button down, dragging the child's name into the proper position. You can also rearrange a person by highlighting the person, then clicking the "Move up" or "Move down" buttons. Repeat this for each child that needs to be rearranged, and then click the OK button to close the child list.

You can also click the "Sort by birth date" button to have RootsMagic automatically rearrange the children by their birth date.

Rearranging Spouses

To rearrange a person's spouses, highlight the person and select "Edit > Rearrange > Spouses" from the menu. A list of spouses similar to the list of children in the previous section will appear.

The spouses in the list can be rearranged by clicking your mouse on a spouse's name, and while holding the mouse button down, dragging the spouse's name into the proper position. Repeat this for each spouse that needs to be rearranged, then click the OK button to close the spouse list.

Editing People

History is only a confused heap of facts. - Lord Chesterfield

The RootsMagic edit screen is the place where you will enter everything you know about a person. To edit a person, simply double click on the person's name on the main screen. You can also highlight the person on the main screen and press the **Enter** key to bring up the edit screen.

If you want the edit screen to be a little larger, you can resize it by clicking the edge of the edit screen and dragging it.

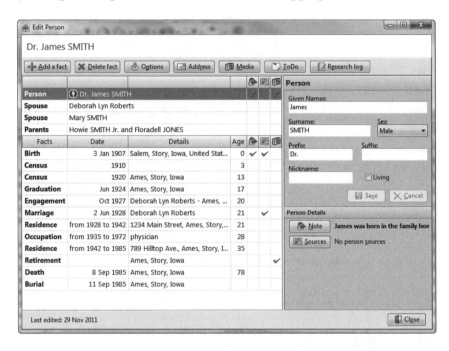

The edit screen is divided into two main sections. The left half of the screen is a list of all the pieces of information you have for the person. This list can include the person's name, spouses, parents, events, alternate names, DNA tests, and more. The right half of the screen is a live-edit panel. When you select an item in the list on the left, RootsMagic will display an edit panel for that type of information on the right.

Names, Titles and Sex

Selecting the "Person" row will set the live edit panel to include fields where you can just type in the person's name, titles and sex. When you finish filling in one field, you can move to the next field by pressing the Enter or Tab key. If you make a mistake, you can press Shift+Tab to move back to the previous field. You can also click your mouse on any field to move the cursor there for editing.

The Given names field is where you enter the person's given names (first, middle, etc). You should separate each given name with a space, like this: John Michael.

The Surname field is where you enter the person's last name. If the person is female, you should enter their maiden (unmarried) name here.

The Sex field is a list that you can select "Male", "Female" or "Unknown" from. You can click your mouse on the list and select the sex, or press the first letter of the sex ("M", "F", or "U").

The Prefix field provides a place to enter titles that come *before* the person's name, such as *Dr.* John Smith.

The Suffix field provides a place to enter titles that come *after* the person's name, such as John Smith *Jr.*

The Nickname field provides a place to enter a nickname that the person was (or is) known by.

The Living checkbox lets you mark whether the person is still living. This is used if you choose to "privatize" data for living people when creating GEDCOM files or websites. This is useful if you know the person is deceased and you don't have a death date.

Spouses

RootsMagic will add a row for each spouse you have entered for the person. When you highlight a spouse in the list you will be able to set the label used for the person and spouse. This is mainly just for reports, but you can choose from Father, Husband, Mother, Wife, or Partner.

You can also optionally choose whether you feel you have proven this relationship with the "Proof" setting. You can choose from:

- Proven
- Disproven
- Disputed

You can also select whether you want to make this relationship private.

Parents

There are many different relationships a child can have with their parents, and RootsMagic allows you to set that relationship for each of the child's parents. Highlight the parents row on the edit screen and choose from birth, adopted, step, foster, related, guardian, sealed or unknown.

As with the spouse row, you can also select a proof for this relationship as well as mark it private if desired.

Facts and Events

RootsMagic allows you to enter unlimited facts to each person. A fact can be **an event** like a birth or death, **a phase in the person's life** like an occupation or military service, or **a descriptive item** like an ID number or physical description.

A fact can contain a date (or date period), a place, a description if necessary, a note and unlimited source citations.

You can enter multiple copies of each fact type, so you can, for example, enter all 10 occupations in Uncle Joe's life. By adding all these facts (along with fact notes and fact sources) you are building a complete personal history for each person in your database.

Adding a Fact to a Person

To add a fact to an individual, click the **"Add a fact"** button on the person's edit screen, or press **Alt+A** as a shortcut key. RootsMagic will display a list of fact types that you can choose from.

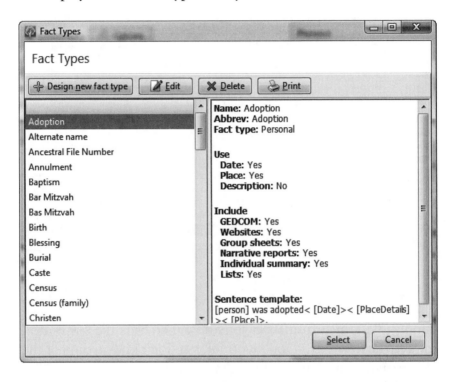

Simply highlight the type of fact you want to add. As with any list in RootsMagic, you can use the arrow keys to highlight the item, or can just begin typing the fact name and RootsMagic will move to the matching fact type for you.

> **Note**
>
> If you want to add a fact that isn't in the list, you can create your own fact types. This is discussed in the next chapter titled "Facts and Events" (page 62).

Once you have highlighted the type of fact you want to add to the person, just click the **Select** button and RootsMagic will add a blank fact of that type to the person's edit screen where you can enter the details for the new fact. You can enter the date and place for the fact, as well as a note and sources.

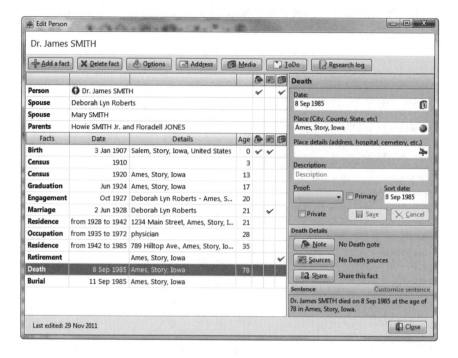

Simply fill in the information you know then click the **Save** button to save the new fact. Don't worry if you don't know some of the information. Just enter as much as you can. You can always come back to make changes or add more information.

If you have "conflicting" information about a fact (for example, two different birth dates), you can enter two different birth facts to the person, and use the "Primary fact" checkbox to tell RootsMagic which fact is the main one to use.

RootsMagic will show you what a sentence using that data with that fact will look like. You can click the **"Customize sentence"** button to change the sentence for that single fact.

For more information on facts and how they work, see the next chapter titled "Facts and Events" (page 62).

Editing a Person's Facts

To edit a fact for a person, bring up the person's edit screen, click your mouse on the fact you want to edit, then begin editing the information on the right side of the screen. You can change any information or add new information. When you are satisfied with the changes, click the **Save** button to save the changes.

Deleting a Person's Facts

To delete a fact from a person, bring up the person's edit screen, click your mouse on the fact you want to delete, then click the **"Delete fact"** button. RootsMagic will ask you to confirm that you really want to delete the fact. Click **"Yes"** to remove the fact from the person's list.

Alternate Names

Many people don't go by the same name their entire life. For these people RootsMagic lets you add "Alternate name" facts. You add them just the same way you add any other fact to a person (by clicking the "Add a fact" button).

The live edit panel on the right will display name fields for an alternate name fact. You can even enter a date or date range in case the person only went by that name during a particular period in their life.

You can also select what type of name the alternate name is; AKA (also known as), birth, immigrant, maiden, married, nickname, or other spelling. Just select the type from the list, although you can just leave it blank too if you want.

DNA Tests

Over the past few years, great advances have been made in the field of genetic genealogy. Genetic genealogy involves comparing DNA markers in living (or in some special cases, deceased) individuals against the markers of others, stored in a database. By looking for common DNA markers, people may find common ancestors and make contact with other descendants of those ancestors.

You can track these DNA tests (along with their markers) just like you would enter any other fact type. On the person's edit screen, click the "Add a fact" button and select "DNA test" from the list of fact types. RootsMagic will ask you to choose which type of DNA test you want to enter.

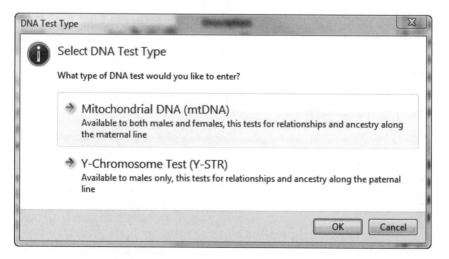

Select the desired test type and RootsMagic will display an entry screen for the DNA test.

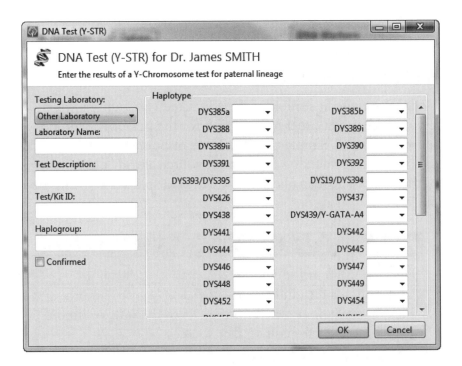

The entry screen will look a bit different depending on whether you are entering a Mitochondrial or Y-Chromosome test, but they both let you select which lab performed the test, the test description, kit ID, Haplogroup, and the results of the test.

After entering and saving the DNA test information, RootsMagic will display the general information about the test in the live edit panel on the right, along with a "DNA Test Results" button which will bring up

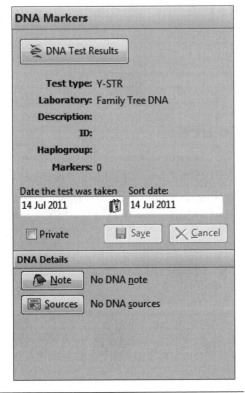

the test results screen if you need to edit or view the results. You can also enter the date the test was taken.

Notes and Sources

Under the live-edit section of the edit screen are buttons which let you add or edit other information for the person; notes and source citations. Simply click the Note or Sources buttons to add or edit this information. If a note or source already exists in any of these areas, a green check mark will be displayed in the list on the left.

> **☺ Tip**
>
> Here's a shortcut for editing these items. Instead of highlighting a fact and clicking the **"Note"** button, simply click on the little box next to the fact in the note column. This also works for editing fact sources.

Notes

The "Notes" button lets you enter and edit the note for the highlighted row. This is a note that is associated with that person, family, or fact. For details on notes, see the chapter titled "Notes – Telling Your Story" (page 82).

Sources

The "Sources" button lets you enter and edit the sources for the highlighted row. These are sources that are associated with that person, family, or fact. For details on sources, see the chapter titled "Sources – Proving It" (page 86).

Other Items

Media

The "Media" button shows the media album for the person. The media album allows you to enter and scan photos for a person, family, or fact, and attach documents, sound and video clips. Photos attached to a person can be printed in many of RootsMagic's reports and charts. For more information on the media album, see the chapter titled "Pictures, Sound, and Video" (page 115).

Address

The "Address" button lets you enter and edit the current addresses for the highlighted person or family. You only need to enter an address for the head of a household, not for each person in the household. This address is intended only for the "current" address. You can add "Residence" facts to the person if you want to track all the places the person ever lived. These addresses can be printed in the form of an address list or address labels, or can be exported to a mail-merge file that you can import into your word processor.

The address page and list work exactly the same as the "Repository" page and list described on page 112.

To Do List

The "To Do" button shows the to do list for the highlighted person or family. The to-do list provides a place to save all those tasks you need to accomplish. For details on the to do list, see the chapter titled "Research Aids" (page 246).

Facts and Events

History is only a confused heap of facts. - Lord Chesterfield

What Is a Fact?

RootsMagic allows you to track every detail in a person's life in the form of "facts". A fact can be **an event** like a birth or death, **a phase in the person's life** like an occupation or military service, or **a descriptive item** like an ID number or physical description.

When you highlight a fact on a person's edit screen RootsMagic will display a live-edit panel where you can enter the information for the fact. A fact can contain of any or all of the following parts: a date (or date period), a place (including details), a description, a note and unlimited source citations.

You can also choose whether a fact is a primary or private fact. **A primary fact** is useful when you have multiple facts of the same type (like more than one birth fact when you have conflicting information). **A private fact** is one you may not want included in reports or other uses. Most reports offer the option to print or ignore private facts.

You can also optionally choose whether you feel you have proven this fact with the "Proof" setting. You can choose from:

- Proven
- Disproven
- Disputed

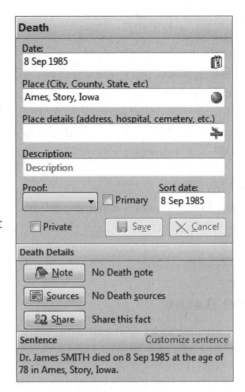

Dates

RootsMagic will accept just about any date you type, and will convert it into a standard format for displaying and printing. While you should enter the full date (day, month and year) if you know it, RootsMagic will also accept partial dates, like **"Feb 1780"**, **"13 Feb"**, **"Feb"**, or **"1780"**. You can even use BC if you are lucky enough to have information back that far.

Double Dates

RootsMagic also supports double dates, which were used in England prior to the adoption of the Gregorian calendar. You would enter these double dates with a slash separating the two years, like **"13 Feb 1729/30"**.

Quaker Dates

RootsMagic has built-in date support for Quaker dates. Quaker date are written referring to days of the weeks and months of the year by their number rather than the names which were based on "pagan" gods.

RootsMagic accepts these dates as "12day 5month 1588" or "12da 5mo 1588", and displays them as "12da 5mo 1588". Note that Quaker dates before 1752 were based on the Julian Calendar, so the first month refers to March, not January.

Date Modifiers

RootsMagic provides **date modifiers**, which you can add to your dates to alter their meaning. You can use them with full dates, partial dates, or a combination of the two. Here is a list of the date modifiers supported by RootsMagic.

Sort Dates

The sort date is a "non printing" date which you can enter to force RootsMagic to sort the facts in the order you want.

When you enter the normal date for the fact, RootsMagic will automatically fill the sort date, but you can change it if you want. This is useful in situations like when you have a death fact with a place but don't know the date. Instead of putting in a fake date like "after 1 Jan 1900" in the date field, you can go ahead and leave the date field blank but put in a sort date to force the fact into the position you desire.

> ☺ **Tip**
>
> If you happen to have multiple events which happened on the same date you can use the sort date to force them into the desired order. You can enter the actual date in the sort date, but append a dash date to force the sort order between them. For example, if you have a death and burial both on 15 Jun 1850, you can enter:
>
> 15 Jun 1850 - 15 Jun 1850 for the death sort date
>
> 15 Jun 1850 - 16 Jun 1850 for the burial sort date

Modifier	Description	Example
Before	Before a date	before 1 Jan 1900
By	Happened by this date	by 1 Jan 1900
To	End date of an unknown period	to 1 Jan 1900
Until	Until a date	until 1 Jan 1900
From++	Start date of an unknown period	from 1 Jan 1900
Since	Since a date	since 1 Jan 1900
After	After a date	after 1 Jan 1900
Between/And	A date which is between two dates.	between 1 Jan 1900 and 5 Jan 1900
From/To	A date period. Useful for spans like the period of time a person held an occupation.	from 1 Jan 1900 and 5 Jan 1900
- (dash)	Date period	1 Jan 1900-5 Jan 1900
Or	Conflicting dates	1 Jan 1900 or 5 Jan 1900
About	Near a date	abt 1 Jan 1900
Estimate	An estimated date	est 1 Jan 1900
Calculated	A calculated date	calc 1 Jan 1900
Circa	Near a date	ca 1 Jan 1900
Say	An estimated date	say 1 Jan 1900
Certainly	Little doubt about the date	cert 1 Jan 1900
Probably	More than likely date	prob 1 Jan 1900
Possibly	Some evidence supports the date	poss 1 Jan 1900
Likely	Odds favor the date	lkly 1 Jan 1900
Apparently	Presumed date	appar 1 Jan 1900
Perhaps	Could be the date	prhps 1 Jan 1900
Maybe	Date might be correct	maybe 1 Jan 1900

Places and Place Details

RootsMagic facts allow you to enter the place where the fact or event occurred. When you enter a place, separate each part with a comma, and enter it from specific to general like this:

Albuquerque, Bernalillo, New Mexico, United States

By separating each part of the place with a comma, RootsMagic can abbreviate the place when it needs to fit the place name in a tight area of a report.

> ☺ **Tip**
>
> When entering place names, it is best to spell out the different parts. While abbreviations (like the post office abbreviations for states) are standard in their country of origin, they are not standard throughout the rest of the world.

Every time you enter a new place, RootsMagic adds the place you enter to a master place list. Whenever you need to enter a place, RootsMagic will autofill the place as you type. As you type each letter of the place name, RootsMagic tries to match the letters you've typed with existing names in the place list. Just continue typing characters until the correct place appears.

You can also click the "Place list" button (which looks like a globe on the right end of the place field) to bring up a list of previously entered places to choose from. The master place list is described on page 105.

RootsMagic also provides a second field called the "Place Details". This is where you can enter more specific information about the place, like the hospital, cemetery, or street address where the event took place. You can click the street sign button at the right end of the place details field to open the place details list.

Descriptions

Some facts have what is called a "description". This is where you enter a specific detail about a fact. For example, in the Occupation fact, you would enter the actual occupation (for example "teacher").

Shared Facts

You will often come across facts or events that are actually shared by more than just the person you add the fact to. For example, you may have a census record which includes a father, mother, and a number of children. You don't want to have to retype that fact over and over into each person's edit screen, so RootsMagic offers a feature called "Shared facts".

This is also useful for facts like Residence, and can also be used to add "witnesses" to events, like the best man for a marriage event, or a witness to a baptism.

Any time you are highlighting a fact in a person's edit screen, the live edit panel on the right will have a button called "Share this fact". Click that button and RootsMagic will allow you to select other people who will share that particular fact.

You can click "Add a person" to add the person who shares this event. You can choose someone who is in the database (by selecting them from a list) or you can just type in the name of a person (this is useful for neighbors and others that you don't actually want to enter into the file).

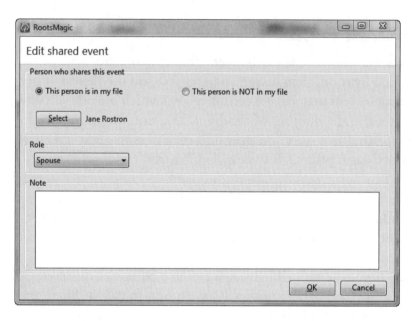

Once you have selected the person, there are two extra pieces of information you can enter:

1. **The person's role in the event.** For example, if the shared fact was a census, the role might be "Spouse", "Child", "Boarder", or any other role you might want to include. Just select the role you want from the list. These role types aren't all automatically built in, so there is an item in the list called "Add new role type". Select that item and you can create a new role. Just enter a name for the role, and an optional sentence template. The sentence template is used to write the sentence in books when a person with this role is talked about.

2. **A note about the person's role in the event.** This
    optional note is a place where you can put more details
    about this person's specific role in this event.

You can also add multiple people at once who share the fact.
RootsMagic will open a list of all the people in the database and
you can mark the ones you want to share the fact. After you
have selected the group of people RootsMagic will ask you to
select the role for that group. While it does let you select
multiple people at once, it will assign the same role to each
member of that group.

You can also make changes to a person's role or role note by
clicking the "Edit" button, and can remove a shared person by
clicking the "Remove person" button.

The Fact List

RootsMagic has a "fact list" with a number of built-in fact types
that are already defined and include the appropriate fields. You
can also create your own fact types that RootsMagic will add to
the fact list. A description of each of the built-in facts can be
found in the Quick Summary at the end of this book.

You can get to the fact list in two different ways: 1) by clicking
the "Add a fact" button on a person's edit screen, and 2) by selecting
"Lists > Fact type list" from the main menu. You can scroll through the
list of fact types and see details about the highlighted fact type on
the right side of the Fact Type List.

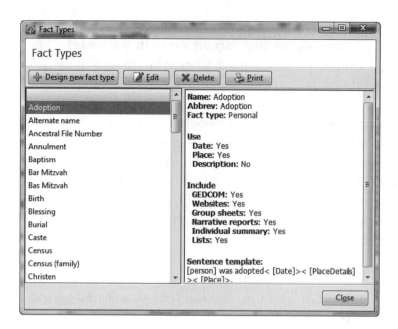

Creating a New Fact Type

To create a fact type that isn't already in the list, click the **"Design new fact type"** button. The following screen will appear so you can tell RootsMagic whether the new fact type will be attached to people (like birth, death, etc), or to families (like marriage, divorce, etc).

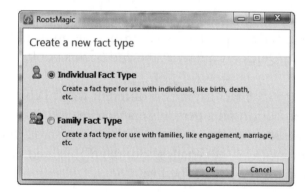

RootsMagic will then display the following dialog so that you can enter the details for the new fact type you want to create.

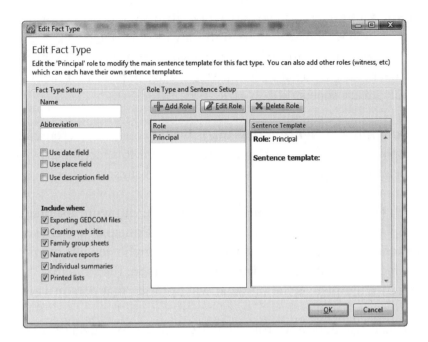

Name is where you enter the name for the new fact.

Abbreviation is where you enter a short version of the fact type name.

Use date field lets you select whether your fact type needs a date. Although you might not think your fact needs this field, you might want to add it anyway. For example, a physical description might not be thought of as needing a date, but you might have facts stating that Aunt Peggy was a brunette from 1960 to 1985, but was a blonde from 1985 to 1987.

Use place field lets you select whether your fact type needs a place. If you include the place field, RootsMagic will also include the place details field automatically.

Use description field lets you select whether your fact type needs a description field. This is useful for fact types like Occupation or Religion where the fact has a value as well as a date and place.

Include when lets you specify where RootsMagic uses your new fact. If you uncheck an item in this area RootsMagic will ignore the fact when performing that function. For example, if you uncheck "Family group sheets", RootsMagic will not print that fact in family group sheets.

Role Type and Sentence Setup is where you enter a "sentence templates" to tell RootsMagic how you want this fact type to appear when printing books or creating websites.

Each fact can have multiple "roles" that you can write a sentence template for. Every fact has a role called "Principal" which is the sentence that will be printed for the person who actually owns the fact. So if you add a birth fact to a person, the Principal sentence template is the one that will print for that person's birth.

You can also add other roles that are used when you share a fact with someone else. So if you wanted to share that person's birth fact with his godmother, you could create a new role type called "Godmother" and enter a sentence template that would print for the godmother in her paragraph in the book.

To create a sentence template you need to tell RootsMagic how to put a fact's information together to create a readable sentence. Edit a role to create the sentence template for that role.

To create the templates you can use field names which RootsMagic provides for the different kinds of information. For example [person], [date], and [place]. Notice that field names have square brackets around them. Simply put these field names together and include any additional words or punctuation you want between them. For example:

[Person] was born [Date] [Place].

When RootsMagic has to write that sentence, it will replace [Person] with the person's name, [Date] with the date entered for the fact, and [Place] with the place entered for the fact. So when the actual sentence is printed it will look something like this:

John Doe was born on May 1, 1820 in Avon, Polk, Iowa.

Notice that when RootsMagic replaces [date] with the date, it adds the word "on" or "in" as appropriate, so you don't need to take that into account in your template. Also, when RootsMagic replaces [place] with the place, it adds the word "in" so that you don't have to add the word "in" to the sentence template. This ensures that the sentence will still read properly even if the date or place are blank for a particular fact.

There are dozens of different fields you can use in a sentence template, with modifiers to change how the fields work, and switches which let you handle any situation you can think of.

Let's say you wanted to create a sentence template for an occupation. You might enter something like this:

[person] was a [desc] [date] [place].

But what if you had information that a person was working but didn't know what the job was? If you left the description field blank your sentence would look like this:

John Doe was a from 1820 to 1830 in Avon, Polk, Iowa.

RootsMagic lets you use angle brackets < > to tell the source template not to print something unless the user actually fills in the field. It even lets you put a bar | separator in to have a default value if the field is blank. So if you did this:

[person] was <a [desc]|employed> [date] [place].

those angle brackets tell RootsMagic to only print the description if it isn't blank, otherwise print "employed". So the sentence would look like either:

John Doe was a farmer from 1820 to 1830 in Avon, Polk, Iowa.

or

John Doe was employed from 1820 to 1830 in Avon, Polk, Iowa.

There are a **ton** of other things you can do with sentence templates (way too many to talk about here). There is an appendix at the end of the book (page 330) which describes the entire template language available.

Editing an Existing Fact Type

To edit an existing fact type, highlight the name of the fact you want to edit, and click on the **"Edit"** button. RootsMagic will display the "Edit Fact Type" dialog with the current settings for the fact. If you are editing one of RootsMagic's built-in fact types, some of the fields will be disabled so that you can't change them. Make any changes you want, then click the **"OK"** button to save the changes.

Deleting an Existing Fact Type

To delete a fact type from the fact list, simply highlight the fact name in the fact list, and click the **"Delete"** button. RootsMagic will ask if you really want to delete the fact type. You can only delete fact types that you have added yourself. RootsMagic won't let you delete any of the built-in fact types.

Searching for Information

Searching for needles in a haystack

Although you can move through your family on the various views, there are times when you need to find someone buried deep in your database.

 To find a person in your database, simply click the "Search" button on the toolbar and the RootsMagic Explorer will appear. You can also select **"Search, Person list"** from the main menu, or press **Ctrl+F** to bring up this screen.

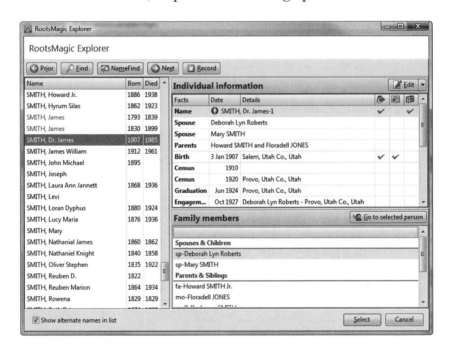

The left side of the Explorer is an alphabetical list of every person in your database. You can use the up and down arrow keys to move the highlight bar from one name to another. The **PgUp, PgDn, Home** and **End** keys also move the highlight bar.

The right side of the Explorer displays information about the person highlighted in the left column. The top list displays all the facts (events) in the person's life, while the lower list displays the family (parents, siblings, spouses, and children) of the highlighted person. As you move the bar in the left column to different individuals, the information in the right side of the screen changes. When the person you are looking for is highlighted, click the OK button (or press Enter) to close the search screen and display the person on the main screen.

Finding a Person by Name

To find a person when you know their name, just begin typing the name in the Explorer, last name first. As you type the name, the highlight bar will move through the list to highlight the closest matching name. Just type the last name, then a comma, then begin typing the first name.

RootsMagic also includes a feature called NameFind. When you click the "NameFind" button RootsMagic will display a dialog where you can enter a given name and a surname.

When you fill in the name fields and click OK, RootsMagic will search for the first person that matches the name you enter. The nice thing is that it doesn't just search for the name entered in a person's edit screen. It will also search for married names as well. So if you search for Mary Smith, it will find Mary Ann Jones if she is married to William Smith.

> ☺ Tip
>
> When typing a name in the search screen, you can type a comma to finish out a surname. For example, if you are typing **"Christiansen, John"** and **"Ch"** has placed you on the first **"Christiansen"** in your database, just type a comma and RootsMagic will let you start typing the first name without typing the rest of the surname.

Finding a Person by Other Information

To find a person (or group of people) when you don't know their name, click the **"Find"** button at the bottom of the RootsMagic Explorer and the "Search" dialog will appear.

Don't be intimidated by the search dialog. It simply wants you to tell it how to find a person. You tell it something about the person you are looking for, and RootsMagic will search through the entire database looking for someone that matches what you entered.

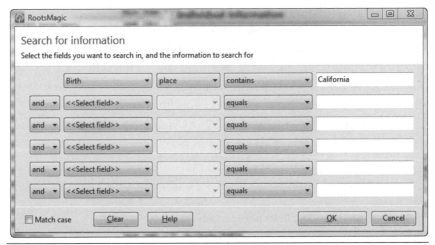

You can search just about any information for a person; names, dates, places, facts, sex, notes, and sources. When the search examines each person's information, it compares that information with whatever you enter in the "Search for?" field. You even get to select "how" it is compared.

Let's try an example. If you wanted to find everyone born in California, this is what you would do.

1) Click the drop arrow on the first field that says "<<Select field>>". A list of search fields will appear.
2) Select "Birth" from the list.
3) From the next field select "Place".
4) We now need to tell RootsMagic what we want to look for in people's birth place. Since we want to find people whose birth place contains California, select "contains" from the next field, and enter "California" in the last field on the line.
5) **That's it.** Just click the OK button and RootsMagic will move the highlight bar in the search screen to the first person whose birth place contains the text "California". You can then click on the "Next >>" button to have RootsMagic find the next person who matches that criteria. The "<< Prior" button can be used to move back to the previous match that RootsMagic found.

Although we only completed one row in the "Search" dialog, RootsMagic provides 6 such rows, so your search can be as complex as you want. To the left of each row is another list box where you can select between "And" and "Or". This tells RootsMagic how to handle the multiple "criteria" rows. "And" means that RootsMagic must find each item to consider the person a match. "Or" means that RootsMagic should consider the person a match if any of the items match.

For example, if you entered these two lines of criteria:

Birth place contains Utah AND Death place contains Iowa

Then RootsMagic will only find people who were born in Utah AND died in Iowa. Both parts have to be true.

If you entered:

Birth place contains Utah OR Death place contains Iowa

then RootsMagic will find people who were born in Utah or people who died in Iowa. Only one part has to be true, although both can be.

In our example above, we used a "condition" of **"contains"**. Any time you select a field to search, RootsMagic provides a large number of ways to search the field. These "comparison" types depend on the type of field you select.

If search field is a...	You can compare in these ways...
Date	equal to, not equal to, is before, is after, is blank, is not blank, contains, does not contain
Place, Name, or Text	equal to, not equal to, contains, does not contain, less than, greater than, less than or equal, greater than or equal, sounds like, is blank, is not blank
Note	Contains, does not contain, is blank, is not blank
Source	Exists, does not exist, contains, does not contain, is blank, is not blank (for each part of the source or citation)

Editing From the Explorer

RootsMagic also allows you to edit a person from the Explorer. Just click the Edit button and RootsMagic will open the person's edit screen. This is especially useful when you need to edit a number of people and don't want to keep switching back and forth between the search screen and the main screen.

If you click the little down arrow on the right side of the Edit button a menu will appear where you can edit notes, sources, and other pieces of information. If you are highlighting a specific fact you will be able to edit that fact's note, source or media.

If you have LDS options turned on, an LDS button will display next to the Edit button and will let you edit the LDS facts from a template.

There is a button in the header of the Family members section which will move the selection in the Explorer to the currently highlighted family member when you click it.

Finding a Family

RootsMagic provides a family list that you can bring up by selecting **"Search, Family list"** from the main menu.

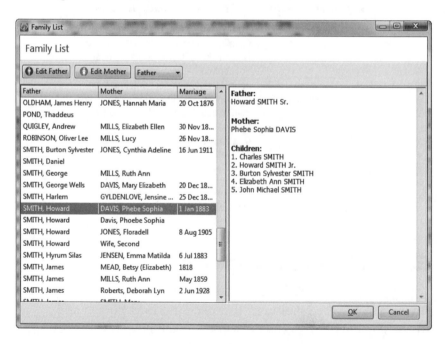

The family list will list the husband, wife, and the marriage date. As you move the highlight in the list from family to family, the right side of the screen will show the parents and children in the family. The data for the family list needs to be collected and regenerated each time you select it.

You can sort the family list by the husband's name or by the wife's maiden name by selecting from the **"Sort by"** drop list.

You can search for individuals in the family list by typing the name of the husband or wife (depending on the sort order).

You can edit the highlighted husband or wife by clicking on the "Edit father" or "Edit mother" button.

If you click the **OK** button, RootsMagic will bring that couple up on the main screen.

Finding a Previously Viewed Person

You may often find yourself wanting to return to a person you just recently viewed or worked on. RootsMagic maintains a "history list" of the most recently visited individuals in your database. Select **"Search > History"** from the menu to open the history panel on the side list.

Finding a Person on the Internet

To find a person on the internet, just switch to the WebSearch view as described on page 19.

Notes – Telling Your Story

Anybody can make history. Only a great man can write it.
- Oscar Wilde

If names, dates and places are the bones of your family history, notes are the meat on those bones. **A note** is where you enter stories or more details about a person, family, or fact. For example, a birth note might include the name of the doctor that delivered the person, who witnessed the birth, how much the person weighed at birth, or other stories about the birth.

Where Can I Use Notes?

Notes can be associated with people, families, or facts in a person's life.

> ➤ **Individual notes** are tied to a person. These notes are where you enter information about a person that won't fit in one of the facts for the person. To enter or edit an individual note, open the person's edit screen, highlight the first row (their name) and click the "Notes" button.

> ➤ **Family notes** are tied to a family. These notes are where you enter information about a family that you don't want to enter separately for the father, mother and children. To enter or edit a family note you can open the person's edit screen, highlight the row with the desired family, and click the "Notes" button.

> ➤ **Fact notes** are tied to a fact in a person's life. These notes are where you enter more detailed information about the fact. To enter or edit a fact note open the person's edit screen, highlight the fact, then click the "Notes" button.

And finally, you can edit any note from the RootsMagic Explorer
by highlighting the desired person, family, or fact and clicking the
"Note" button to the right of it.

Note Editor

When you edit a note, the note editor will appear. You can just
begin typing in the note. The title bar of the note dialog will tell
you what type of note you are entering, and who you are entering
it for. In the dialog below, we are entering a "Birth" note for Dr.
James Smith.

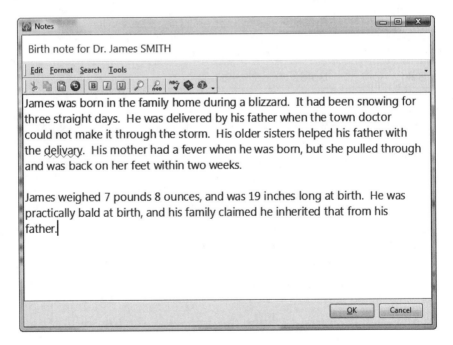

You can access the edit commands from the editor menu,
toolbar, or by right clicking the mouse button.

Edit Command	Command Description	Hot Key
Cut	Places the marked text on the clipboard, then removes the marked text from the note.	Ctrl+X
Copy	Places the marked text on the clipboard.	Ctrl+C
Paste	Inserts any text from the clipboard to the note at the position of the blinking cursor.	Ctrl+V
Undo	Undoes the last editing command.	Ctrl+Z
Find	Lets you search for text within the note.	Ctrl+F
Find Next	Repeats the last search.	Ctrl+N
Replace	Lets you do a search and replace within the note.	Ctrl+H
Open	Read text into the note from a file.	Ctrl+O
Save	Save the note to a text file.	Ctrl+S
Spell check	Spell checks the current note. The spell checker is described in more detail in the chapter titled Tools (page 271).	F7
Bold	**Bolds** the selected text.	Ctrl+B
Italics	*Italicizes* the selected text.	Ctrl+I
Underline	<u>Underlines</u> the selected text.	Ctrl+U
Character map	Opens the character map to let you select special (accented) characters.	Ctrl+T

If you want to change the font used in the note editor (to make it larger for example) do "Tools > Program Options" from the menu and you can choose a new font. This font is only used for the data entry screen. The font for printing notes is selected in the separate report dialog screens.

When you are finished editing the note, click the OK button and RootsMagic will save the note and attach it to the appropriate person, family, or fact.

Private Notes

RootsMagic allows you to make parts of your notes private. Just place curly brackets { } around any text in the note that you want to be considered private.

When you print reports, export GEDCOM files, or create websites, RootsMagic will give you the option to include or ignore private notes. If you don't include private notes, RootsMagic will strip out everything between the curly brackets, including the brackets themselves.

If you do include private notes, you will also have the option whether to strip out the brackets when printing.

For example, if you have the following note:

This is a line of text.{ This is a private note.} This is another line of text.

choosing to ignore private notes would result in:

This is a line of text. This is another line of text.

Including private notes would result in either:

This is a line of text.{ This is a private note.} This is another line of text.

or

This is a line of text. This is a private note. This is another line of text.

depending on whether you chose to strip the brackets.

Sources – Proving It

Opinion has a significance proportioned to the sources that sustain it - Benjamin Cardozo

One of the most important things you can do when researching your family history is to document your information. Without proper documentation, the data you hand down to your descendants will probably have to be checked all over again.

Sources allow you to document where your information about a person, family, or fact came from. For example, a birth source might be a birth certificate, a baby announcement, or a family bible with details of the person's birth.

Where Can I Use Sources?

Sources can be associated with individuals, families, or facts in a person's life.

> ➢ **Individual sources** are tied to a person. These sources are where you enter information about a person that won't fit in one of the facts for the person. To enter or edit individual sources, open the person's edit screen, highlight the first row (their name) and click the "Sources" button.
> ➢ **Family sources** are tied to a family. These sources are where you enter information about a family that you don't want to enter separately for the father, mother and children. To enter or edit family sources open the person's edit screen, highlight the row with the desired family, and click the "Sources" button.
> ➢ **Fact sources** are tied to a fact in a person's life. These sources are where you enter more detailed information about the fact. To enter or edit fact sources open the person's edit screen, highlight the fact and click the "Sources" button.

> **☺ Tip**
>
> **To quickly edit a fact source**, just click your mouse in the source column of the fact list next to the desired fact.

And finally, you can edit any source from the RootsMagic Explorer by highlighting the desired person, family, or fact and clicking the source button to the right of it.

Sources and Citations

To use sources to document your family, you need to understand the difference between a Source and a Citation.

A Source is the actual paper or document that provides information about your family. For example, a source might be a birth certificate, a book, or a tombstone. When you enter a source, you will enter information about the source, like a description, title, author, publisher, etc. You can also select a "Repository", which is just a fancy word for the place where the source is stored (like a library, courthouse, or even your own home).

A Citation is a reference to a source. By "citing" a source, you can allow a source to be entered just once, but cited many times. For example, if you cite a book as a source, you only enter the details about the book once (title, author, publisher), but you can cite it as many times as you want. The citation includes both the source, and also "source details" that are specific to that reference, such as the page number, volume, or film number.

As an example, if a person's birth were mentioned on page 93 of a book, you would cite the book as a source, and put "page 93" as the citation details. Citations for other people or facts might also cite the same source, but would likely have different details (page numbers). You can also enter actual text from the source, as well as any comments you have about this usage of the source.

Entering Sources for People or Facts

When you click the **"Sources"** button for a person, fact or family, RootsMagic will display the Citation Manager for that item. This screen is a list of all the sources that have been cited (referenced) for that item. For example, a birth Citation Manager screen might look like the one below, with 2 sources being cited: a birth certificate and a journal entry.

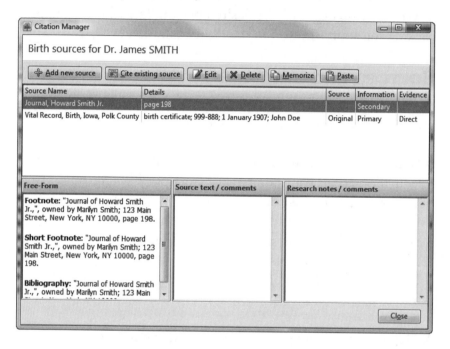

When you highlight a citation in the list, RootsMagic will display the detailed information on that citation in the panels below. You can resize the window or the panels to see the information better if desired.

To add a source citation you can either click the **"Add new source"** button, which lets you add a brand new source, or the **"Cite existing source"** button, which lets you select from a list of sources which have already been entered. This list of existing sources is known as the "Master Source List" and is described on page 96.

To edit a source, highlight the citation in the list and click the "Edit" button. RootsMagic will bring up the "Edit Source" screen described in the next section.

To delete a citation, highlight the citation in the list, and click the "Delete" button. RootsMagic will ask you to confirm that you want to delete the citation. Deleting the citation will not remove the source itself, just this reference to the source.

The Citation Manager also offers **"Memorize" and "Paste" commands**, which will memorize the highlighted citation (including both source and citation details). You can then paste it into the citation list for other people, families, or facts.

Adding a New Source

To add a new source, click the "Add new source" button on the Citation Manager or Master Source List. RootsMagic will bring up a list of source types to choose from. Don't be intimidated by the sheer number; there are some shortcuts RootsMagic offers to help you out.

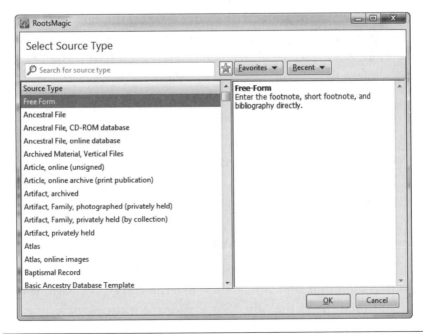

Search for source type   Rather than scroll through the long list of source types, enter what you are looking for in the "Search for source type" field. RootsMagic will filter the list down to only those source types that match what you are looking for. For example, if you want to enter a birth certificate, type "birth certificate" into that field and the list will filter to only those source types.

Favorites ▼   Although there are over 400 different source types built in, most of us will only use a very small number of them. When you find a source type you think you will be using on a regular basis, highlight it in the list and then click the star button to make it a favorite. You can then select that source type quickly by clicking the Favorites button rather than scrolling through the long list.

Recent ▼   Any time you use a new source type, RootsMagic will keep track of it. You can access these recently used source types by click the Recent button.

As you scroll through the list of source types, RootsMagic will display information about that source type on the right side of the screen, including the reference that the source type is based on. Here is a list to tell you which reference each of those cryptic codes refers to.

- EE = Evidence Explained
- E! = Evidence
- CYS = Cite Your Sources
- QS = Quick Sheet
- AQS = Ancestry Quick Sheet

Free Form vs. SourceWizard

Notice that the first source type in the list is called "Free Form" (even though that isn't alphabetical like the rest of the list). It is a little different from the other SourceWizard source types.

If you select a free form source, RootsMagic will let you enter the footnote, short footnote, and bibliography directly for that source.

If you select one of the SourceWizard source types (those that aren't free form), RootsMagic will provide specific fields for you to fill in for that source type. Just fill in the blanks and RootsMagic will write the properly formatted footnote, short footnote, and bibliography for you.

Free Form Sources

Free form sources require you to enter the footnote, short footnote, and bibliography directly. If you want your sources to be entered in a proper format, this does require you to have some knowledge of how to put together a footnote or bibliography entry. When you select a free form source, you will get a screen that looks like this.

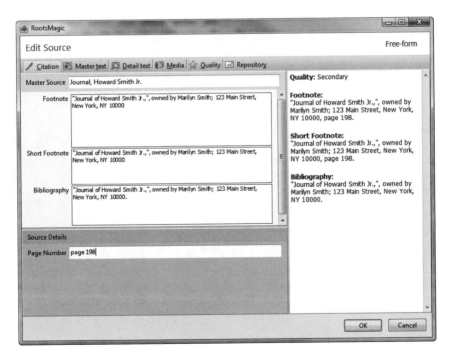

You do have some basic formatting features available (bold, italics, underline) by clicking the right mouse button in those fields.

A footnote is a note of text which cites a source for something in the report. The footnote can appear at the bottom of a page (which is why it is called a "footnote"), but it can also be at the end of the report, in which case it is often called an "endnote". It is usually tagged to the text in the report with a superscript number.

A bibliography is an alphabetical list of the sources used in a report that appears at the end of the report. A source is only listed once in the bibliography regardless of how many times it is "cited" in the report.

SourceWizard Sources

But what if you don't know how to write a footnote or bibliography? The SourceWizard is RootsMagic's tool that will write properly formatted sources for you. When you choose a non-freeform source you just choose the type of source, fill in the blanks, and RootsMagic writes the footnote, short footnote and bibliography.

SourceWizard source types are based on a number of different references: Evidence Explained, Evidence! and the various Quick Sheets by Elizabeth Shown Mills, and Cite Your Sources by Richard Lackey.

When you select a source type, you will get a screen that looks like this (of course the fields will be different depending on which particular source type you choose).

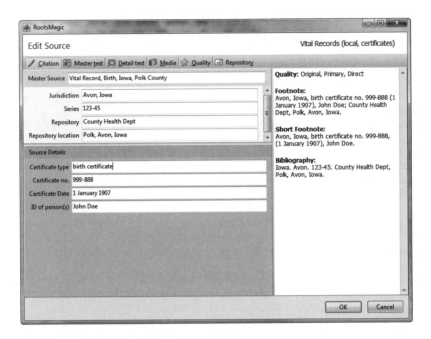

Source and Detail Fields

As you fill in the fields in the Master Source and Source Details sections, the SourceWizard will write the properly formatted footnote, short footnote and bibliography on the right side of the screen.

Each field will have a gray text hint in the field to let you know what kind of data it is expecting. Some fields have more options than will fit in a short hint. Those fields will have a blue button with a question mark that you can click to get more help.

As you enter text in various fields you will notice the fields are actually quite smart. For example, a name field (like author) knows how to display the name as "John Doe", "Doe", or even "Doe, John" depending on how it needs to be formatted. But you only have to enter it as "John Doe".

When you save the new source, RootsMagic will ask you to enter a name for the source. This the text you want displayed in the master source list. This is a required field (meaning you can't leave it blank). Since RootsMagic sorts the master source list alphabetically, you can use this name to make the sources sort the way you want. For example, you could enter the names of census sources so that they group in an understandable fashion, like:

Census, Iowa, 1870
Census, Iowa, 1880
Census, Iowa, 1900
Census, New Mexico, 1910
Census, New Mexico, 1920
Census, Utah, 1910

Master Text

The Master Text tab lets you enter text or comments which apply to the source itself. Actual text from the source might be a transcription of the preface of a book. Any comments would apply to the book as a whole, such as a description of the quality of the book. You can also enter an optional source reference number to tie your master source to your physical filing system. If you assign file numbers to the hard copies of your certificates, books, and other sources, you can enter that number here.

Detail Text

The Detail Text tab lets you enter research notes or comments about the specific citation. You might want to enter a summary, transcription, or extraction of the part of the source you are using in this instance. You can also enter any comments about the research notes as well. Entering a detail reference number on this page lets you tie this detail to your physical filing system. This is useful if (for example) you assign file numbers to page numbers within books, rather than just to the book itself.

Citation Quality

RootsMagic also allows you to enter a "quality" for the citation. This quality follows the standards set down by the Board for Certification of Genealogists (BCG).

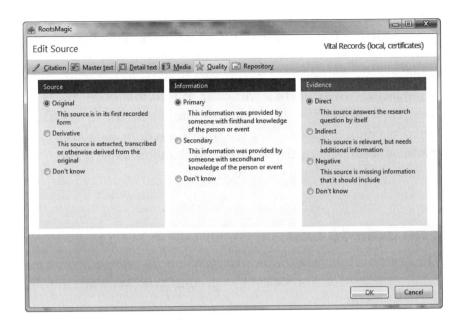

Rather than just a "good" or "bad" type of quality rating, RootsMagic lets you choose the quality of the source itself, the information in the source, and the evidence the source is attempting to answer.

The Quality tab will only show when you are editing a citation (not when editing from the master source list). The reason the quality is assigned to the citation rather than the source is because a single source can have varying reliability depending on why it is cited. For example, a birth certificate might include primary information for the person's birth, but only secondary information when used for the parent's birth date.

Repository

When adding or editing a source, you can click the "Repository" tab and RootsMagic will let you enter both a primary and a secondary repository for the source. The repository is the place where the source was found; the library, archive, courthouse, etc. You can also enter the "Call number" within the repository where the source can be found. More information on this can be found on page 112.

Media

If you have a scanned image of the source or details, you can add it on the Media tab. Source media might be an image of a certificate, tombstone, or a picture of a book. Detail media might include an image of a particular page in that book that is being cited. When you are editing a source citation you can filter the media item to show either the source media or the detail media, and can add media to either. Multimedia albums are described in more detail on page 115.

The Source List

The heart of RootsMagic's source capabilities is the Source list. You can access the Source list by selecting **"Lists > Source list"** from the main menu.

The left side of the Source list is a list of all your sources. The right side of the screen displays information about the source highlighted in the left column. As you move the bar in the left column to a different source, the information in the right side of the screen changes.

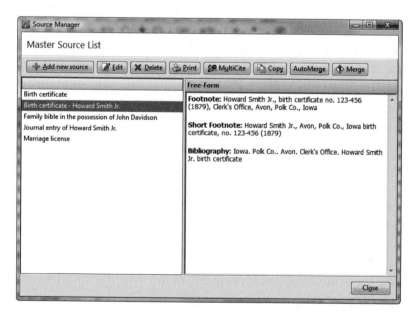

Adding a Source

To add a source click the **"Add new source"** button, which lets you add a brand new source (see page 89) for more details on adding sources).

Editing a Source

To edit a source, highlight the name of the source in the Source list, then click the **"Edit"** button. RootsMagic will display the same dialog that you used when entering the source. Any changes you make here will be applied every place this source is used. Simply make the changes or additions you want and then click the **OK** button.

Deleting a Source

To delete a source, highlight the name of the source in the Source list, then click the **"Delete"** button. RootsMagic will ask if you really want to delete the source. If you select **"Yes"**, then RootsMagic will check if there are any people, families, or facts that cite the source. If there are, you will again be asked if you really want to delete the source. If you delete a source that has been cited, all the citations of that source will be deleted from the database as well. If you want to see which people, families, or facts are citing the source, you can use the Print command described below.

Printing Your Sources

If you want to find which people, families, and facts are citing a particular source, highlight the source in the Source Manager, then click the **"Print"** button. RootsMagic will print up the report dialog for the Source list (described on page 172).

Adding a Source to a Group of People

If you have a source that you need to add to more than one person, highlight the source in the Source list and click the "Multi-Cite" button. RootsMagic will bring up the selection screen (page 210) so that you can mark all the people you want to add the source to. RootsMagic will add the source to everyone you select.

Copying a Source

You may find a need to add a source that is very similar to another source already entered in the source list. In this case you can highlight the similar source in the source list and click the Copy button. RootsMagic will make an exact copy of the source which you can edit. The new source will have the same name as the original source except with (copy) added to the end of the name.

Merging Duplicate Sources

There may be times when you find multiple copies of the same source in the Source Manager. This sometimes happens when importing a GEDCOM file that came from a program that doesn't allow you to reuse sources.

RootsMagic offers two options for merging duplicate sources.

1. To merge all exact duplicate sources into a single source open the source list (**"Lists, Source list"** from the menu) and click the AutoMerge button. RootsMagic will merge all the exact duplicate sources in your database. If there is any difference in the source footnote, short footnote, bibliography, actual text or comments field, the sources will not be merged.

2. To merge two sources (even if one is a little different from the other), highlight the primary source in the source list and click the "Merge" button. The "Merge" button will change to "Select dup". You can then highlight the duplicate source in the source list and click the "Select dup" button. RootsMagic will ask if you want to merge the duplicate source into the primary source. RootsMagic does not combine the text from the two sources. It only keeps the text from the primary source and merges citations of the duplicate source into the primary source.

Creating New Source Types

While RootsMagic provides over 400 different source types, there may be times when you want to create your own source type that isn't already built in.

To see a list of all the built-in source types, select **"Lists > Source templates"** from the RootsMagic menu.

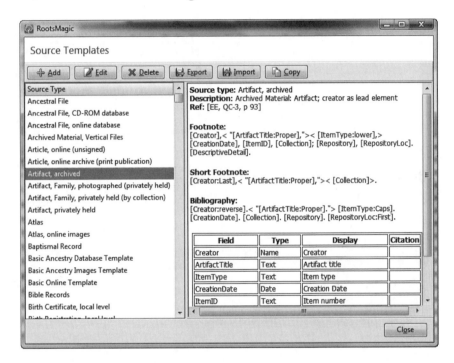

Adding a New Source Type

To create a new source type, click the "Add" button to open the Source Template Editor.

There are two steps to creating a new source template; adding the fields which the user will fill in with data, and telling RootsMagic how to put those fields together to make a proper source citation.

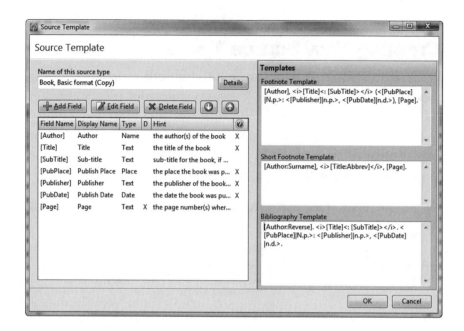

Adding Fields to the Source Template

To add a field, click the "Add Field" button and fill in the screen that appears.

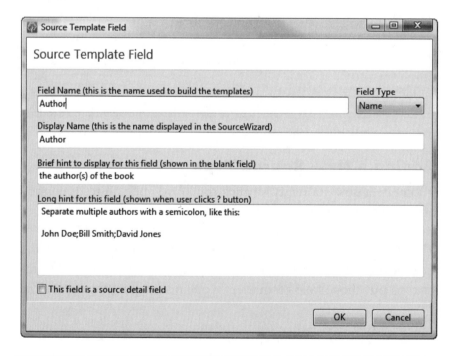

There are several pieces of information you need to enter for each field:

- **Field Name** - This is the name that you will use when creating the templates. It can't contain any spaces, and you might want to keep it kind of short but readable.
- **Field Type** - Choose from Text, Name, Date, or Place. This determines what features RootsMagic will apply to this field.
- **Display Name** - This is the name of the field as it is displayed in the SourceWizard when entering a source of this type.
- **Brief Hint** - This is the gray text which is shown in the field when it is blank. Try to keep it short so it will fit and display in the field.
- **Long Hint** - This can be used to enter a hint that is longer. If you enter a long hint, RootsMagic will display a help button when the user is entering the source.
- **This field is a source detail field** - This is a very important option. It tells RootsMagic whether this field is part of the Master Source, or part of the source details. This is useful for fields like page numbers which are different for each use of that source.

You can edit or delete fields from the Source Template Editor, as well as rearrange the order of the fields using the up and down arrow buttons.

Creating the Source Templates

After you have added the fields for your new source type, you need to tell RootsMagic how to put them together to create the footnote, short footnote, and bibliography. The Source Template Editor has 3 fields for you to do just that.

To create the templates you can use the fields you created in the first step (put them in square brackets) and include the punctuation you want between them. For example:

[Author], [Title] ([PubPlace]: [Publisher], [PubDate]), [Page].

When RootsMagic has to put that source together, it will replace [Author] with whatever you enter into the author field on the source screen, [Title] with whatever you enter into the title screen, and so on.

Now of course that is a very basic template, and you will want to fix it up some more. Since you would want the title to be displayed in italics you can put <i> and </i> around it, like this:

[Author], <i>[Title]</i> ([PubPlace]: [Publisher], [PubDate]), [Page].

Those two little symbols tell RootsMagic to turn italics on and then off.

But what if there were cases where a page number (the [Page] field) might not be entered by the user? RootsMagic lets you use angle brackets < > to tell the source template not to print something unless the user actually fills in the field. So if you did this:

[Author], <i>[Title]</i> ([PubPlace]: [Publisher], [PubDate])<, [Page]>.

those angle brackets tell RootsMagic not to print the comma or the [Page] field unless the [Page] field actually contains something.

There are a **ton** of other things you can do with source templates (way too many to talk about here). There is an appendix at the end of the book (page 330) which describes the entire template language available.

Editing and Deleting Source Types

You can click the Edit button to edit a source type that you have created. You can't edit one of the built-in source types since they are custom designed based on *Evidence Explained*, *Evidence!*, and several other standard formats.

> ☺ **Tip**
>
> If you want a source type that is very much like one of the existing ones, highlight that source type and click the "Copy" button. RootsMagic will make an exact copy of that source type which you can then edit (and rename so that you know it is yours).

When you edit a source template, you will use the exact same screens and techniques described in the previous section (Adding a New Source Type).

If you want to delete one of your own source templates, highlight it in the list and click the "Delete" button. As with editing, you can't delete any of the built-in source types.

Importing and Exporting Source Types

RootsMagic makes it possible to share a source template you have created with other people. Just highlight the template in the list and click the Export button. RootsMagic will open the standard File Save dialog so that you can save that template to a file.

You can then give a copy of that file to another RootsMagic user and they can click the Import button on the Source Types list to import that new source type into their file.

Places - Mapping, Geocoding, and Gazetteers

RootsMagic includes a worldwide place database with over 3.5 million place names. This place database can be directly accessed in the Gazetteer, and is also used by RootsMagic's geocoding and mapping features.

Gazetteer

The Gazetteer is an easy way to look up places around the world. Select **"Tools > Gazetteer"** from the menu, then enter part of a name to search for (it can be a city, state, country, etc). The gazetteer will display places in the world which match what you entered.

You can select a place in the list and copy it to the clipboard so you can paste it elsewhere, or you can view an online map showing where in the world that place is located.

Place List and Geocoding

Whenever you enter a place in RootsMagic, that place is added to a list so that you can reuse it over and over.

RootsMagic allows you to make changes to the Place List by selecting "Lists > Place list" from the main menu. The following list will appear.

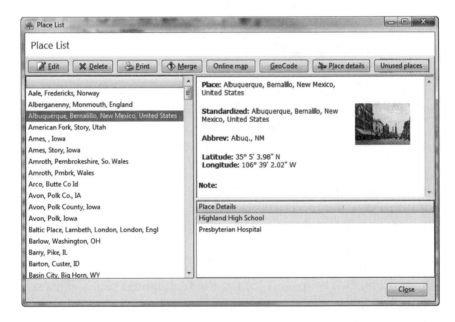

To edit a place in your place list, highlight the name of the place by clicking on it with your mouse, then click the **"Edit"** button. A dialog will appear where you can edit the place name, the latitude and longitude for the place, a "standardized" or abbreviated place name, a note or place history for the place and media items (pictures) of the place. All items except the actual place name are optional.

You can click the GeoCode button to automatically fill in the latitude, longitude, and standardized place name if RootsMagic can find it in its 3.5 million name place database. Then you can click the "Use standardized place" button if you want to replace the original place you entered with the standardized version.

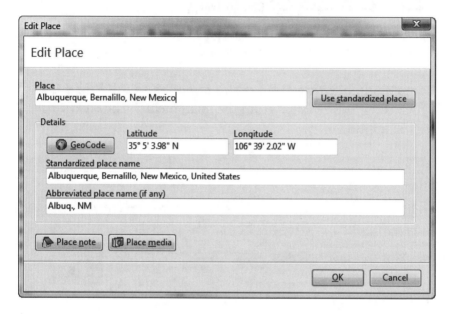

Just change the place name the way you want, then click the OK button to save the modified place name. Every fact that uses that place name will be adjusted to use the modified place name.

You can also click the "Place media" button to open the media album (described on page 115) for the highlighted place. This is useful for adding a picture of a home, cemetery plot, or other landmark to a place.

To delete a place in your place list, highlight the name of the place in the list, then click the "Delete" button. RootsMagic will ask if you really want to delete the place name. If you do delete the place name, any facts that happened in that place will have their place field erased.

To print information from your place list, highlight the name of a place in the list, then click the "Print" button. This dialog will appear which will let you pick one of 4 types of place list printouts. Select the type of printout you want, then click the OK button.

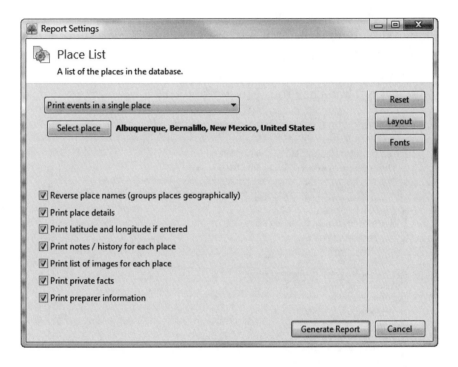

1. **Print all places in database** will print a list of every place in your database.
2. **Print all places (including events)** will print a list of every place in your database, along with all the events which occurred in each of those places.
3. **Print events in a single place** will print a list of every fact in your database that occurred in the highlighted place. It will list the person's name, fact type, and date for each fact.
4. **Print events near a place** will print a list of every event which happened within a selected distance. For example, you can print every event which happened within 50 miles of Dallas, Texas.

RootsMagic can also print the latitude and longitude (if entered), place notes or a list of images linked to each place. You can also use the "Print private facts" checkbox to tell RootsMagic whether to print facts that you have marked as private.

You can combine duplicate entries in your place list with the "Merge" button. At some point you may find your place list cluttered with multiple copies of the same place, each spelled just a little differently. This is especially common after importing information from a GEDCOM file. Highlight the place you want to keep and click the "Merge" button.

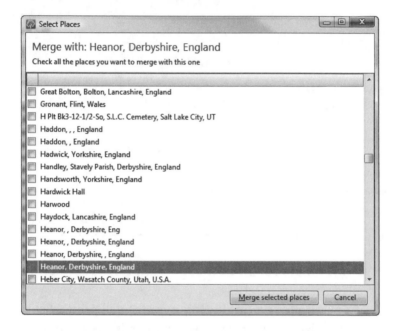

RootsMagic will display a list of the places in your file. Just put a checkmark next to the places you want to merge into that place and click the "Merge selected places" button.

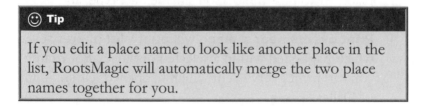

😊 Tip

If you edit a place name to look like another place in the list, RootsMagic will automatically merge the two place names together for you.

To view where a place is located on a map, highlight the place in the place list and click the "Online Map" button. RootsMagic will open a browser window with a map showing the location.

You can geocode all the places in your place list at once by clicking the GeoCode button on the place list. RootsMagic will look up every place in your file in the 3.5 million name place database. If it finds a match it will fill in the latitude, longitude, and standardized place name for each place. After it has processed every place in your list, it will display a list of any places that it couldn't geocode. You can select a match manually for those places.

If a place in your place list has place details, you can click the "Place details" button to bring them up in a list. Place details are the specific locations you might have entered when editing a person. So while the place may contain the city, county, state, and country, the place details might be the name of a hospital, cemetery, or other specific location within that place. You can edit individual place details, including the latitude, longitude, note, and media items for the detail.

To view a list of places in your place list which aren't being used by any event, click the "Unused places" button. You can delete any unused place from this list.

CountyCheck

RootsMagic's CountyCheck feature uses a different (specialized) database than the other place features. CountyCheck can tell you whether a county, state, or country existed on a particular date. Currently the CountyCheck feature is limited to places in the USA, Canada, United Kingdom, and Australia.

Live CountyCheck

As you enter events, CountyCheck will look at the date and place of the event and let you know whether the county, state or country existed on that date. If possible, RootsMagic will offer a suggestion for you to use. You can turn the live CountyCheck feature on or off in the Tools > Program options screen.

CountyCheck Report

If you prefer to see all of CountyCheck's recommendations all at once, you can choose the CountyCheck report. This report is described in more detail on page 153.

Mapping

RootsMagic makes it easy to view online maps of places in your database, as well as where events in people's lives occurred. This feature does require an internet connection. Select "Tools > Mapping" from the menu and the RootsMagic Mapping screen will appear.

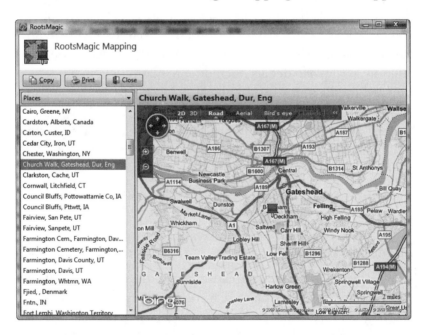

The left side of the mapping display is a list of all the places in your database. Just click on a place in the list and RootsMagic will display the map of that place.

You can switch between the "Road" view which looks like most maps, and the "Aerial" view which is a satellite image of the map. You can zoom in or out to see more or less detail in either of these views. You can also print the map or copy it to the clipboard with the "Print" and "Copy" buttons.

To see where events in a person's life occurred, click the drop list above the list of places and change it from "Places" to "People".

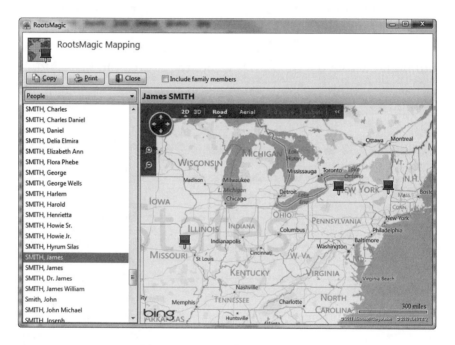

RootsMagic will change the list to display all of the people in your database. Just click on a person and RootsMagic will display the map with red pins where the events in that person's life happened. You can move your mouse over any of those pins to see a list of the events that happened in that location. If you mark the checkbox named "Include family members" (above the map), RootsMagic will also display events from the lives of the selected person's immediate family members.

Repositories – Where Is It?

Now where did I find that source?

Almost as important as documenting where you found your information, is where that information is located. These locations, whether they be libraries, archives, courthouses, or even your own home, are called "repositories".

The Repository Page

When adding or editing a source, you can click the "Repository" tab and RootsMagic will let you enter both a primary and a secondary repository for the source. You can also enter the **"Call number"** within the repository where the source can be found.

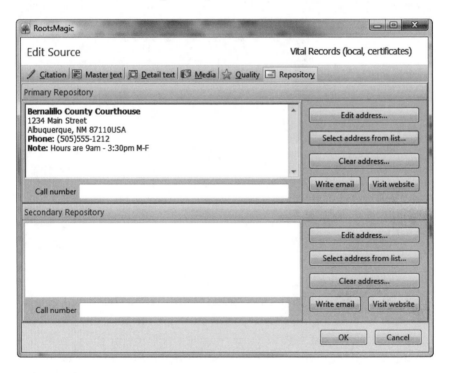

To enter (or edit) a repository, click the "Edit repository" button to the right of the repository area. RootsMagic will open an entry screen where you can add the name, address, phone number, fax, email and website of the repository. You can also add notes about the repository like directions, business hours or names of employees you need to work with.

The "Send Email" and "Visit website" buttons make it quick to send an email or visit the website of the repository.

When you have filled in the blanks, click the **OK** button and RootsMagic will return to the source's repository page.

If the source is in a repository that you have already entered, click the "Select repository from list" button, and RootsMagic will open the Repository list, described in the next section. You can choose the repository from the list.

The Repository List

The Repository list is simply a list of places, such as libraries, archives, courthouses, fellow researchers; or any place that a source might be found. **To access the Repository list**, select "Lists, Repository list" from the main menu.

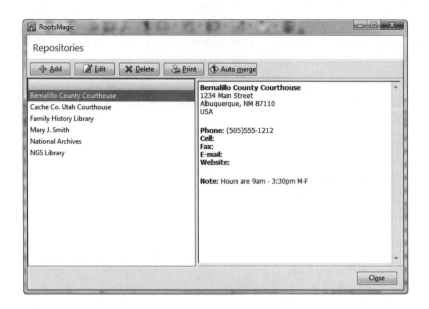

To add a new repository click the "Add" button, and enter the repository as described in the previous section.

To edit a repository, highlight the name of the repository in the list, then click the "Edit" button. RootsMagic will display the same dialog that you used when entering the repository. Simply make the changes or additions you want, then click the OK button.

To delete a repository, highlight the name of the repository in the list, then click the "Delete" button. RootsMagic will ask if you really want to delete the repository. If you delete a repository that has a source, to do task, or correspondence referencing it, the source, task, or correspondence will have their repository or contact field cleared.

To print a list of all information associated with a repository, highlight the repository and click the "Print" button. RootsMagic will open the report dialog for you to print the repository list for that repository (see page 171 for more details).

To merge duplicate repositories, click the "Auto merge" button.

Pictures, Sound, and Video

One picture is worth a thousand words. - Fred R. Barnard

As computers become more powerful, and the cost of scanners and digital cameras come down, it becomes easier to add photos to your computerized genealogy. RootsMagic provides a Multimedia Album for each person, family, fact, source, citation and place in your database. This album can hold scanned photos, files, sound clips, and video clips.

To view the media album for a person, open the person's edit screen then click the Media button. The media album will display all media attached to the person, his families, and facts. You can filter the media album to only show the media items for a single fact or family by clicking the drop list labeled "All media" above the images. As a shortcut to this filtering, you can click the box in the media column next to a fact instead of clicking the Media button on the person's edit screen.

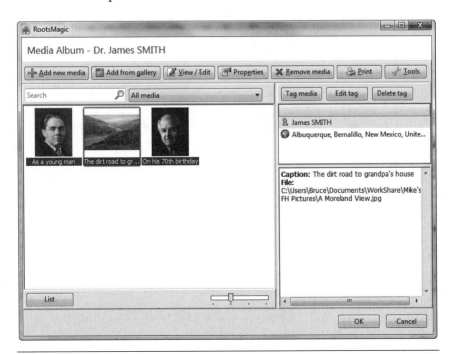

From the media album you can add, edit, print and remove media, enter captions and descriptions, and tag images with the records that they apply to.

Adding Media

There are two ways to add an item to the media album; adding it as a new item, or linking to one you have previously added to another person, family, fact, source, citation or place.

Adding a New Media Item

To add a new media item click the **"Add new media"** button on the album. The following screen will appear.

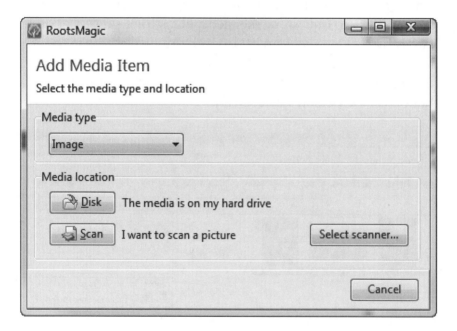

Select the type of media you want to add (Image, File, Sound or Video), then choose whether the file is already on your disk, or if you want to run your scanner to scan it in.

If the media is on the disk, click the **"Disk"** button to find the media using the Windows file dialog.

If the photo hasn't been scanned yet, and you have a scanner attached to your computer, just click the **"Scan"** button, and RootsMagic will run your scanner's software for you. When the scanner software is finished, RootsMagic will ask you to save the scanned photo. Just enter a filename and image file type, and RootsMagic will do the rest. It may be necessary to use the "Select scanner" button if your scanner isn't set as the default on your system.

☺ **Tip**

To bring a photo into RootsMagic, you need to "scan" the photo using a scanner. A scanner scans the photo (much like a copy machine) and then saves that scanned image in a graphics file. If you don't have a scanner yourself, you may have a friend or relative who does. If not, there are many copy centers that offer scanning services. You can take your photos in and leave with a disk of scanned images that can be used in RootsMagic and other programs.

For some great tips on scanning, you can visit the website at: **http://www.scantips.com**.

Adding a document, sound clip or video clip to a person's album works exactly the same way as adding a photo, except that the **"Scan"** button is not available, nor are the **"Primary photo"** or **"Include in scrapbook"** checkboxes.

Adding a Previously Added Media Item

To reuse a previously added media item click the **"Add from gallery"** button on the album. The Gallery is an album of all the media items you have added to the current database. Just highlight the desired item and click the "Select" button.

Entering the Media Properties

After you have selected or scanned the desired media item, RootsMagic will display the properties form so that you can enter a caption, description and other information about the media item.

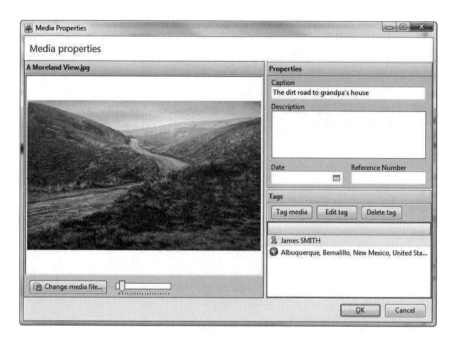

"Caption" allows you to enter a one line description of the photo, like "John on his first birthday".

"Description" allows you to enter a more detailed description of the photo. This is especially useful for listing the names of all the people in a family photograph.

"Date" lets you enter a date for the media. This can be the date the photo was taken.

"Reference number" lets you enter a personal file number which ties this record to your own filing system.

Once you have everything entered the way you want, click the OK button and RootsMagic will add the photo to the album.

If you ever want to change the caption, description, or other settings for the photo, simply click on the photo in the album, then click on the **"Properties"** button at the top of the album. RootsMagic will open up the same dialog you used when adding the photo, and you can make the changes desired.

Tagging Media Items

RootsMagic knows that a picture can contain more than just a single person, place or thing. RootsMagic lets you "tag" a picture or media item with the person, family, event, source, citation, or place the media item refers to. A media item can have more than one tag, so you can, for example, tag a census image with the people and family mentioned in the image, the source or citation for the census, and the place the census image refers to. To tag a picture, click the "Tag media" button on the Media Gallery, Media Album, or Media Properties screen. Select the type of item you want to tag the media with and then select the item itself.

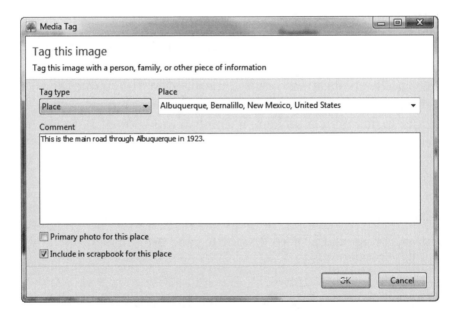

You can enter a comment for the tag to provide more details about that particular item in the picture.

"Primary photo" lets you tell RootsMagic which photo in an album is the one that you want printed on charts, since RootsMagic allows you to add unlimited photos to an album. The primary photo is also displayed on the main screen for the person.

"Include in scrapbook" lets you tell RootsMagic whether you want this photo to be included when you print the scrapbook.

> **⚠ Warning**
>
> RootsMagic only stores links to multimedia items, not the items themselves. Therefore, moving the items to another directory will cause RootsMagic to lose track of them and report the links as invalid.
>
> If this happens, open the Media Gallery (**Lists > Media Gallery** from the menu) and click **"Tools > Fix broken media links"**.

Removing Media

To remove an item (photo, document, sound or video clip) from RootsMagic, highlight the item, then click the **"Remove media"** button. RootsMagic will ask if you really want to remove the item. Click on **"Remove media"** to remove the item. When RootsMagic removes an item, it simply removes the link to the item. It doesn't actually remove the image, document, sound or video file from the hard drive itself.

Removing a media item will also remove all tags for the media item. If you just don't want the media item in a particular media album, you should just remove the tag and not the media item itself.

Rearranging Media in an Album

Since you may not always add your photos in the same order you want them displayed or printed, RootsMagic allows you to rearrange them any way you want (for example, from baby picture to 100th birthday photo). Just click **"Tools > Rearrange media items"** on the album, and RootsMagic will bring up a list of all media in the current scrapbook, which you can drag and drop into the desired order.

Editing Photos

When the album is displayed, the photos displayed are "thumbnails" of the actual photo. A thumbnail is a small, low-resolution copy of the image that is designed to display fast on the screen.

To edit the photo, click your mouse on the photo you want to see, then click the **"View / Edit"** button. You can also just double click your mouse on the photo in the album. Although RootsMagic isn't (and doesn't claim to be) a graphics editing program, it does allow you to perform some editing of your photos. Simply make any desired changes, then close the editor, and RootsMagic will ask if you want to save the modified photo.

The "View" menu in the Photo Editor provides options for viewing the photo. You can view it full (actual) size, or you can have RootsMagic fit it to the editor window. If you select full size, and the image is too large for the window, scroll bars will appear for your use. You can also zoom the photo in and out from this menu.

The "Image" menu allows you to manipulate the photo. You can flip or rotate the photo. You can also adjust the color settings for the image. You can adjust the contrast, hue, saturation, and gamma of the image. Simply select one of the tabs and adjust the value. The preview photo will change to show what the image will look like if you press OK. To accept the changes, press OK. To cancel without making any changes, press Cancel.

Printing Scrapbook Photos

RootsMagic allows you to print your photos in a variety of ways.

If you simply want to print a single photo, open the album, click on the photo you want to print, then click the "Print" button.

If you want to print your photo with data, just choose any of the RootsMagic printouts that offer a checkbox to include photos, and make sure that box is checked. RootsMagic will print photos in books, individual summary, family group sheet, scrapbooks, or photo tree).

Viewing and Editing a File

When you add a file to an album, RootsMagic displays the icon for the file type in the album. **To view or edit a file**, click your mouse on the icon, then click on the "View / Edit" button. You can also double click your mouse on the icon. RootsMagic will open the file using the program which is associated with that file type in Windows Explorer.

Playing Sound and Video Clips

When you add a sound clip or video clip to an album, RootsMagic displays the icon of the media type. **To play a sound or video clip**, click your mouse on one of these pictures, then click on the **"View / Edit"** button. You can also double click your mouse on the icon for the clip.

Putting Your Family on Paper

There is no such thing as a paperless world.

One of the main reasons a person buys a genealogy program is to print out their family on paper. Not surprisingly, everybody wants his or her family displayed in a different format.

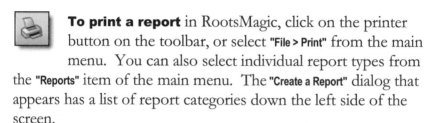 **To print a report** in RootsMagic, click on the printer button on the toolbar, or select **"File > Print"** from the main menu. You can also select individual report types from the **"Reports"** item of the main menu. The **"Create a Report"** dialog that appears has a list of report categories down the left side of the screen.

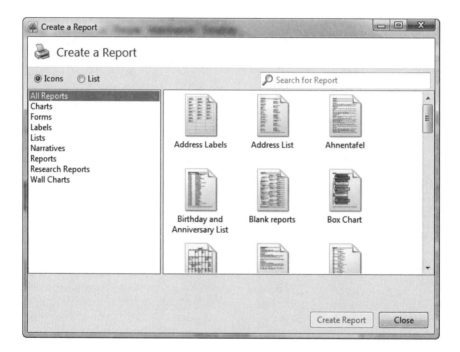

You can click your mouse on any of the report categories to see the report types in that category. When you have the report type selected, just click the **"Create Report"** button at the bottom of the dialog to select the options for the report.

Report Options

While each type of report will have its own options, most report types will use some or all of the following options. Rather than repeatedly discuss these options for each and every report, we'll mention them here. Of course the "Reset" button is to reset the various report settings back to their default, so have fun experimenting with the options.

Report Title

Several reports allow you to customize the title for the report. You can click the "Title" button to change or reset the title.

Page Layout

Many of the various printout dialogs have a button that lets you change the margins, headers and footers, page orientation and starting page number for the selected report type. For example, if you change the page layout for group sheets, it doesn't affect the page layout of pedigree charts. Clicking the "Layout" button on the report dialog will open the following dialog.

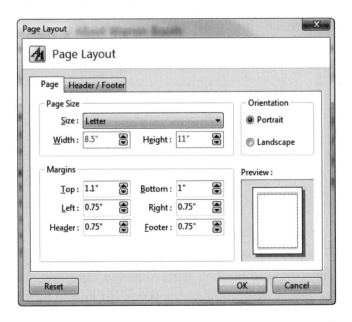

Page Size lets you select the size of the page. You can choose from a list of preset sizes, or enter a custom width and height.

Margins allows you to enter the top, bottom, left and right margins for the printout.

Orientation lets you tell RootsMagic which direction to print on the paper. Portrait prints the standard way on the page, while landscape prints "sideways" on the page.

Reset is a button which simply restores RootsMagic's defaults for the current page layout.

To change the header or footer for the report, click the Header/Footer tab in the Page Layout dialog.

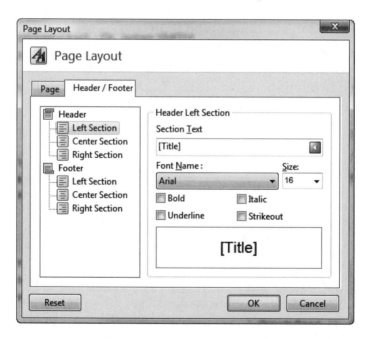

Check the "Print header" box (in the Header section) if you want RootsMagic to print a header at the top of each page. The header will consist of the text entered in the **"Left section"**, **"Center section"**, and **"Right section"** along with a separator line. These "sections" tell RootsMagic where to print the text within the header. For example, anything entered in the "Center section" will be centered in the header. You can also select different fonts for each section.

You can enter text into any section, or special "codes" that RootsMagic will convert when printing. These codes are:

[Date]   RootsMagic will replace this with the current date.

[Page]   RootsMagic will replace this with the current page number.

[Title]   RootsMagic will replace this with a title designed specially for this printout.

[File]   RootsMagic will replace this with the name of the database.

[Total]   RootsMagic will replace this with the total number of pages in the report. This is useful for creating page numbering like "Page [Page] of [Total]".

You can also swap the left and right header sections (mirror header) on even pages. This is useful for example when you are printing double sided and want the header to be a mirror image on facing pages.

The footer works exactly the same way as the header, except that it is printed at the bottom of each page.

Selecting the Fonts for the Report

"Fonts" lets you select the fonts that RootsMagic will use for the selected report. You can highlight a font in the list and click the "Change font" button to select the font and point size to be used. The "Reset defaults" button will reset all the fonts for the report back to their original settings.

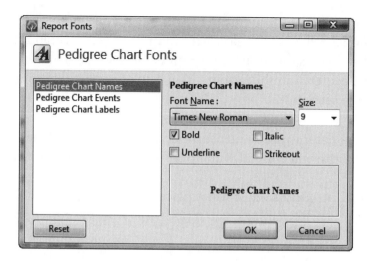

Source Options

Many of the reports let you print your sources as part of the report. RootsMagic provides a lot of options for you to customize the way those sources will print. For those reports you can click the "Sources" button on the right side of the report form.

The Citation Type lets you choose where you want the sources to print; Endnotes will print at the end of the document, while footnotes will print at the bottom of each page. You can also choose to just not print any sources at all for the report.

Print research notes with each citation tells RootsMagic to print the research notes after the source.

Print detail comments of sources with each citation tells RootsMagic to print the source detail comments following the source.

Reuse endnote numbers where possible causes RootsMagic to not print exact duplicate sources over and over when using endnotes. If RootsMagic encounters an exact citation that it has already printed, it will reference the already printed citation again. This has no affect when printing footnotes since the previously printed footnote would likely not be on the same page.

Use "Ibid." in consecutive duplicate citations tells RootsMagic to use the Latin term "Ibid." when multiple exactly the same citations appear in a row. The first time the full citation will be printed, but each consecutive identical citation will use "Ibid.".

Combine all citations for a single fact will combine all the citations for each fact into a single citation. This can greatly reduce the number of footnotes or endnotes that are printed. Be careful combining this with the "Reuse endnote numbers" option above, because combined citations will rarely be exactly the same as other combined citations.

There are a couple of additional options in the Bibliography, Options, and Fonts tabs of the Source Settings form.

Print bibliography of sources used will print an alphabetical list of all the sources used in the report. This is independent of the foonotes and endnotes, and can be printed in addition to or instead of them.

Hide private data in the endnotes, footnotes, and bibliography tells RootsMagic whether to hide private information in certain sources when they are printed. Some of the source templates provide the ability to have certain sensitive data (like personal addresses) replaced with privacy text like "ADDRESS FOR PRIVATE USE". This option tells RootsMagic whether to print that sensitive data or to print the privacy text.

Indexes

Many reports offer the option to print an index at the end of the report. You can print a name index, which is a list of the people who are in the report, or a place index, which is a list of the places mentioned in the report.

The name index is a list of the people mentioned in the report. There are several different formats you can choose from. You can also choose how many columns to print for the index.

You can specify whether you want the surnames in the index uppercase. This is useful to make the surnames stand out better. And finally you can tell RootsMagic whether you want to color code the names in the index. If you choose this option, RootsMagic will print the index using any color coding you have set for the people in the index.

The place index is a list of the places mentioned in the report. You can choose whether to reverse the place names in the index. When you reverse the places it groups them together geographically and makes it easier to find a place in the index.

You can also choose how many columns to use for the place index.

You can also select the fonts to be used for both indexes by selecting the Fonts tab and making your selections.

The Report Viewer

When you create any report, RootsMagic will open it in the Report Viewer. This preview lets you scroll through the entire report, zoom in or out, and print, save, and email your report. The left side of the Report Viewer is a set of thumbnails to give you an overview of what the report contains. When you are finished with your report, just click the "Close" button.

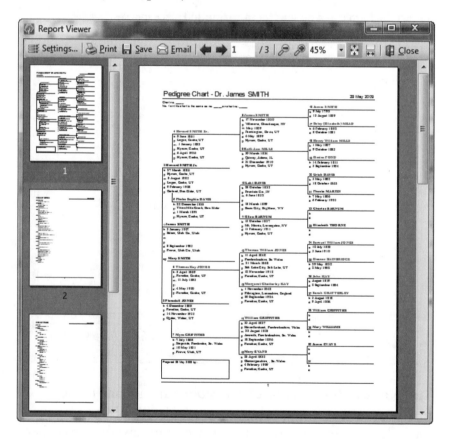

Modifying the Report

 Sometimes you will create a report and find out you didn't use the exact settings you wanted. Click the "Settings" button and RootsMagic will display the original report form where you can change any settings and regenerate the report.

Printing a Report

 To print the displayed report, just click the "Print" button. You will be able to select from the standard print options:

> ➤ Printing the entire document, the currently displayed page, or a range of pages.
> ➤ Selecting how many copies to print.

Saving a Report to File

 If you want to save the displayed report to a file, click the "Save" button on the Report Viewer. RootsMagic supports a number of different file formats, but some may not be available depending on the type of report.

- Rich Text (RTF) is a text format that preserves the formatting of the file, such as fonts, tabs, indents, superscripts, etc. Most current word processors can read RTF files, so this is a good way to get a RootsMagic report into your word processor for extra editing.
- Acrobat PDF is a (mostly) non-editable format that is very useful for sending to family members. It retains all formatting, images, etc. and can be printed by the recipient to look exactly as if you had printed it yourself.
- Text files will retain the text itself, but will lose most formatting. This format can be useful if you want to send a report to somebody by electronic mail (email).

- HTML is useful for putting on a website. It will retain some formatting like bold and italics, but won't always do a good job of preserving layout formatting.

Emailing a Report

There may be times that you want to email a report to someone. Just click the Email button on the Report Viewer and RootsMagic will let you select what format you want for the report (they will be the same ones as saving a file in the previous section). Select the file format and RootsMagic will generate the report and open your email program with that report already attached.

You just need to fill in the subject, email address, write a note and send the email.

Pedigree Charts

The pedigree chart is a visual display of the direct ancestors of the person on the far left of the chart. It is one of the most commonly used charts in genealogy.

To generate a pedigree chart for a person, highlight the start person on the main screen, then click the Print button on the toolbar, then click **"Pedigree Chart"** on the report list.

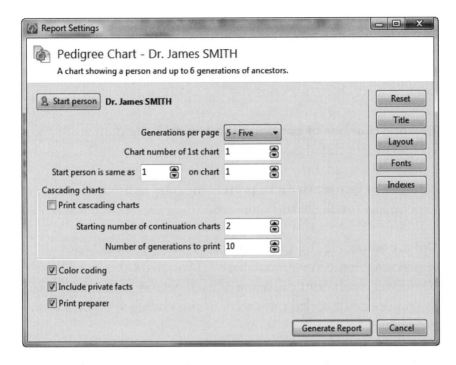

Start person is the person who the pedigree chart will begin with. You can click the "Start person" button to change this person.

Generations per page lets you print 4, 5, or 6 generations of ancestors on each page of the printout.

Chart number of 1st chart is the number of the first chart printed (usually 1).

Start person is same as X on chart Y lets you specify whether the starting person is already on a chart you have previously printed. These are usually both 1.

Cascading charts makes RootsMagic create a series of pedigree charts that span more generations than will fit on a single page.

RootsMagic will still use the generations per page selected, but will print additional pages as necessary and number the pages. Each person in the farthest right generation of a chart will become person number 1 on subsequent charts.

If you select cascading charts, the following options become available. Although you should usually just use the default values, RootsMagic allows you to change them in case you need to print continuation charts for ones you have printed previously.

Starting number of continuation charts is the number of the second chart printed (usually 2).

Number of generations to print is the total number of generations for all charts combined.

Color coding lets you print any color coding you may have applied to people in your database. If you mark this checkbox, RootsMagic will print the name of each person in the same color as they are color coded on screen. Color coding is described on page 265.

Include private facts lets you choose whether RootsMagic should include any facts (birth, marriage, or death) that you have marked as "private".

Print preparer tells RootsMagic whether you want your name and address printed on the pedigree chart. You can enter that address information in the File Options screen described on page 314.

Family Group Sheets

The Family Group Sheet is probably the most heavily used printout in genealogy. It is essentially a table that lists all of the facts for a father, mother, and children in a family.

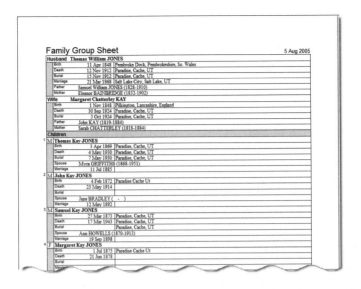

To generate a family group sheet, highlight the father or mother of the family on the main screen, then click the Print button on the toolbar, then click **"Family Group Sheet"** in the report list.

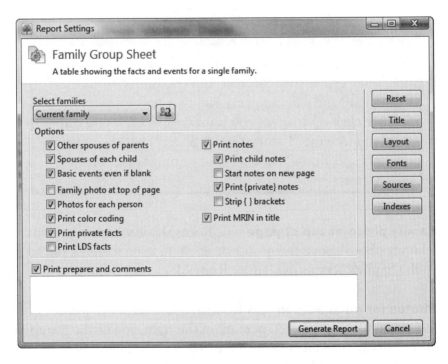

Select families lets you decide if you want to print a single group sheet for the current family, or if you want to print a bunch of group sheets all at once. If you pick the second option, RootsMagic will bring up a list of every family in your database to choose from.

Other spouses of parents lets you specify whether RootsMagic should print other spouses of the parents on the group sheet.

Spouses of each child lets you specify whether RootsMagic should print spouses of each child on the group sheet.

Basic events even if blank determines whether RootsMagic will print birth, marriage, death and burial facts for each person even if they are blank. If this box is unchecked, RootsMagic will only print facts that have been entered for the person. If a person doesn't have a death fact entered, RootsMagic will not print a blank one for them.

> ☺ **Tip**
>
> It is possible to turn off certain facts from ever printing in the family group sheet. Select **"Lists > Fact type list"** from the main menu and a list of every fact type will appear. Double click on the fact you want to turn off. You can then uncheck the "Family Group Sheet" checkbox for that fact and RootsMagic will not print that fact on any group sheets.

Family photo at top of page tells RootsMagic whether to print a family photo above the group sheet. You need to add a photo to the family's scrapbook before RootsMagic can print it.

Photos for each person tells RootsMagic whether to print individual photos for each person on the right side of the group sheet. In order to line photos up nicely, RootsMagic will print a blank box for people who do not have a photo entered.

Print color coding lets you print any color coding you may have applied to people in your database. If you mark this checkbox, RootsMagic will print the name of each person in the same color as they are color coded on screen. Color coding is described on page 265.

Print private facts lets you choose whether RootsMagic should include any facts (birth, marriage, death, etc.) that you have marked as "private".

Print LDS facts lets you choose whether RootsMagic should include any LDS facts (baptism, endowment, sealings, etc).

Print notes determines whether RootsMagic will print any notes with the group sheet. If this box is checked, RootsMagic will print all the family, individual, and fact notes associated with the family. You can select whether the notes will begin on a separate page following the group sheet, or whether they will immediately follow the last child on the group sheet. You can also disable printing of the children's notes, in case you are printing multiple group sheets and don't want to duplicate the children's notes on multiple group sheets.

Print private notes and **Strip brackets** let you choose whether RootsMagic should print any private notes you have entered. Private notes are described in more detail on page 85.

Print MRIN in title causes RootsMagic to print the marriage record number at the end of the title of the group sheet.

Print preparer and comments allows you to enter text that will be printed at the bottom of the family group sheet. The preparer information will also be included.

Narrative Reports

Narrative reports allow you to print a family history of a person. The narrative report can include the ancestors of the person (parents, grandparents, etc) or the descendants (children, grandchildren, etc).

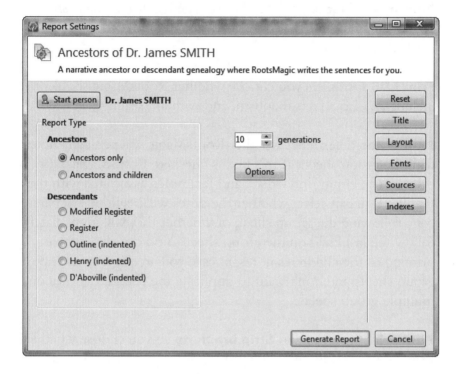

Start person is the person the report will begin with. You can click the "Start person" button to change this person.

Report type lets you select what type of book you want to print.

➤ **Ancestors only** - Prints a narrative history of the starting person and his/her ancestors. Only direct ancestors are included in the book.
➤ **Ancestors and children** - Same as the ancestor book, except that children of each ancestor are also included.

- ➤ **Modified Register** - Prints a narrative history of the starting person and his/her descendants. The book is broken into chapters by generation.
- ➤ **Register** - Prints a narrative history of the starting person and his/her descendants. The book is broken into chapters by generation.
- ➤ **Outline (indented)** - Prints a narrative history of the starting person and his/her descendants grouped by family. Many non-genealogists find this book format easier to follow. Each generation is indented from the previous generation, and is numbered in an outline format (I, A, 1, i, a, etc).
- ➤ **Henry (indented)** - Same as the indented outline descendant book, except that the numbering system follows the Modified Henry format. The first person is number 1, and each generation receives an additional digit stating the order of that child in that generation. If there are more than 9 children in a family, the modified Henry system uses the letters of the alphabet. For example, the person with Henry number 1.b.3 is the third child of the eleventh child of the starting person.
- ➤ **D'Aboville (indented)** - The D'Aboville numbering format is similar to the Henry format, except that a period is added between generations, so that digits instead of letters can be used beyond 9. For example, the person with D'Aboville number 1.11.3 is the third child of the eleventh child of the starting person.

Generations lets you specify how many generations you want to include in your report.

The **Options** button will display a dialog with a number of options for customizing your narrative report.

- ▪ **Date format** lets you select how RootsMagic will print dates in the report. Month names can be abbreviated or fully spelled out.

- **Start each generation on a new page** specifies whether RootsMagic will start each new generation (chapter) on a new page.
- **Print uplines** is only available when printing Modified Register or Register reports. This option will print a list of ancestors (and generations) following the name of each descendant in the report. For example:

John Doe (David-3, Samuel-2, William-1) was born in 1820.

- **Print preparer** lets you specify whether RootsMagic should print the preparer's name and address at the bottom of the printout. You can set the preparer's name and address in the options screen (page 314).
- **Print color coding** lets you print any color coding you may have applied to people in your database. If you mark this checkbox, RootsMagic will print the name of each person in the same color as they are color coded on screen. Color coding is described on page 265.
- **Print notes** specifies whether RootsMagic will include notes in the report. If notes are included, RootsMagic will insert them in the text. For example, a birth note would immediately follow the sentence about the person's birth · date and place.
- **Include photos** specifies whether RootsMagic will include photos of individuals in the report. RootsMagic will use the primary photo for the person as entered in their multimedia scrapbook. You can also choose the size RootsMagic should print the photos. Photos are not included when printing to a text file.
- **Include private facts** lets you choose whether RootsMagic should include any facts (birth, marriage, death, etc.) that you have marked as "private".
- **Include private notes** and **Strip brackets** let you choose whether RootsMagic should print any private notes you have entered. Private notes are described in more detail on page 85.

- **Sentence template for people with no entered facts** lets you tell RootsMagic what to write for people with no facts. When creating the narrative report, RootsMagic will write sentences for each fact entered for a person. If a person has no facts, then RootsMagic can't normally write anything about the person. If you don't want anything written about the person, then you can leave this field blank. Some suggestions for this template are:

[person] was born.

[person] was born (date unknown).

No further information is known about [person].

☺ Tip

When printing a report to a Rich Text (RTF) file RootsMagic will not actually build the index at the end of the report (since RootsMagic has no way of knowing how your word processor will paginate the report). Instead, RootsMagic will "mark" each person in the RTF file so that your word processor can build the index itself. This is extremely useful in case you want to add more text, photos, or make other changes.

For example, to build the index in Microsoft Word after you have imported the RTF file, move to the end of the file, then select "Insert > Index and Tables" from Word's main menu. Select whatever options you want, then click OK and Word will generate the index for you. WordPerfect users can generate an index in a similar manner.

Box Chart Reports

Box chart reports let you print ancestor or descendant box charts which can be used in books because they print on standard size pages. They can also be selected when publishing your information using the RootsMagic Publisher described later.

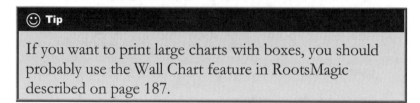

> ☺ **Tip**
>
> If you want to print large charts with boxes, you should probably use the Wall Chart feature in RootsMagic described on page 187.

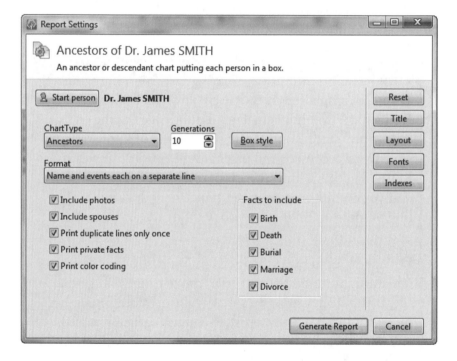

Start person is the person who the report will begin with. You can click the "Start person" button to change this person.

Chart type lets you select what type of chart you want to print.

- ➤ **Ancestors** - Prints a box chart of the starting person and his/her ancestors. Only direct ancestors are included in the chart.
- ➤ **Descendants** - Prints a box chart of the starting person and his/her descendants. Each generation is indented a bit to the right, and connecting lines are drawn to show the links between generations.

Generations lets you specify how many generations you want to include in your box chart.

Box style lets you select the style of the border which RootsMagic draws around each person. When you click the "Box style" button, the following dialog box will appear. From this dialog, you can choose what style you want, whether you want the box to have a shadow, and what color the box and shadow should be.

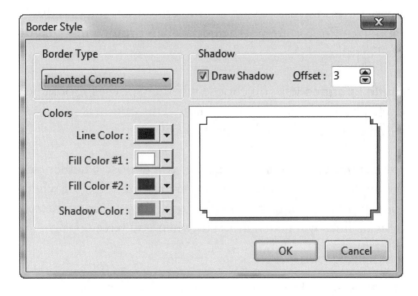

Just play with the various settings and see what the box will look like. Pick a style you like then click the OK button. If you decide you don't want to change the box style after all, you can click the Cancel button and RootsMagic won't modify the box style.

Format lets you select how RootsMagic will print each person's information in the chart. You can choose from:

> - **Single line** – RootsMagic will print the name of each person followed by their birth and death date on the same line. This is intended to be a compact format and no boxes are drawn around the single line for each person.
> - **Name and events each on a separate line** – RootsMagic will print the name of each person on a line, then print each fact type you choose to print on a separate line under the name.
> - **Name and events word wrapped** – RootsMagic will print the name followed by the facts you choose word wrapped to fit inside the box.

Include photos specifies whether RootsMagic will include photos of individuals in the chart. RootsMagic will use the primary photo for the person as entered in their multimedia scrapbook. Photos are not included when printing to a text or Rich Text file.

Include spouses lets you choose whether spouses should be included in the descendant box chart. This option is not applicable when printing an ancestor chart.

Print duplicate lines only once lets you choose whether to print duplicate lines every time they are encountered, or whether to only print duplicate lines the first time they are encountered. Duplicate lines will generally occur when you have cousin marriages.

Print private facts lets you choose whether RootsMagic should include any facts (birth, marriage, etc.) that you have marked as "private".

Print color coding lets you print any color coding you may have applied to people in your database. If you mark this checkbox,

RootsMagic will color a person's box in the same color as they are color coded on screen. The boxes of non color coded people will be printed in the color chosen in the "Box style" dialog. Color coding is described on page 265.

"Facts to include" lets you choose which facts you want to include in each person's box. You can choose from birth, death, burial, marriage, and divorce.

Address Labels

RootsMagic will print mailing labels using any number of standard Avery labels.

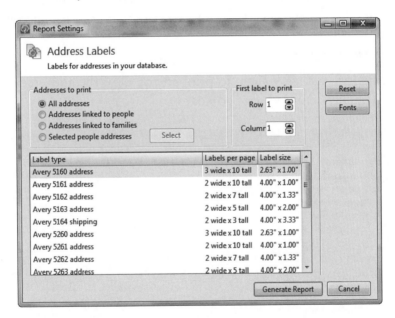

Addresses to print lets you decide which people you want to include in the list. If you pick "Select individuals", RootsMagic will bring up a list of every person in your database when you click the **"OK"** button. This selection screen is described in the chapter titled "Custom Reports" (page 210), and allows you to select the people you want to print labels for.

First label to print is especially useful when you have a partially printed label sheet, and need to start printing your labels somewhere in the middle of the sheet.

Label type lets you select what type (and size) label you want to print on. Just highlight the desired label type.

Lists

RootsMagic provides a large assortment of printable lists from the report dialog. Just highlight the list type and RootsMagic will display an option dialog specific to the list you want to print.

All lists offer the ability to print to the screen or printer, a text file, or a Rich Text file. You can also select the font for each list.

Address List

The address list allows you to print any or all of the addresses that you have entered for people.

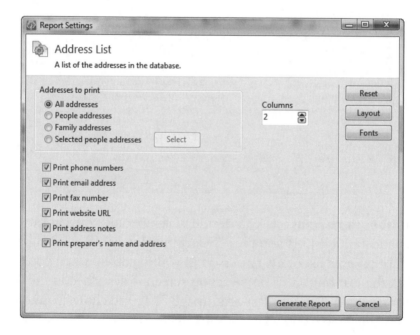

Addresses to print lets you decide which people you want to include in the list. If you check "Select individuals", RootsMagic will bring up a list of every person in your database when you click the **"OK"** button. This selection screen is described in the chapter titled "Custom Reports" (page 210), and allows you to select the people you want in your list.

Print preparer's name and address lets you specify whether RootsMagic should print the preparer's name and address at the bottom of the printout. You can set the preparer's name and address in the options screen (page 314).

The remaining checkboxes let you tell RootsMagic which additional address information (phone number, fax, etc) you want to print for each person.

Columns lets you choose how many columns to print the address list in.

Ahnentafel

The Ahnentafel (which means "Ancestor Table" in German) is an ancestor report. The Ahnentafel is in narrative form, and each individual in the report is assigned an "Ahnentafel number." This numbering system makes it easy to determine a person's parents. The Ahnentafel number of a person's father is exactly twice the person's number and the mother's number is twice the person's number plus one.

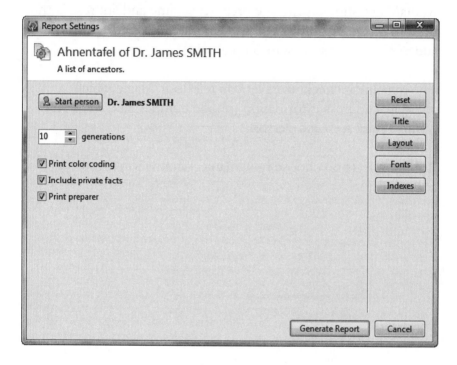

Start person is the person who the report will begin with. You can click the "Start person" button to change this person.

Generations lets you specify how many generations you want to include in your report.

Print color coding lets you print any color coding you may have applied to people in your database. If you mark this checkbox, RootsMagic will print the name of each person in the same color as they are color coded on screen. Color coding is described on page 265.

Include private facts lets you choose whether RootsMagic should include any facts (birth, marriage, death, etc.) that you have marked as "private".

Print preparer lets you specify whether RootsMagic should print the preparer's name and address at the bottom of the printout. You can set the preparer's name and address in the options screen (page 314).

Birthday and Anniversary List

The birthday and anniversary list prints birthdays and / or anniversaries sorted by date. You can choose to include everyone in your database, or just selected individuals. If you choose "Selected individuals", RootsMagic will bring up a list of every person in your database when you click the **"OK"** button. This selection screen is described in the chapter titled "Custom Reports" (page 210), and allows you to select the people you want in your list.

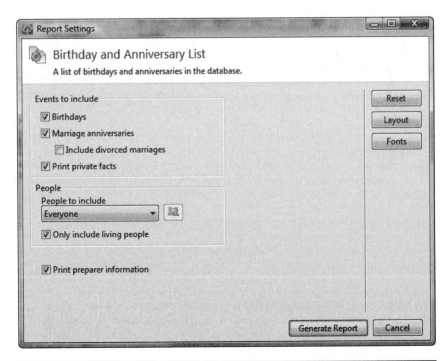

You also have several options which can be used to filter out individuals, such as only including living people and including (or ignoring) marriages with divorces entered. You can also have RootsMagic print the preparer's name and address at the end of the list. You can set the preparer's name and address in the options screen (page 314).

Correspondence List

The correspondence list is a report of all correspondence you have entered using the **"Lists > Correspondence list"** command.

You can select which types of correspondence you want to print (mail, phone, email, fax, other, sent or received). You can even have RootsMagic print the full address of each correspondent.

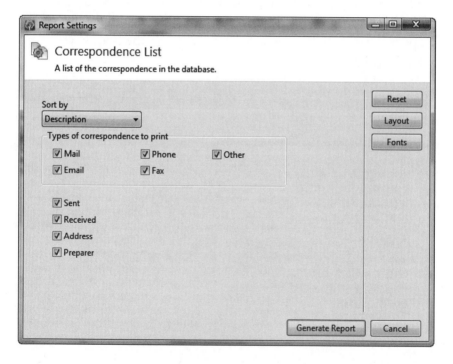

Sort by lets you sort the correspondence by either the description, the correspondent's name or the correspondence date.

Preparer lets you specify whether RootsMagic should print the preparer's name and address at the bottom of the printout. You can set the preparer's name and address in the options screen (page 314).

CountyCheck Report

The CountyCheck report is a list of events with place problems like a county which didn't exist on the date of the event.

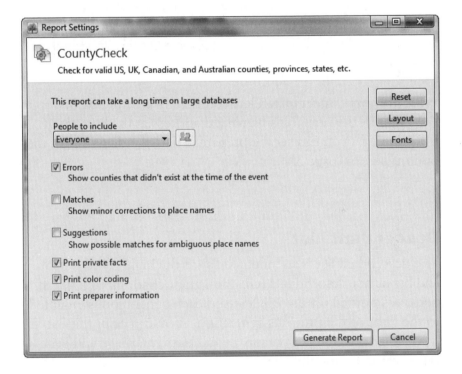

People to include lets you decide which people you want to include in the list. You can print everyone in the database, or select people from a list. If you check "Select from a list" RootsMagic will bring up a list of every person in your database. This selection screen is described in the chapter titled "Custom

Reports" (page 210), and allows you to select the people you want in your list.

Information to include lets you choose which messages you want printed: errors (like a county not existing on a date), suggestions (for possible missing parts of the place), or matches.

Print private facts lets you choose whether RootsMagic should include any facts (birth, marriage, death, etc.) that you have marked as "private".

Print color coding lets you print any color coding you may have applied to people in your database. If you mark this checkbox, RootsMagic will print the name of each person in the same color as they are color coded on screen. Color coding is described on page 265.

Print preparer information lets you specify whether RootsMagic should print the preparer's name and address at the bottom of the printout. You can set the preparer's name and address in the options screen (page 314).

Descendant List

The descendant list is an indented list of the highlighted person and his or her descendants (children, grandchildren, etc). Each person is printed on a single line and each generation is indented to the right of the previous generation. You can print this list with either one line per person, or full birth, marriage and death information on multiple lines.

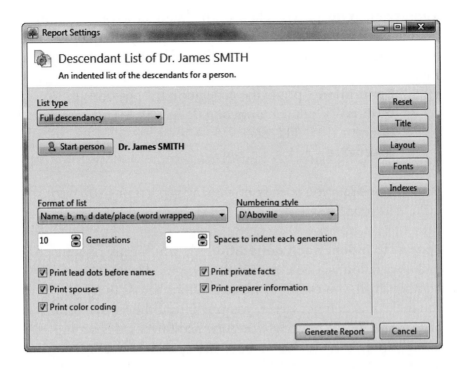

List type lets you choose whether to print a full descendancy (all descendants of the starting person), or a direct line descendancy (only those descendants from the starting person to a specific descendants).

Start person is the person who the report will begin with. You can click the "Start person" button to change this person.

Descendant only appears when you print a direct line descendancy, and lets you select the end person on the report.

Format of list lets you print each person:
1. on a single line with just their birth and death date
2. on a single line with just the birth and death year
3. on up to 4 lines for each person (name, birth date and place, marriage date and place, and death date and place)
4. on a single line but with the name, birth dates and death dates in columns
5. with the name, birth, marriage, and death date and place wordwrapped

Numbering style lets you choose what number to print in front of each person in the report. The outline, Henry, and D'Aboville numbering systems are described in Narrative Reports on page 140.

1. **Generation** – prints the generation the person is in
2. **Outline** – Outline numbering (I, A, i, a, etc)
3. **Henry** – 1, 11, 111, etc.
4. **D'Aboville** – 1, 1.1, 1.1.1, etc

Generations lets you specify how many generations you want to include in your list.

Spaces to indent each generation lets you specify how much each generation will be indented to the right. If you make this number small, you can fit more generations across the page. If you make this number larger, you can spread the list across the page more. When printing wordwrapped format, this setting doesn't apply because the wrapped paragraphs have a hanging indent.

Print lead dots before each person's name tells RootsMagic whether it should print a string of dots before each person's name in the list. This can sometimes make the list easier to read.

Print spouses specifies whether RootsMagic should print the spouses of the descendants in the list.

Print color coding lets you print any color coding you may have applied to people in your database. If you mark this checkbox, RootsMagic will print the name of each person in the same color as they are color coded on screen. Color coding is described on page 265.

Print private facts lets you choose whether RootsMagic should include any facts (birth, marriage, death, etc.) that you have marked as "private".

Print preparer information lets you specify whether RootsMagic should print the preparer's name and address at the bottom of the printout. You can set the preparer's name and address in the options screen (page 314).

Duplicate Record List

The duplicate record list is a report of possible duplicate records in your database. The list will contain pairs of records that might be duplicates. This report is particularly useful when you want to merge individual records and want a list of records that need merging.

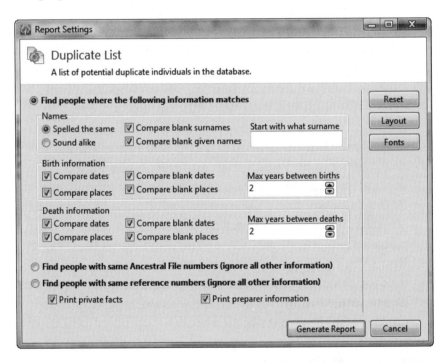

RootsMagic offers three different kinds of duplicate searches.

Find people where the following information matches lets you set options to have RootsMagic compare people using.

➤ **Names** lets you tell RootsMagic how people's names must match to be considered duplicates. You can specify whether matching names have to match exactly, or if they just need to sound alike. You can also choose whether blank names (both given and surnames) will be considered as matches with non blank names. Checking these boxes often leads to many false duplicates.

➤ **Starting surname** lets you tell RootsMagic where in the database to start the duplicate search. If you leave this blank, then RootsMagic will search the entire database for duplicates. If you enter "D", then RootsMagic will start with surnames beginning with the letter "D". If you enter "Jones", then RootsMagic will start with people with the last name "Jones".

➤ **Birth information** tells RootsMagic whether to compare birth information of people when checking for duplicates. You can choose to compare birth dates and / or birth places. You can also enter a maximum number of years between birth dates. If you set this value to 0, RootsMagic will only consider two individuals duplicates if they were born the exact same year. A value of 5 means that two individual's birth dates can be 5 years apart and still be considered duplicates. The smaller this number, the fewer duplicates RootsMagic will find. You can also tell RootsMagic whether you want to consider individuals without birth dates or birth places as possible duplicates. If you don't check these boxes, RootsMagic will not consider any individuals whose birth date (or place) is blank, even if they match in other ways.

➤ **Death information** works the same as the birth options (except with death data of course).

Print private facts lets you choose whether RootsMagic should include any facts (birth, marriage, death, etc.) that you have marked as "private".

Find people with the same Ancestral File Numbers finds individuals with matching Ancestral File numbers. All other criteria is ignored.

Find people with the same reference numbers finds individuals with matching Reference numbers (REFN). All other criteria is ignored.

Fact List

The Fact List is one of the most useful printouts available in RootsMagic. It allows you to print lists of people associated with any fact in your database (including any user-defined facts you have created).

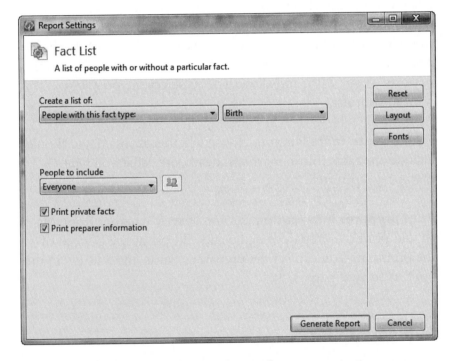

You can print a list of people who have or don't have a specific fact. Simply select the desired fact type from the drop list, and you can print a list of everyone with that fact, everyone without that fact, or everyone with more than one of that fact. For example, if you wanted a list of everyone in your database that you have not entered a birth for, select birth from the list, select "People without this fact type", and click Create.

You can print a list of facts that have or don't have sources. You can even print facts that have sources of a certain quality.

You can print a list of facts with text dates. These are dates that are either invalid dates, or are dates that RootsMagic can't figure out.

You can print a list of private facts. These are facts that you have marked the "private" checkbox for.

People to include lets you decide which people you want to include in the list. You can print everyone in the database, or select people from a list. If you check "Select from list" RootsMagic will bring up a list of every person in your database. This selection screen is described in the chapter titled "Custom Reports" (page 210), and allows you to select the people you want in your list.

Print private facts lets you choose whether RootsMagic should include any facts (birth, marriage, death, etc.) that you have marked as "private".

Print preparer information lets you specify whether RootsMagic should print the preparer's name and address at the bottom of the printout. You can set the preparer's name and address in the options screen (page 314).

Individual List

The Individual list is an alphabetical list of any or all people in your database. It can be as simple as just the names of the individuals, or can include the facts, parents, spouses, and children for each individual as well.

People to include lets you decide which people you want to include in the list. You can print everyone in the database, or select people from a list. If you check "Select from a list"

RootsMagic will bring up a list of every person in your database. This selection screen is described in the chapter titled "Custom Reports" (page 210), and allows you to select the people you want in your list.

You can also print several specialized lists, including people who have no parents entered in the database, people who have more than one set of parents entered in the database, and people who aren't linked to anyone else in the database (no spouses, children, or parents).

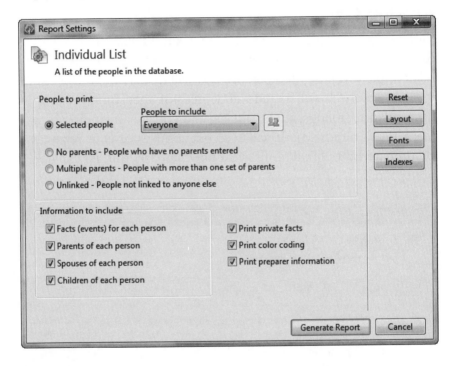

Information to include specifies what information you want printed for each person in the list, including facts for each person, or the parents, spouses, or children of each person.

Print private facts lets you choose whether RootsMagic should include any facts (birth, marriage, death, etc.) that you have marked as "private".

Print color coding lets you print any color coding you may have applied to people in your database. If you mark this checkbox, RootsMagic will print the name of each person in the same color as they are color coded on screen. Color coding is described on page 265.

Print preparer information lets you specify whether RootsMagic should print the preparer's name and address at the bottom of the printout. You can set the preparer's name and address in the options screen (page 314).

Kinship List

One of the coolest lists in RootsMagic is the Kinship list. RootsMagic will print a list of every person in the database that is related to the highlighted person, and will display the relationship to that person. It will include all degrees of ancestors, descendants, siblings, aunts, uncles, and cousins (including how many times removed). It will even get spouses of your relatives. Be prepared though, if you have a big database, this list can get pretty long!

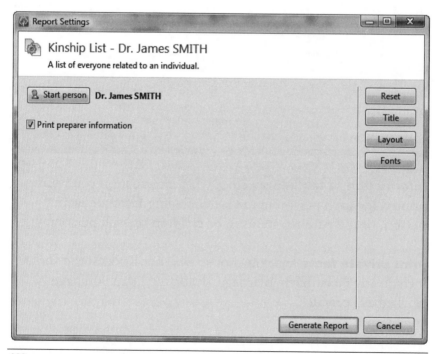

Start person is the person who the report will find relatives for. You can click the "Start person" button to change this person.

Print preparer information lets you specify whether RootsMagic should print the preparer's name and address at the bottom of the printout. You can set the preparer's name and address in the options screen (page 314).

LDS Ordinance List

The LDS ordinance list (there are actually two of them) will print LDS ordinance information for the people in your database.

Report type lets you select which ordinance list to print.

➢ **Individual ordinances** - lists individuals and the dates for LDS baptism, endowment, and sealing to parents.
➢ **Marriage sealings** - lists families and the marriage date and sealing to spouse date.

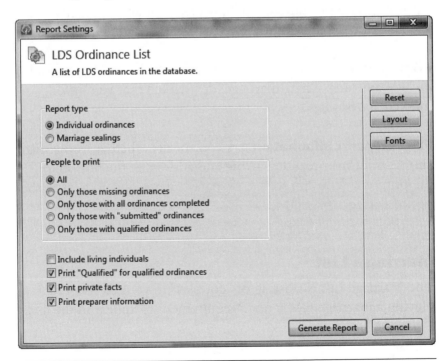

People to print lets you select which individuals to include in the selected list.

> **All** – prints everyone in the database
> **Only those missing ordinances** - prints only individuals who are missing at least one ordinance
> **Only those with all ordinances completed** - prints only individuals who are not missing any ordinances
> **Only those with "submitted" ordinances** - prints only individuals who have at least one ordinance with a status of "Submitted".
> **Only those with "qualified" ordinances** - prints only individuals who have at least one ordinance which is qualified for temple work.

Include living individuals gives you the option to ignore living individuals (since you can't do temple work for them anyways).

Print 'Qualified' for qualified ordinances will cause RootsMagic to print the word "qualified" for any ordinance that is qualified for temple work.

Print private facts lets you choose whether RootsMagic should include any facts (birth, marriage, death, etc.) that you have marked as "private".

Print preparer information lets you specify whether RootsMagic should print the preparer's name and address at the bottom of the printout. You can set the preparer's name and address in the options screen (page 314).

Marriage List

The Marriage List is a listing of "couples" in your database. Having a marriage fact is not a requirement to appear in the list.

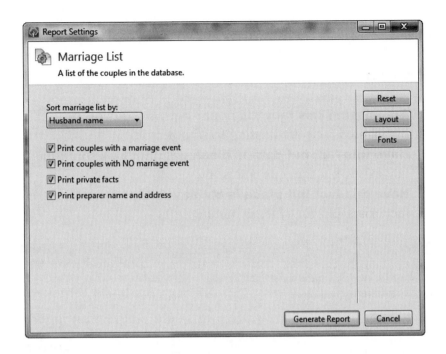

Sort marriage list by lets you sort the marriage list by the husband's surname, the wife's surname, the marriage date, or the marriage place.

You can have RootsMagic print couples with a marriage event, or those without a marriage event, or both.

Print private facts lets you choose whether RootsMagic should include any facts (birth, death, etc.) that you have marked as "private".

Print preparer name and address lets you specify whether RootsMagic should print the preparer's name and address at the bottom of the printout. You can set the preparer's name and address in the options screen (page 314).

Missing Information List

The Missing Information List creates a list of individuals missing any fact(s) or part of a fact that you choose. You can select multiple fact types in a single report.

Click and highlight as many facts as you want RootsMagic to check for each person. Then select what part of the fact needs to be missing.

➢ **Are missing this fact** will print a person if any of the highlighted facts are missing for the person.
➢ **Have this fact but date is blank** will print a person if the fact exists, but the date is missing.
➢ **Have this fact but place is blank** will print a person if the fact exists, but the place is missing.

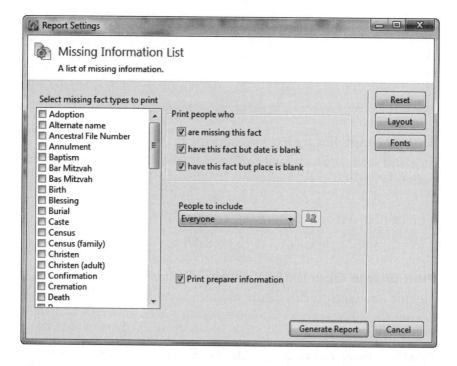

People to include lets you decide which people you want to include in the list. If you check "Select from a list", RootsMagic will bring up a screen for you to select the people you want to include. This selection screen is described in the chapter titled "Custom Reports" (page 210), and allows you to select the people you want in your list.

Print preparer information lets you specify whether RootsMagic should print the preparer's name and address at the bottom of the printout. You can set the preparer's name and address in the options screen (page 314).

Multimedia List

Since the RootsMagic scrapbook links to multimedia items on your hard disk, it is possible to lose track of which photos, video and sound clips you are linking to. The multimedia list generates a printout of multimedia items your database is using, including the full path name and what the item is linked to.

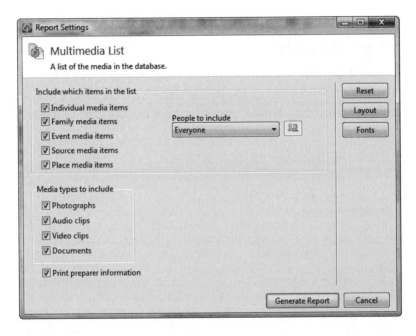

Include which items in the list lets you decide which multimedia items you want to include in the list. You can select any combination of multimedia items connected to people, families, sources, events, or places. If you choose Individual multimedia items, you can futher choose whether to include everyone or just selected people. If you choose "Select from a list", RootsMagic will bring up a list of every person in your database when you click the **"Create"** button. This selection screen is described in the chapter titled "Custom Reports" (page 210), and allows you to select the people you want in your list.

You can further filter the list by choosing whether to include any combination of photos, audio clips, video clips, or documents.

You also have the option to print the caption and description for each multimedia item as well.

Print preparer information lets you specify whether RootsMagic should print the preparer's name and address at the bottom of the printout. You can set the preparer's name and address in the options screen (page 314).

On This Day List

The "On This Day" report will list all the events from your database that occurred on a selected day. You can also choose to print famous births, deaths, and historical events that occurred on that same day.

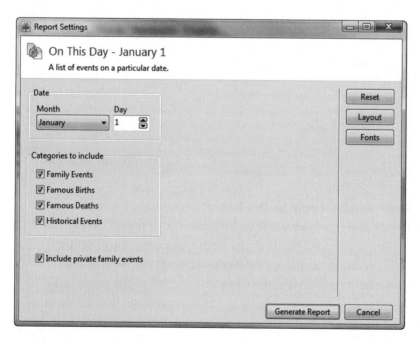

Date lets you select which date to print the events for.

Categories to include lets you select which items RootsMagic will include in the report.

Include private events lets you choose whether RootsMagic will print events from your database which you have marked as private.

Place List

The place list can potentially be one of the longest reports you generate.

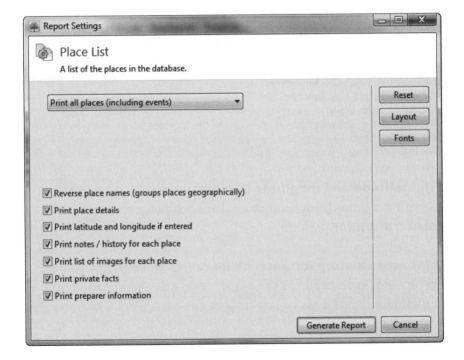

You can:

1. **Print all places in database** will print a list of every place in your database.

2. **Print all places (including events)** will print a list of every place in your database, along with all the events which occurred in each of those places.

3. **Print events in a single place** will print a list of every fact in your database that occurred in the highlighted place. It will list the person's name, fact type, and date for each fact.

4. **Print events near a place** will print a list of every event which happened within a selected distance. For example, you can print every event which happened within 50 miles of Dallas, Texas.

When places are printed, RootsMagic can reverse them so that the general part of the place name is first to sort places geographically. For example, if you mark the checkbox to reverse place names, places will be listed like:

New Mexico, Bernalillo Co., Albuquerque
New Mexico, Santa Fe Co., Santa Fe
Utah, Salt Lake Co., Draper
Utah, Salt Lake Co., Salt Lake City
Utah, Utah Co., Orem
Utah, Utah Co., Provo

Print latitude and longitude if entered will cause RootsMagic to print the latitude and longitude for each place that you have entered that information.

Print notes/history for each place causes RootsMagic to print any notes you entered for the place. You can also have RootsMagic print a list of any images the each place's multimedia scrapbook.

Print private facts lets you choose whether RootsMagic should include any facts (birth, death, etc.) that you have marked as "private".

Print preparer information lets you specify whether RootsMagic should print the preparer's name and address at the bottom of the printout. You can set the preparer's name and address in the options screen (page 314).

Repository List

The repository list will print either a single repository (libraries, archives, etc) or all repositories in the database. You can also have RootsMagic include all the sources, to-do tasks, and correspondence for each repository. This is especially useful if you want to print a list of things you need to do at a repository.

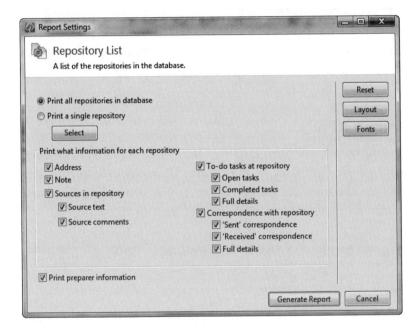

Address tells RootsMagic to print the full address for each repository.

Note tells RootsMagic to print any notes you have entered for each repository.

Sources in repository will print all sources which reside in each repository. Additionally you can include the actual text and comments about each source.

Todo tasks at repository will print all to-do tasks for each repository. You can choose whether to print open or completed tasks (or both), and can ask RootsMagic to print the full details for each todo task.

Correspondence with repository will print any correspondence you have had with each repository. You can choose to print correspondence you have sent to or received from the repository, and can ask RootsMagic to print the full details for the correspondence.

Print preparer information lets you specify whether RootsMagic should print the preparer's name and address at the bottom of the printout. You can set the preparer's name and address in the options screen (page 314).

Source List

The source list will print either a single source, or a list of every source in the database. You can also have RootsMagic print every use (citation) of each source. If you print all sources you can also tell RootsMagic how to sort the printed sources.

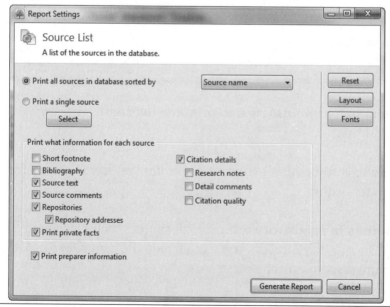

Short footnote will print the short version of the source if it has been entered.

Bibliography will print the bibliography version of the source if it has been entered.

You can also choose to print the actual source text and comments about the source.

Repositories will print the primary and seconday repository for each source in the list. You can also have RootsMagic print the full address for each repository.

Print private facts lets you choose whether RootsMagic should include any facts (birth, death, etc.) that you have marked as "private".

Citations details specifies whether all citations for each source should be printed. The citation includes the person (or family) and the fact. You can also choose to include the research notes, citation comments, and citation quality for each citation.

Print preparer information lets you specify whether RootsMagic should print the preparer's name and address at the bottom of the printout. You can set the preparer's name and address in the options screen (page 314).

Statistics List

The statistics list is a fun little list that will calculate various statistics about a group of people in your database. It will calculate the minimum, maximum, and averages for age at first marriage, age at death, marriages per individual, and children per marriage. It also breaks these categories down by sex.

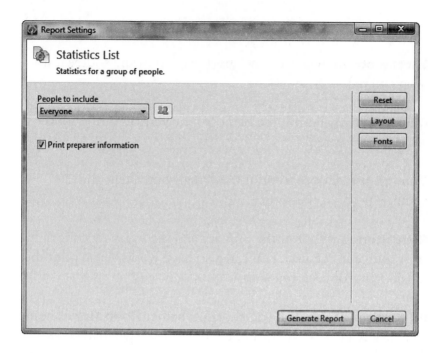

People to include lets you decide which people you want to include in the list. If you check "Select from a list", RootsMagic will bring up a list of every person in your database. This selection screen is described in the chapter titled "Custom Reports" (page 210), and allows you to select the people you want in your list.

Print preparer information lets you specify whether RootsMagic should print the preparer's name and address at the bottom of the printout. You can set the preparer's name and address in the options screen (page 314).

Surname Statistics List

The Surname Statistics List prints a list of every surname in your database. Each surname is listed only once, along with the number of people with that surname (broken down by males and females), and the earliest year and most recent year the surname appears in your database.

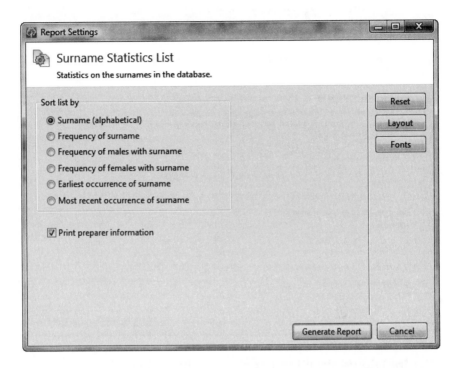

You can sort the surname statistics list: 1) alphabetically, 2) by the number of people with that surname (frequency), 3) by the number of males with that surname, 4) by the number of females with that surname, 5) by the earliest occurrence of the surname, and 6) by the most recent occurrence of the surname.

Print preparer information lets you specify whether RootsMagic should print the preparer's name and address at the bottom of the printout. You can set the preparer's name and address in the options screen (page 314).

Timeline List

The Timeline list is actually two different lists that print a chronological list of events for a group of people (including your entire database if desired).

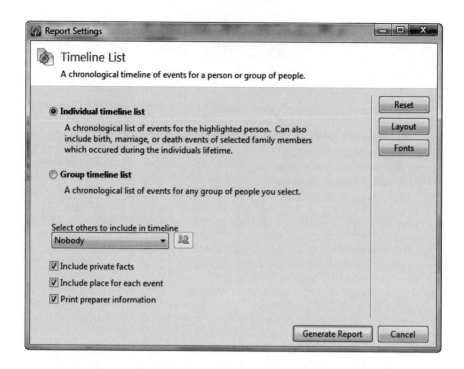

The Individual timeline list prints a chronological list of the events in the highlighted person's life, along with the birth, marriage, and death information for any other group of people that you select (but only those that fall within the lifetime of the primary person). By selecting the family members of the highlighted person, you can get an informative list of all family events which occurred within his or her lifetime.

The Group timeline list simply prints a list of every event for any group of people you select. This is especially useful for printing a list of all events for a family.

RootsMagic will display a list of all the people in your database, and you can select which people you want to include in your group timeline list. This selection screen is described in the chapter titled "Custom Reports" (page 210).

RootsMagic will then chronologically list all events in the selected person's lives (if they have a date).

Include private facts lets you choose whether RootsMagic should include any facts (birth, death, etc.) that you have marked as "private".

Include place for each event tells RootsMagic to print the place for each event.

Print preparer information lets you specify whether RootsMagic should print the preparer's name and address at the bottom of the printout. You can set the preparer's name and address in the options screen (page 314).

To Do List

The to-do list will print a list of the to-do tasks in your database. It will include the task description, the person the task is for, the soundex code for the person, the repository where the task needs to be done, and the date the task was created.

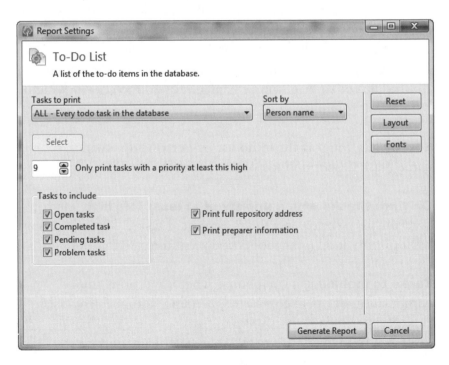

Tasks to print lets you tell RootsMagic which to-do tasks to print. You have a wide range of choices.

> **All** – This option will print every todo task in your database.
> **General** – This option will print to-do tasks which are not tied to a person or family. These would be tasks you added directly to the To do list ("Lists, To do list").
> **People** – This option will print to-do tasks which are linked to people. RootsMagic will display a list of all the people in your database, and you can select which people you want to include. This selection screen is described in the chapter titled "Custom Reports" (page 210).
> **Person** – This option will print all the todo tasks for a single person. The "Select" button will be enabled for you to choose which person's tasks to print.
> **Family** – This option will print all the todo tasks for a family. The "Select" button will be enabled for you to choose which family's tasks to print.
> **Repository** – This option will print all the todo tasks for a repository. The "Select" button will be enabled for you to choose which repository's tasks to print.
> **Single** – This option will print a single todo task. The "Select" button will be enabled for you to choose which task to print.

Sort by lets you sort the to do list by Person (alphabetical by name), task description, repository, or date.

Only print tasks with a priority of at least this high lets you filter the list to print only the most urgent tasks. You can choose what priority level (and above) you are interested in.

Tasks to include lets you choose whether to print any combination of open, completed, pending, and problem tasks.

Print full repository address tells RootsMagic to print the full street address for each repository.

Print preparer information lets you specify whether RootsMagic should print the preparer's name and address at the bottom of the printout. You can set the preparer's name and address in the options screen (page 314).

Calendars

If you are always forgetting birthdays and anniversaries, then this is the report for you. You can print a calendar with birthdays and anniversaries for any month or year.

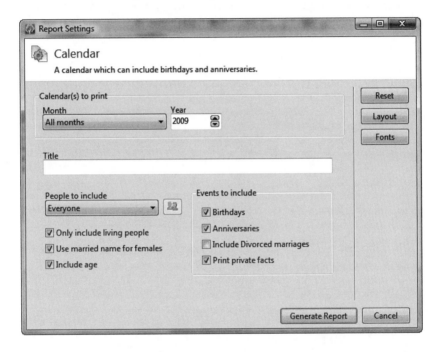

Calendar(s) to print lets you select which month (or all months) and which year to print a calendar for. If you choose "All months" then RootsMagic will print a calendar for each month in the year you choose.

Title lets you enter a title for your calendar.

People to include lets you print everyone in your database, or just selected people. If you choose to select a group of people, RootsMagic will display a list of all the people in your database, and you can select which people you want to include. This selection screen is described in the chapter titled "Custom Reports" (page 210). You can also filter to include only living people, print females with their married name, and include the age of each person.

Events to include lets you choose whether to print birthdays, anniversaries, or both. You can even choose to ignore anniversaries of marriages with divorces entered.

Print private facts lets you choose whether RootsMagic should include any facts (birth, death, etc.) that you have marked as "private".

Individual Summary

The Individual Summary prints just about everything you have entered for a person. You can print a summary for the highlighted person, or you can print multiple summaries all at once. If you choose "Select from a list", RootsMagic will display a list of all the people in your database, and you can select which people you want to include. The selection screen is described in the chapter titled "Custom Reports" (page 210).

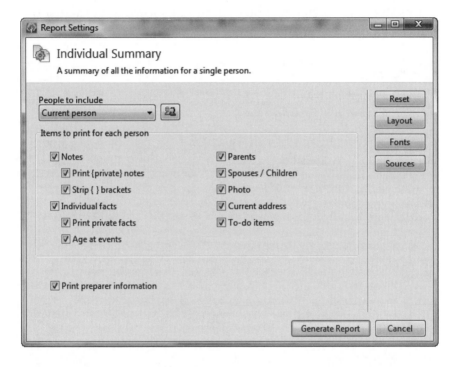

Items to print for each person lets you select which items to print for the person. You can include notes, facts (birth, death, etc), the person's age at each event, parents, spouses and children, a photo, to-do list items, and the person's current address. You can also choose whether to print private notes or facts.

Print preparer information lets you specify whether RootsMagic should print the preparer's name and address at the bottom of the printout. You can set the preparer's name and address in the options screen (page 314).

Relationship Chart

If you have ever wondered how two people in your database are related, then the Relationship Chart is the printout for you. Select the "Relationship Chart" item in the Report dialog. You can select any two people from your database, set some options, and RootsMagic will generate a box chart that shows you exactly how the two people are related.

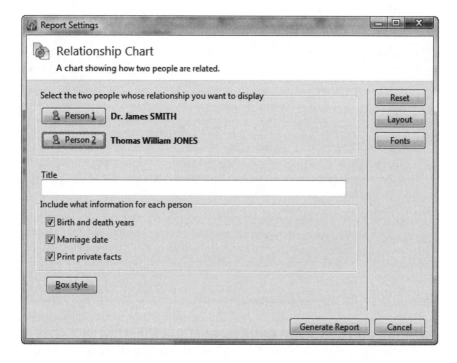

Select the two people whose relationship you want to display - Click on each button to select the two people you want to find the relationship for. RootsMagic will bring up a list of everyone in your database for you to select from. By default, the first person will be set to the person who was highlighted on the main screen, but you can change to a different person if you want.

Title lets you enter the title you want printed at the top of the chart.

Birth and death years tells RootsMagic to print the life span for each person (like "1780 – 1843").

Marriage date tells RootsMagic to print the marriage date for each couple in the relationship chart.

Print private facts lets you choose whether RootsMagic should include any facts (birth, death, etc.) that you have marked as "private".

Box style lets you choose the format of the borders RootsMagic draws around people. This is described in detail on page 145.

Wall Charts

As you add more people to your database, you will find that the connections between people can become blurred in your mind. Wall charts let you print huge family trees which can help you visualize these complicated relationships. While they are easy to create, RootsMagic provides numerous customization tools, so we will cover them in detail in the chapter titled "Wallcharts and Timelines" (page 187).

Timeline Charts

The Timeline chart displays a graphical representation of how the lives of people in your database relate to each other. RootsMagic prints color bars for the lifetime of each person (all or selected) in your database. While they are easy to create, RootsMagic provides numerous customization tools, so we will cover them in detail in the chapter titled "Wallcharts and Timelines" (page 187).

Scrapbook

The Scrapbook is designed to print all the photos for the highlighted person, family, source or place. If you print a scrapbook for a person or family, you can also choose whether you want to include photos attached to the facts for that person or family.

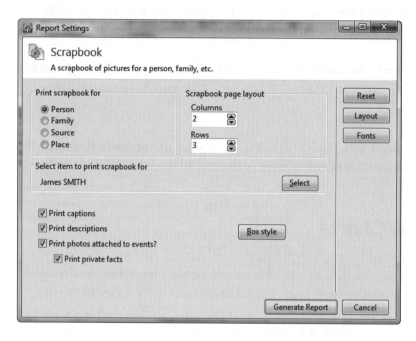

You can select how many rows and columns to print on each page, and whether you want to print the captions or descriptions for each photo. You can tell RootsMagic whether you want a photo included in the scrapbook when you add or edit it in the multimedia scrapbook.

Print private facts lets you choose whether RootsMagic should include any facts (birth, death, etc.) that you have marked as "private".

Select item to print scrapbook for lets you select the person whose scrapbook you want to print. You can click the "Select" button to change this person. When you choose to print a scrapbook for a family, source, or place, this will let you select the family, source or place to print the scrapbook for.

Box style lets you choose the format of the borders RootsMagic draws around photos. This is described in detail on page 145.

Photo Tree

The Photo tree will print a tree (with leaves) with three generations of photos superimposed on it. The tree includes the starting person, his parents, and grandparents. In addition, you can include the brothers and sisters of the start person at the base of the tree.

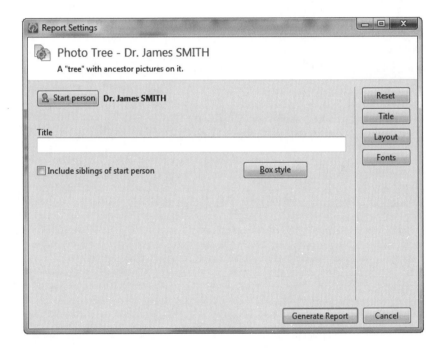

Start person is the person who the report will begin with. You can click the "Start person" button to change this person.

Title lets you enter the title you want printed at the top of the photo tree.

Include siblings of start person tells RootsMagic to print all the children at the base of the tree. RootsMagic will reduce the size of the children's photos as necessary to fit them all in the space available.

Box style lets you choose the format of the borders RootsMagic draws around the photos. This is described in detail on page 145.

Custom Reports

Custom reports allow you to create your own lists. While they are easy to create, there are also sophisticated techniques that can be applied, so we will cover them in detail in their own chapter titled "Custom Reports" (page 203).

Wallcharts and Timelines

Call it a clan, call it a network, call it a tribe, call it a family.
Whatever you call it, whoever you are, you need one.
- Jane Howard, "Families"

While most printouts are limited to standard sized pages, RootsMagic wallcharts and timelines are designed to be as large as you need them to be (they aren't called *wall*charts for nothing). And while they are easy to create, RootsMagic gives you full control over every aspect of the chart, including the positioning, size, colors, fonts, and other aspects of every object in the chart.

Wall Charts

Wall charts let you print huge family trees which can help you visualize these complicated relationships. You can create ancestor, descendant, or hourglass wallcharts. To create a wallchart, click the "Reports" button on the toolbar, or choose "Reports > Charts > Wallcharts" from the menu.

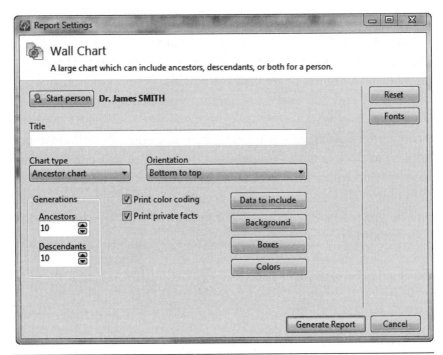

Start person is the person who the chart will begin with. You can click the button to change this person.

Title lets you enter the title for the top of your chart.

Chart type lets you select what type of chart you want to print.

> ➢ **Ancestor chart** - Prints a chart of the starting person and his/her ancestors (parents, grandparents, etc). Only direct ancestors are included in the chart.
> ➢ **Descendant chart** - Prints a chart of the starting person and his/her descendants (children, grandchildren, etc).
> ➢ **Hourglass chart** - Prints a chart which includes both the ancestors and descendants of the starting person.

Orientation lets you choose which direction the chart is laid out. For example, ancestor charts can go from left to right (the default), or from right to left, top to bottom, or bottom to top. The options will vary depending on which Chart type you select.

Generations lets you specify how many generations you want to include in your chart. If you choose an ancestor or descendant chart the appropriate generations field will be enabled. If you choose an hourglass chart you will be able to select the number of ancestor and descendant generations separately.

Print color coding lets you print any color coding you may have applied to people in your database. If you mark this checkbox, RootsMagic will color a person's box in the same color as they are color coded on screen. The boxes of non color coded people will be printed in the default color chosen in the "Colors" dialog. Color coding is described on page 265.

Print private facts lets you choose whether RootsMagic should include any facts (birth, death, etc.) that you have marked as "private".

Data to include is where you can choose exactly what information to put in each person's box. RootsMagic will always print the person's name in the box, and you can choose how that name is formatted.

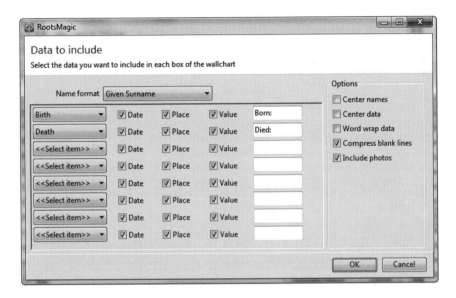

You can also choose which other information to include. You can select up to 8 facts to print for each person, and can specify whether to include the date, place, or value for each fact you choose. You can also change the default label RootsMagic uses for each fact type.

If you choose a lot of information to include, you probably will want to increase the size of the boxes as described earlier, or reduce the size of the fonts using the "Fonts" button on the wall chart dialog. The "Include photos" checkbox lets you include the primary picture for each person. If you include pictures, you might want to consider widening the boxes.

By default, RootsMagic will display each fact on its own line in the person's box, but you can mark the "Word wrap all data" checkbox to cause the data to wrap in the box. If you don't word wrap data, you can choose whether events with no information will print as blank lines or not.

Finally, you can choose to center the person's name and data in the box. If you don't mark these checkboxes, RootsMagic will left justify the name and data.

The Background button lets you choose the background for your chart.

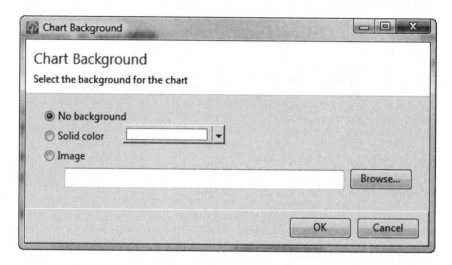

You can choose no background, a solid color, or even select an image as the background. Just remember that while a colored or image background can really look nice, it can also use a huge amount of ink when printing. Companies that print wallcharts on large plotters almost always charge much more for charts with color or image backgrounds.

> **☺ Tip**
>
> RootsMagic Chart will stretch background images to fit the canvas, so the image needs to be proportional to the canvas size so it isn't distorted, and also needs to be a high enough resolution so that it isn't grainy when it is stretched to fit the canvas.

The Boxes button lets you select the size of the boxes for each person, the spacing between the boxes (both horizontally and vertically), as well as whether you want the box to have a drop shadow. When RootsMagic generates the wall chart it will make all of the boxes the size you specify. After the chart is generated you can adjust the size of individual boxes if you want.

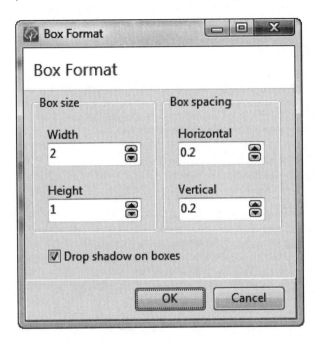

The Colors button lets you choose the colors for the various parts of the wall chart. Simply click on one of the buttons and you can select the desired color for each aspect of the chart.

Timeline Charts

The Timeline chart displays a graphical representation of how the lives of people in your database relate to each other. RootsMagic prints color bars for the lifetime of each person (all or selected) in your database.

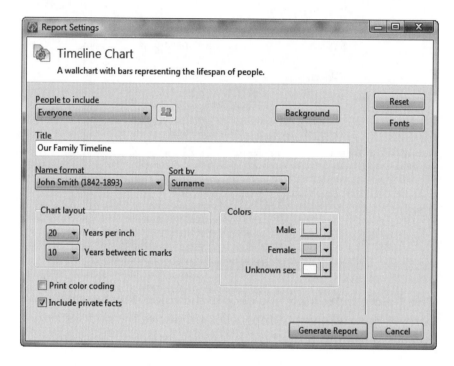

People to include lets you choose whether to include everyone or to choose a group of people. If you choose to include only selected people RootsMagic will bring up the selection screen described on page 210.

Title lets you enter the title you want to print at the top of your timeline chart.

Name format lets you choose how you want each person's name printed on the chart.

Sort by lets you choose the order (from top to bottom) of the bars for each person. You can choose to sort by the person's surname or birthdate.

Chart layout lets you choose the spacing which RootsMagic will use between tic marks.

Colors lets you select the color of the bars for males, females, and people with no sex entered.

Print color coding lets you print any color coding you may have applied to people in your database. If you mark this checkbox, RootsMagic will color a person's bar in the same color as they are color coded on screen. The bars of non color coded people will be printed in the default color chosen in "Bar colors". Color coding is described on page 265.

Include private facts lets you choose whether RootsMagic should include any facts (birth, death, etc.) that you have marked as "private".

The **Background** button lets you choose the background for your chart. This is the same as the wallchart background button described on page 190.

RootsMagic Chart

After RootsMagic creates a wallchart or timeline, another included program called RootsMagic Chart will open the chart so that you can customize it, print it, or save it to disk to work on later.

RootsMagic Chart gives you full control over the positioning, size, colors, fonts, and other aspects of every object in the chart. With simple mouse control you can resize an individual's box, or drag it to another location on the canvas without breaking the family links. You can change colors of individual boxes, or change the font or color of the text in the boxes.

You can even customize your chart by adding additional text, pictures, or shapes to the chart, and you can change the background image or color.

The Canvas

The canvas is the actual drawing area for your chart. All objects, including person boxes, links between boxes, text, images, and shapes are displayed on the canvas.

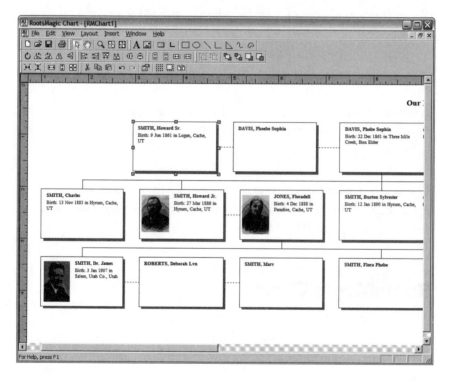

When RootsMagic creates a chart it will use the background image or color you chose when generating the chart, and will automatically size the canvas to fit the chart. If you want to change the size or background in RootsMagic Chart, you can do that as well.

To change the size of the canvas, do "Layout > Canvas size" from the menu, then enter the height and width of the canvas in inches. This is useful when you rearrange the items in the chart and need more (or less) room to handle the changes.

To change the background of the canvas, do "Layout > Background" from the menu, and RootsMagic Chart will display the same dialog as when you originally created the chart (page 190). RootsMagic Chart also provides a number of modes for viewing your data on the canvas. Simply click one of the buttons on the zoom toolbar to choose what mode you are in.

Select – Changes the cursor to the default "Select" cursor which lets you select, move, and size objects.

Pan – Changes the cursor to the "Pan" cursor (which looks like a hand). When this cursor is selected you can click and drag the entire canvas rather than individual objects. To exit from Pan mode just click on the Select button on the toolbar.

Zoom – Changes the cursor to the "Zoom" cursor (which looks like a magnifying glass). When this cursor is selected, clicking the mouse button will zoom in on the canvas, while right clicking the mouse button will zoom out from the canvas.

Zoom to fit – Causes RootsMagic Chart to zoom so that the entire chart is visible on the screen. For large charts this can be used as an overview, but can be very difficult to use for actual work.

Zoom to selection – Causes RootsMagic Chart to zoom so that all selected objects fill the screen.

Toggle grid – Turns the "grid" on or off. The grid is simply a grid of dots which displays on the canvas, but does not actually print. It is useful to help line things up when you are moving objects.

Snap to grid – When snap to grid is enabled, objects will snap to the nearest grid dot (both horizontally and vertically) when moving and resizing the object. This limits the precision of how boxes are sized and positioned, but is very useful for keeping items exactly lined up.

Toggle page bounds – When this is enabled, lines will be drawn to show how the chart would be broken if printed to a regular (small page) printer. This can be useful if you want to print a chart that will be printed on smaller pages and taped together to help you avoid printing boxes or other objects over a page break.

Manipulating Objects

The ability to manipulate any individual item or object on the canvas gives you the flexibility to completely customize any RootsMagic chart. These objects can be person boxes, pictures or text that you may have added, or other shapes like rectangles and circles.

Adding Objects

To add a new object on the canvas, choose Insert from the menu, or click one of the buttons on the drawing toolbar.

> **Text** – Lets you add a text object to the canvas. The cursor will turn into the "add text" cursor, and clicking on the canvas will drop the new text object onto the canvas.
> **Picture** – Lets you add an image to the canvas. A file dialog will open to let you select the image you want to add. Select the desired image and click "Open" and RootsMagic Chart will change the cursor to the "Add picture" cursor, and clicking on the canvas will drop the picture onto the canvas.

- ➢ **Person box** – Lets you add a new person box to the canvas. The cursor will turn into the "add object" cursor, and clicking on the canvas will drop the new person box onto the canvas. You can then double click the name text or event text to change it.

- ➢ **Link** – Lets you link two person boxes together. The cursor will turn into the "add link" cursor (which looks like a little plus sign). When you move the cursor over a spot that the link can be attached (on the middle of any side of a person box) the cursor will change to a circle with a plus sign in it. You can then click the mouse and the link will attach to the person box in that location. You can then move the cursor to the side of another person box (where the circle cursor again appears) and click to finish the link.

- ➢ **Rectangle** – Lets you add a rectangle to the canvas. You can then click on the canvas, and while holding the mouse down drag out the size of the rectangle you want. When you release the mouse the rectangle will be added to the canvas. If you want a perfect square, hold the shift key down while sizing the rectangle.

- ➢ **Ellipse** – Lets you add an ellipse to the canvas. You can then click on the canvas, and while holding the mouse down drag out the size of the ellipse you want. When you release the mouse the ellipse will be added to the canvas. If you want a perfect circle, hold the shift key down while sizing the ellipse.

- ➢ **Line** – Lets you add a line to the canvas. You can then click on the canvas, and while holding the mouse down drag out the line you want. When you release the mouse the line will be added to the canvas.

- ➢ **Line (multi-segment)** – Lets you add a multi-segment line to the canvas. You can then click on the canvas where you want the line to start. Then move the mouse and click on the endpoint of each segment. When you are ready to finish, double click the mouse to set the last segment of the line.

➢ **Polygon** – Lets you add a polygon to the canvas. You can then click on the canvas where you want the polygon to start. Then move the mouse and click on the endpoint of each segment. When you are ready to finish, double click the mouse to set the last segment of the line.

➢ **Curve** – This works almost exactly the same as adding a multi-segment line, except that RootsMagic Chart will "fit" a curve to the line segments.

➢ **Closed curve** – This works almost exactly the same as adding a polygon, except that RootsMagic Chart will "fit" a curve to the line segments.

Selecting Objects

To select an object, simply click on the object with your mouse. RootsMagic Chart will display sizing handles (tiny squares on each side and corner of the object) to show that the object is selected.

To select multiple objects you can click on the first object, then hold down the Shift key on the keyboard while you click the remaining objects. If the objects are close together you can click and drag a region around the objects and all objects inside that rectangular region will be selected.

Moving Objects

To move any object on the canvas, simply click the object with the mouse and drag it to the new position, then release the mouse button. If more than one item is currently selected, this will move all selected items at once.

Resizing Objects

To resize any object on the canvas, click once on the item to display the sizing handles. You can then click on any of these handles and drag them to resize the object (either larger or smaller).

Changing Object Properties

To change the properties of an object (such as color, font, or line style) right click the mouse on the object and select "Properties" from the pop up menu. For most objects the property dialog will appear where you can change any of the properties of the item. If you select Properties for a person box, a list of the components of the person box will appear (box, shadow, name text, event text) and you can change the properties of each of those parts individually.

Positioning Objects

RootsMagic Chart offers many commands to help you size and position objects on the canvas beyond the click and drag method. You can access these commands from the "Layout" menu or by clicking the appropriate button on the toolbar.

Align – The align functions will align all selected objects with the "primary" selected object (the one with the gray sizing handles). You can align the left or right sides, the tops, the bottoms, or the centers (either vertically or horizontally).

Space evenly / Make same size – These commands will evenly space multiple objects, or will make all the selected objects the same size.

- **Across** – Will horizontally space all of the selected objects between the left-most and the right-most selected object.

- **Down** – Will vertically space all of the selected objects between the upper-most and lowest selected object.

- **Width** – Will make all selected objects the same width as the "primary" selected object (the one with the gray sizing handles).

- **Height** – Will make all selected objects the same height as the "primary" selected object (the one with the gray sizing handles).

- **Both** – Will make all selected objects the same size (both height and width) as the "primary" selected object (the one with the gray sizing handles).

Nudge – The nudge commands will move the selected object (or objects) just a tiny bit. This is useful when an object is very close to the position you want but just needs a little bit of a "nudge". You can nudge objects up, down, left or right.

Grouping / Order – Moves the selected object in front of or in back of other objects on the canvas.

- **Group** – Combines all selected objects into a single new object (group). When this new grouped object is moved, sized or otherwise manipulated, all parts of the group are manipulated equally.

- **Ungroup** – Breaks apart a group of objects which were combined using the Group command.

- **To Front** – Moves the selected object in front of all other objects on the canvas.

- **To Back** – Moves the selected object behind all other objects on the canvas.

- **Forward one** – Moves the selected object one step towards the front of the canvas.

- **Backward one** – Moves the selected object one step towards the back of the canvas.

Rotate / Flip – The rotate and flip commands let you rotate the selected object.

- **Rotate** – Lets you rotate the selected object. After selecting this option the mouse pointer will change to the rotate pointer. Clicking and dragging on the corner of an object will rotate the object as desired.

- **Rotate left** – Rotates the selected object 90 degrees to the left.

- **Rotate right** – Rotates the selected object 90 degrees to the right.

- **Flip vertical** – Flips the selected object vertically.

- **Flip horizontal** – Flips the selected object horizontally.

Working with RootsMagic Chart Files

One of the biggest advantages of a separate charting program like RootsMagic Chart is that you can save your modified chart to disk, and later reopen it to print it or edit it some more. RootsMagic Chart offers all the standard file commands, like:

- **New** – Opens a new blank chart / canvas on the screen.
- **Open** – Brings up a file dialog where you can select an existing RootsMagic chart to be opened on screen.
- **Close** – Closes the currently active window.
- **Save** – Lets you save the current chart to disk. If you have not yet saved the chart, a file dialog will come up where you can enter the file name for the chart. If the chart has already been saved once, this button will just save the modified chart with the existing name.
- **Save as** – Lets you save a copy of the current chart with another name. This is useful if you want to make a copy of a chart for special modification.

- **Export** – Lets you export the chart to a number of graphics formats. You can export to an Enhanced Meta File (*.emf) file, which is a resizable format that can be used to print on large plotters. There are also a number of standard image formats (.jpg, .png, etc) so you can create images of your chart.

If you want to run RootsMagic Chart to open a previously created chart, simply start the program with the icon installed on your desktop or in the Windows Start menu.

Printing Your Chart

Of course the final destination for your wall chart is the printer. RootsMagic Chart offers several options for printing your chart.

If you print your chart to a regular printer, the chart will be broken up and printed on pages which you can then tape together into a larger chart. If you want to see how the pages will be broken up before you print the chart, choose "View, Page bounds" from the menu to toggle lines on the screen which show where the pages would fall. You can also do "File, Print preview" to see exactly what each page will look like when printing.

If you are lucky enough to own a printer capable of printing a chart the size you need, you can do "File, Page setup" to choose the printer and the larger paper size to print on. RootsMagic Chart will automatically print to the larger page size.

Finally, you can also go to www.PrintMyChart.com, or do "Reports, PrintMyChart.com" from the RootsMagic menu (not the RootsMagic Chart menu) and take advantage of the chart printing service offered by RootsMagic, Inc. The price to print your chart will depend on the size of the chart, and whether the chart has pictures and / or a background color or image. You can see the size of the chart by doing "File, Properties" from the RootsMagic Chart menu.

Custom Reports
Have it your way...

If you want to get a list of information from RootsMagic in a particular format, but it isn't available in the program, then the custom report creator is the place to go.

The Custom Report creator is probably one of the most powerful features of RootsMagic. You can create your own customized lists that include almost any information about anyone in your database, sorted in any order and laid out in any position.

Let's Create One

The easiest way to learn about custom reports is just to create one. Let's say you want a list of people in your database along with their birth date and place. When it is finished, you want it to look something like this:

Name	Birth Date	Birth Place
Doe, John	3 Sep 1906	Albuquerque, New Mexico
Doe, Mary	10 May 1943	Provo, Utah
Jones, David	8 Aug 1920	Phoenix, Arizona
Smith, William	4 Feb 1872	Columbia, Missouri
Thomas, Bill	12 Jul 1889	Pittsburgh, Pennsylvania

To design such a report, you will need to tell RootsMagic that for each person, you want to print from left to right the name, then the birth date, and finally the birth place. You will also need to tell RootsMagic to print the words "Name", "Birth Date", and "Birth Place" in the header at the top of each column. Let's create this report now.

To create a custom report, click the Printer button on the toolbar, then select the "Reports" category, then "Custom Report" from that category, or select **"Reports > Custom Reports"** from the RootsMagic menu.

The two main aspects of creating a custom report are designing the report layout, and selecting the people to print in the report.

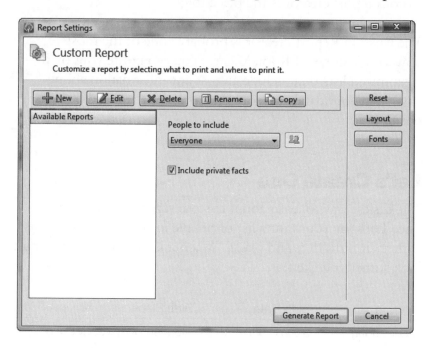

Designing a Custom Report

To start creating our custom report, click the **"New"** button on the dialog. RootsMagic will display the screen where we will design our report. On this screen, we will tell RootsMagic what information we want to print for each person, and where to print it on the page.

The Designer Screen

The designer screen is kind of like a spreadsheet. It has "cells" laid out in rows and columns, and your job is to tell RootsMagic what you want printed in each of those cells.

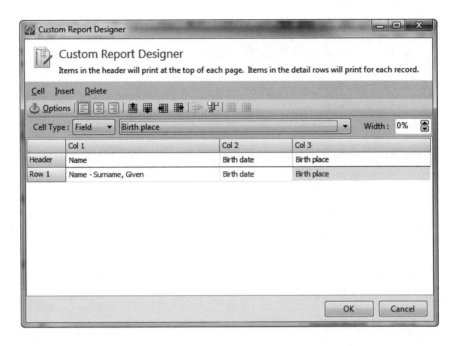

There are several sections that make up the Custom Report Designer. At the top is the menu, where you can select from a number of options to modify the layout of the fields.

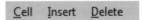

Below that is the toolbar. The toolbar contains buttons for basically the same options as the menu.

Under the menu and toolbar is the cell definition bar. This is where you can set the options for the highlighted "cell" in the custom report.

Below all of that are the rows and columns that will make up
your custom report.

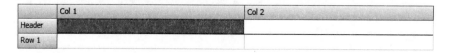

The top row is the "header", and that is where you enter the text
you want printed at the top of each column on each page. The
remaining rows are the "details", and that is where you will tell
RootsMagic which data to print in each cell (a cell is the place
where a column and row intersect).

You can click on any cell in that section to make changes to that
cell, and you can use the arrow keys to move from cell to cell.

When you first start the custom report designer, it will show the
header row, and one data row. It will also show 2 columns.

In our case, we want 3 columns (one each for the name,
birth date, and birth place). We can click on one of the
cells in column 2, and then do **"Insert > Column right"** from the menu to
add a new column (or just click the **"Insert column right"** button on the
toolbar).

The Header

The Header is where you will enter text that you want to print at
the top of each page.

To add text to the header, click your mouse on the first cell in the
header row and begin typing the word **"Name"**. Now just repeat
this action in the other two header cells to add **"Birth Date"** and **"Birth
Place"**.

To edit text once it is on the screen, click on the cell, then
edit the text in the cell definition bar above.

To delete some text, click on the cell, then delete the text in the
cell definition bar above.

The Details

The Details section is all the rows under the Header row, and is where you enter the information that you want to print for each person. Anything you put in these other rows will be printed once for every person that you include in the custom report.

In our case, we want to print the name, birth date, and birth place for every person, so we need to tell RootsMagic to print those three items for each person. We do this by telling RootsMagic which data to print in each cell.

To tell RootsMagic what data to print in a cell, click your mouse on the cell, then select the field type from the cell definition bar.

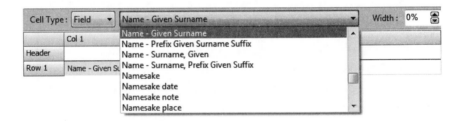

Since the person's name is the first item we want to print, select Name – 'Surname, Given' from the list. The cell will now contain that field name. Now just repeat this action to add fields for Birth date and Birth place in the other two cells in Row 1.

To delete a field, click on the cell and change the field back to "<<Select field>>".

Custom Report Options

RootsMagic offers a number of options that apply to your custom report. Click the **"Options"** button to bring up the following screen. When you have selected the options you want, click the OK button to return to the Custom Report Designer screen.

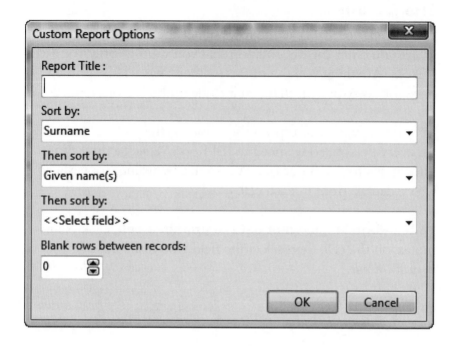

Report Title is where you type the title you want to appear at the top of your custom report. For example, you might enter "Birth List" for the report we are creating now.

Sort by is where you tell RootsMagic how you want your report sorted. Select the sort order from the drop list. We can just pick "Surname" for this list, since we want the list to be sorted alphabetically by last name. If we later wanted to sort the list by birth date or birth place, we can change the sort order here.

Then sort by fields let you further sort the list. For example, if you set the 2nd sort field to "Birth date", then all the "John Smiths" who were grouped together by the "Surname" sort, will be sorted amongst themselves by birth date.

Blank rows between records lets you tell RootsMagic how to space individuals in your custom report. If you use the default value of 0, RootsMagic will print each person's information on one line after another. If you change this value to 1, RootsMagic will put 1 blank line between each person that it prints.

To save your custom report once it is designed, click the "OK" button on the Custom Report Designer. RootsMagic will ask you for a name for your report. RootsMagic will then display the name of the report you designed in the "Available Reports" list. Once you have designed a custom report, you can reuse the same report over and over without having to redesign it.

Modifying a Custom Report

If you ever need to make changes to a custom report, highlight the report in the "Available Reports" list, then click the "Edit" button. RootsMagic will load the selected report and open it in the Custom Report Designer where you can modify any of the report design. When you are satisfied with the changes, click the "OK" button to save the modified report.

If you just want to change the name of the report (instead of changing the way it looks), you can highlight the name of the report in the list and click the Rename button.

If you no longer need a custom report, just highlight it in the list and click the Delete button.

 Tip

If you want to create a new report that is very similar to an existing report, highlight the existing report and click the Copy button. You can then modify that copy.

Printing a Custom Report

When you are ready to print a custom report that you have designed, highlight the report in the "Available reports" list, choose who you want to print the report for, then click

"Generate Report". You can choose from the same font and layout options as with any other report.

Printing a Report of Every Person

If you select **"Everyone"** before clicking the **"Generate Report"** button, RootsMagic will generate the custom report and display it on the screen in the Report Viewer (see page 132). From this viewer, you can zoom, change pages, or print the report.

Printing People in a Named Group

If you have created any named groups (page 256), those groups will be listed for you to select from.

Selecting People to Print in Your Report

If you choose **"Select from list"** RootsMagic will ask you to select the individuals you want to include in the report. The following "selection screen" will appear.

As with the RootsMagic Explorer (page 75) you can type a person's name to highlight them and you can edit the highlighted person. But the main purpose of the selection screen is to select a group of people.

This selection screen allows you to "mark" and "unmark" people to include in your custom report. When a person is marked, an "x" appears in front of their name in the list. When you unmark a person, the "x" is removed from in front of their name. You simply mark and unmark people until you have an "x" next to every person you want to include. Then click the OK button and RootsMagic will generate the custom report for you.

There are two buttons at the top of the selection screen, "Mark people" and "Unmark people". Clicking each button will display a menu of ways you can mark (or unmark) people in the list.

To mark or unmark a single person click the checkbox in front of their name.

To mark or unmark a family, highlight a person and select "Family of highlighted person" from either the "Mark" or "Unmark" menu. If the person is only in one family (whether as a parent or child), RootsMagic will mark (or unmark) each person in the family. If the person is a member of more than one family, RootsMagic will present a list like this and allow you to select which families you want to mark or unmark.

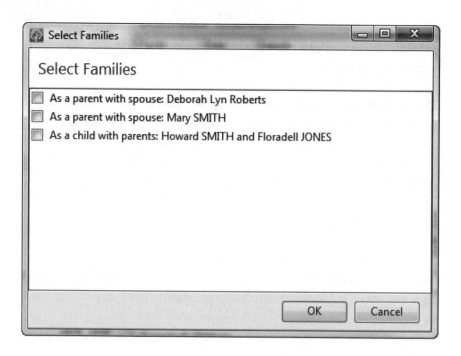

To mark or unmark a person and their ancestors, highlight the person and select **"Ancestors of highlighted person"** from either the "Mark" or "Unmark" menu. The following screen will appear.

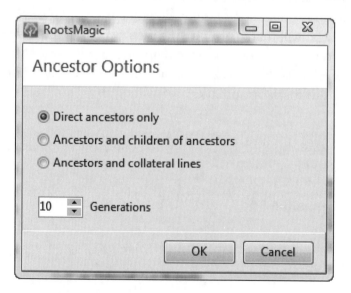

You can choose the number of generations to consider, and whether to include the children of each ancestor as well. You can also choose to print the collateral lines which tries to select all ancestors and their families.

Make your choices, then click OK and RootsMagic will mark or unmark the highlighted person and his or her ancestors.

To mark or unmark a person and their descendants, highlight the person and select "Descendants of highlighted person" from the "Mark" or "Unmark" menu. The following screen will appear.

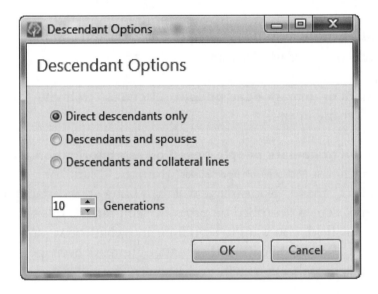

You can choose the number of generations to consider, and whether to include the spouses of each descendant as well. You can also choose to print the collateral lines which tries to select all descendants and their families.

Make your choices, then click OK and RootsMagic will mark or unmark the highlighted person and his or her descendants.

To mark or unmark everyone in the database, select "Everyone in the database" from either the "Mark" or "Unmark" menu.

The "Everyone" option is especially useful when you want to include everybody except for a certain few. You can mark everyone in your database, then use the other options to unmark those few that you don't want included.

To mark or unmark everyone related to the highlighted person, select "Everyone in the highlighted person's tree" from either the "Mark" or "Unmark" menu. RootsMagic will mark or unmark everyone in the same tree as the highlighted person.

To mark or unmark living people, select "Living" from the "Mark" or "Unmark" menu.

To mark or unmark dead people, select "Dead" from the "Mark" or "Unmark" menu.

To mark or unmark people based on any information about them, choose "Select people by data fields" from the "Mark" or "Unmark" menu. RootsMagic will then bring up the exact same "Search" screen described on page 77. You can use this screen to enter any fields you want to search in, and what you want to find in them. RootsMagic will either mark or unmark every person that matches what you enter in this screen.

Publishing Your Family History

This is where is all comes together.

If you have ever tried to print several different narrative reports or charts, and then tried to combine them into a single book, you know what a pain it is trying to get everything working together.

The RootsMagic Publisher allows you to combine multiple reports into a single document (or book). This document can include narrative books (like the modified register), pedigree charts, family group sheets, and several other common printouts. The document can also include cover and title pages, a table of contents, other introductory pages, a shared index and source bibliography covering all the sections in the document.

 To create a book, click the "Publish" button on the toolbar, or select **"Reports > Publisher"** from the main menu, and the following screen will appear.

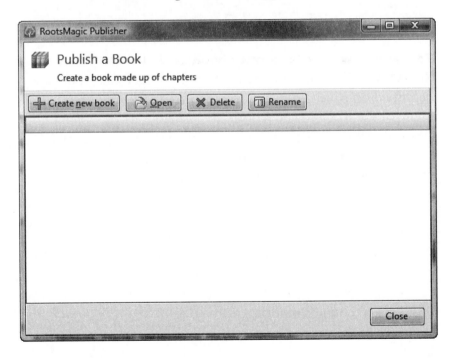

You will first need to create a book template by clicking the "Create a new book" button. If you want to open an existing book template highlight the desired book in the list and click the "Open" button.

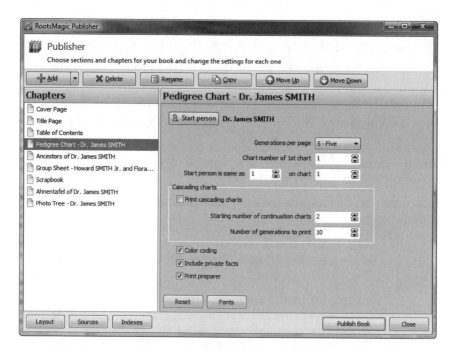

To add a new chapter to your book, click the "Add" button. RootsMagic will open the "Select Report" screen (like the one described on page 124) where you can select the chapter type. Many of the RootsMagic reports are available, as are several "Special sections" like a cover page, title page, text page, table of contents and more. You can even add blank pages, which is useful if you want to add photos or other items to your book which aren't stored in RootsMagic.

RootsMagic will add the selected chapter type to the publisher. When that chapter is selected in the chapter list you can modify its settings on the right side of the publisher. The options for each chapter will be basically the same as when you print a single copy of that chart or report.

The chapter will initially be added at the current position in the chapter list, but you can use the **"Move Up"** and **"Move Down"** buttons to put it in the desired position.

> **Note**
>
> When you create a book template, it is stored in the current database since the chapters you add are specific to people in the current database. For example, you can add a pedigree chart for John Doe, or a narrative book for Mary Smith.

To modify a chapter, highlight the chapter in the list and make any changes on the right side of the screen.

To remove a chapter highlight the chapter and click the **"Delete"** button. RootsMagic will ask you to verify that you want to delete the chapter.

To rearrange the order of chapters in your book click the **"Move Up"** or **"Move Down"** buttons to move the highlighted chapter up or down one spot in the list.

Indexes – Lets you choose whether to print a person index or place index for the book. These are the same options as described on page 130.

Layout – Click this button to bring up the Page layout dialog to set the page margins, headers, and other page settings for the document. This is the same dialog as described on page 125.

Sources - Lets you tell RootsMagic how to print sources for the book (if at all). It will bring up the source print option dialog described on page 128.

To print the book click the "Publish book" button to generate the book using the settings you have chosen.

If you make changes to your database (new people or facts), you can return to the RootsMagic Publisher, and generate the book and it will create the book taking into account any changes you made.

Sharing Data with Others

Share and share alike.

Genealogy is one of the few hobbies where you want to give everything you collect to others (and want them to give theirs to you). RootsMagic lets you share your data with others by providing full GEDCOM import and export, import from Family Tree Maker, PAF, Legacy and Family Origins, and the ability to create shareable CDs of your database.

Creating a Shareable CD

RootsMagic makes it easy to create a CD of your database to share with others. The CD you create and share will automatically display an introduction page with a title, photo, introduction, and contact information. The introduction page will also have a button which will present your database in a read-only version of RootsMagic. To create a shareable CD, select "Tools, Create a shareable CD" from the menu.

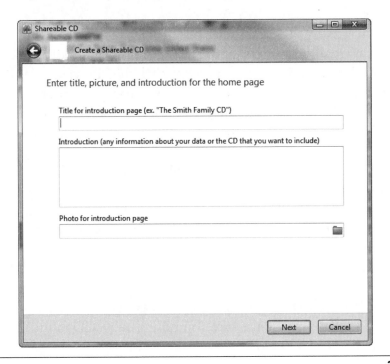

Enter the title, photograph, and introduction for your intro page. If you don't want to choose a photograph, RootsMagic will use a default image. Click the "Next" button to continue.

Enter your contact information; name, address, phone number, email address, and website. You can click the "Preview your CD opening page" button to see what your introduction page will look like. If you see something you need to change, close the preview intro page, make the changes and preview it again.

When you are ready to create your Shareable CD, click the "Next" button. RootsMagic will organize the files to burn to the CD and will ask if you want to burn the CD right now, or if you want to burn it later with your own burner software. This second option is useful if you want to put other files on the CD before burning it.

If you choose to burn the CD now, RootsMagic will display the "Burn CD" dialog. Make sure you have a blank CD in the drive, select which drive to burn to (if you have more than one), and click the "Burn CD/DVD" button. RootsMagic will create the Shareable CD.

Importing Data From Other Programs

RootsMagic can directly import data from Family Tree Maker (version 2006 and earlier), Personal Ancestral File (PAF) version 2 and later, Legacy Family Tree, and Family Origins version 4 and later. All information will be brought in to RootsMagic, including names, dates, places, links, notes, and image links.

To import data from Family Tree Maker, PAF, Legacy or Family Origins, create a new database and do "File > Import" from the main menu.

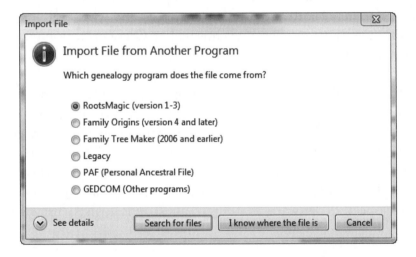

Select which program you are importing from, then ask RootsMagic to search for those files, or tell RootsMagic you know where the files are. RootsMagic will bring up the standard Windows file open dialog where you can select the file you want to import.

☺ Tip

All imports except for GEDCOM import will only read a file into a new (empty) database. This isn't a problem unless you want to combine the data into an existing database. In this case, create a new database and import the file into that database. Then drag and drop the information into your existing database.

Importing a GEDCOM File

Importing a GEDCOM file into RootsMagic has a few extra steps beyond what the direct imports require.

GEDCOM is a file format. It is not a piece of software, although many software programs can read and write GEDCOM files. A GEDCOM filename ends with a .GED extension (like "family.ged").

GEDCOM was developed by the Family History Department of The Church of Jesus Christ of Latter-day Saints (LDS Church) to provide a flexible, uniform format for exchanging computerized genealogical data. GEDCOM is an acronym for **GE**nealogical **D**ata **COM**munication. Its purpose is to foster the sharing of genealogical information and the development of a wide range of inter-operable software products to assist genealogists, historians, and other researchers.

To import a GEDCOM file do "File > Import" from the main menu as described in the previous section and select GEDCOM as the file type, then select the file you want to import.

If you are importing the file into an existing database, RootsMagic will ask if you want to create a new database to import the GEDCOM into, combine the GEDCOM with the current database, or cancel.

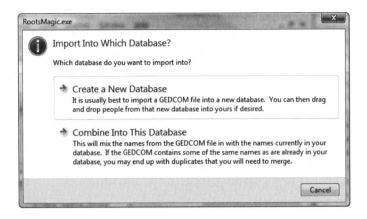

You usually want to create a new database. If you choose to combine the GEDCOM, RootsMagic will mix all the names in the GEDCOM file with the names already in your database. If the GEDCOM contains names which are already in your database, you will end up with 2 copies of each of those people.

RootsMagic will then display the following dialog, which lets you add a source to each person or event in the GEDCOM file so you can tell where the record came from (only one source is added, and every person or event in the GEDCOM file will point to it).

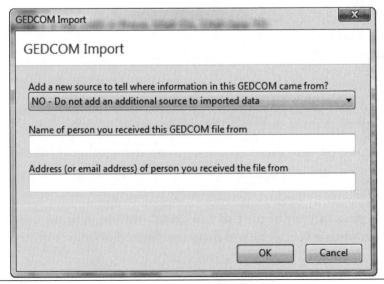

You can choose to add the source to every person, every fact, every person and fact, or to not add a source. If you choose to add a source, you need to enter the name and address of the person you received the GEDCOM from (in order to create the source).

If a GEDCOM file is too large to fit on a single disk, it may be broken into several smaller files. If you ever import one of these multi-disk GEDCOM files, RootsMagic will automatically ask you to insert the disk with the next part.

When you import a GEDCOM file, it is not linked in any way to the names you already had in your database. It is up to you to connect the new names from the GEDCOM with your existing family tree. If you have duplicate copies of individuals in your database, merging those records will link the trees together. Or you can use the "Add > Parents", "Add > Spouse" and "Add > Child" commands to link the individuals together. When RootsMagic asks if you want to create a new person or link to an existing person, select the link option to link the individuals together.

☺ **Tip**

While RootsMagic provides a "merge" feature (page 236) it is really hard to remove or merge a lot of unwanted names from your database if you combine in a GEDCOM file you didn't really want.

Instead, you may want to import the GEDCOM file into a new (blank) database, so that you can view the new information to see if you really want it in your database.

If you do, you can then import the GEDCOM file into your main database. **If you don't**, you can delete the new database and go back to work with your main database.

If you only want part of the GEDCOM file in your database, just drag and drop the desired people from the new database into your main database.

If you import a GEDCOM file that contains data that RootsMagic does not know how to handle, it will be put into what is called a "listing file". The listing file has the same name as the GEDCOM file, except that the file extension is .LST instead of .GED. The listing file is a plain text file that you can look at with the Windows notepad or any other text editor. It will list any lines from the GEDCOM file that it didn't understand.

Creating a GEDCOM File

To create a GEDCOM file do "File > Export" from the main menu. RootsMagic will bring up an options dialog for the GEDCOM file you want to create. Select the options you want, then click OK.

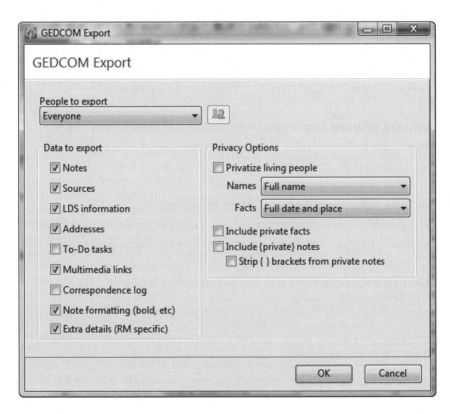

People to export lets you tell RootsMagic whether you want to export everyone in your database, or to select exactly which people you want to export. If you choose **"Select from a list"** RootsMagic will bring up a list of everybody in your database for you to select from. This selection list is the exact same screen described in the chapter titled "Custom Reports" (page 210). Simply select the individuals you want to include in the GEDCOM file.

Privacy options lets you filter the way information is exported for living people. If you don't check the "Privatize living people" box, people will be exported whether they are living or not. If you do check this box, RootsMagic will use the two drop lists to determine exactly how to do the filtering.

➢ Names – Lets you choose whether to export the full name of living people, or whether to export the word "Living".
➢ Facts – Lets you select whether to export the full date and place for each fact, or to not export the fact at all. You can also choose from several other filtering options, like date only, year only, place only, and year and place.

Include private facts lets you choose whether RootsMagic should include any facts (birth, marriage, death, etc.) that you have marked as "private".

Include private notes and **Strip brackets** let you choose whether RootsMagic should export any private notes you have entered. Private notes are described in more detail on page 85.

Data to export allows you to specify what types of data to export for each person.

➢ **Notes** - Check this box if you want notes included in the file.
➢ **Sources** - Check this box if you want sources and citations included in the file. You also have the option whether to

export the short version and bibliography for each source (since most other programs do not support those features).

- ➤ **LDS information** – Check this box if you want to export LDS information like LDS baptisms, endowments, and sealings.
- ➤ **Addresses** - Check this box if you want current addresses included in the file. If you are sending the GEDCOM file to someone else, you probably don't want to include the addresses of all your relatives.
- ➤ **To do tasks** - Check this box if you want your to do items to be exported.
- ➤ **Multimedia links** - Check this box if you want the links to your photos and other scrapbook items to be exported. This does **not** export the photos themselves, just the link information.
- ➤ **Correspondence log** - Check this box if you want your correspondence log to be exported. Since the correspondence log is not part of the official GEDCOM standard, this option is primarily useful when creating a GEDCOM file to be imported back into RootsMagic.
- ➤ **Note formatting** – Check this box if you want RootsMagic to export the bold, italic, and underlining in your notes. Most other genealogy programs can't handle the formatting codes, but this allows you to preserve the formatting when the GEDCOM file will be imported back into RootsMagic.
- ➤ **Extra details (RM specific)** - RootsMagic normally includes data in the GEDCOM that is specific to RootsMagic. But sometimes you may need to turn those items off (like if you are exporting the GEDCOM for a program or website that won't support those extra features).

After you select your options and click OK, RootsMagic will bring up the standard Windows file save dialog where you can enter the name you want to give your GEDCOM file.

Also, while GEDCOM is a very flexible file format, most programs implement it a little differently. Most of this has to do with the types and amount of data each program is capable of storing. If you create a GEDCOM file from RootsMagic and import it into another program which isn't as powerful as RootsMagic, you may lose some of your information simply because the other program has no place to store the information.

☺ **Tip**

RootsMagic allows you to specify whether any particular fact type should be exported when creating a GEDCOM file (they are all exported by default). For example, if you want to create a GEDCOM file but not include Occupation facts, you can do "Lists > Fact type list" from the main menu, highlight "Occupation" in the list, click the "Edit" button, then uncheck the GEDCOM Export checkbox. RootsMagic will then ignore the Occupation facts for everyone when creating a GEDCOM file (until you edit the fact type again and check the GEDCOM Export checkbox).

This is especially useful if you want to get rid of all instances of a fact in your database. For example, lets say you want to get rid of all Ancestral File Numbers in your database. Turn off the Ancestral File Number fact (as described above), then export your database to a GEDCOM file. Then create a new (blank) database and import that GEDCOM file into the new database. You now have the same database minus the Ancestral File Numbers. This works just as well on any other fact type.

☺ **Tip**

If you are transferring your full database back and forth between two computers (for example your desktop and a laptop), it is better to use the "File, Backup" command and "File, Restore" command which will not have any data loss associated with the GEDCOM format.

Should I Send GEDCOM Files by Email?

One of the most commonly asked questions about GEDCOM files is "How can I send a GEDCOM file by email so that the other person can use it" (or vice-versa). Unfortunately, every Internet provider is different, and so is every email package, so there is no easy answer.

The best way to email a GEDCOM to someone, is by sending it as an "attachment". An "attachment" is a way to attach a file (either text or binary) to the email, but it is **not** a part of the email text itself. Although GEDCOM files are basically text files, they have special formatting and can get quite large, and therefore shouldn't be sent as part of the email text itself (in other words, don't paste a GEDCOM into the message part of an email).

Since some email providers don't allow attachments to email messages, this fact alone eliminates those services from being able to dependably send or receive a GEDCOM file.

But (and there is always a "but"), just because an Internet provider can send and receive attachments, doesn't mean that it will work flawlessly. Some Internet providers "encode" attachments when they are sent out (and "decode" them when they are received). If you look at a GEDCOM file you have received, and it looks like total gibberish, then the file has probably been encoded (you may see terms like "MIME", "UUENCODED", etc).

Other systems don't support encoding and decoding, so they will just save the gibberish file, and expect that you will manually decode the file. If this is the case, you can use a program like WinZip (available at www.winzip.com) to decode the file for you.

Another problem you may encounter is the Internet provider breaking the file up into multiple pieces. In this case, you have to know what order the pieces go, and put them back together, and then you may still have to decode the file... what a headache.

Anyway, the bottom line is... if you and the other person can easily send and receive attachments to email messages, then go for it. It doesn't hurt to try sending the file once or twice just to see if it will work. If it doesn't work though, just create the GEDCOM file on a floppy disk and send it by snail mail (US postal service). By the time you fiddle around with all your settings, the disk will have already made its way there.

RootsMagic To-Go

Taking RootsMagic with you

RootsMagic makes it easy to take your program and data along with you. RootsMagic To-Go is a separate utility program that is installed along with RootsMagic. RootsMagic To-Go lets you install the RootsMagic program on your flash-drive, and helps you move your RootsMagic data back and forth between your main computer and the flash drive.

Running RootsMagic To-Go

To run RootsMagic To-Go just click on the icon which was installed on your desktop. It looks like the icon at the beginning of this section.

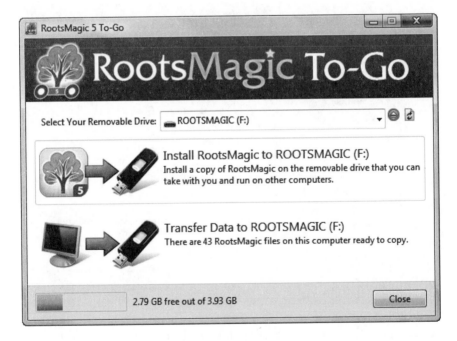

RootsMagic To-Go will display a list of removable drives connected to your computer. If there are none, RootsMagic will ask you to insert one. Select the removable drive that you want to use RootsMagic on. If RootsMagic To-Go doesn't find your flash drive for some reason, you may need to click the "refresh" button (the white button to the right of the removable drive list).

RootsMagic To-Go has two functions; 1) install RootsMagic on your flash drive, and 2) transfer data back and forth between your computer and your flash drive.

When you have finished using RootsMagic To-Go, click the red (circular) button beside the drive field to safely remove your removable drive.

Installing RootsMagic on Your Flash Drive

Click the "Install RootsMagic to Removable Disk" button to open the Install RootsMagic dialog box.

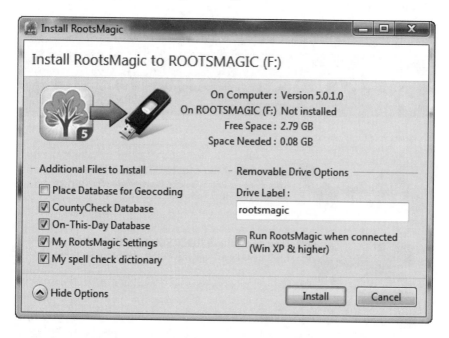

RootsMagic To-Go will display details about your removable drive, and will display an "Install" button that you can click to install RootsMagic on your drive. But if you want to customize the install, click the little round "Show Options" button to see options you can change for the install.

Place Database for Geocoding – Check this option to install the Place Database so you can Geocode your place names while working on the database from the removable drive. (The default is not to install the Place Database.)

CountyCheck Database – Check this option to install the CountyCheck Database which RootsMagic uses to verify whether a county exists on a particular date.

On-This-Day Database – Check this option to install the On-This-Day database that RootsMagic uses for the On-This-Day report.

My RootsMagic Settings – Check this option to install the settings you have set in RootsMagic, such as date format, whether to capitalize surnames, etc. (The default is not to install the RootsMagic settings.)

My spell check dictionary – Check this option to install the dictionary with your additions to the spell checker. (The default is not to install your local spell check dictionary.)

Drive Label – The default drive label is left blank. You can change this by entering a name you would like to use for the drive label.

Run RootsMagic when connected – Check this option to run RootsMagic automatically when the removable drive is inserted into the USB port of another computer. The default is to not start RootsMagic, letting you start RootsMagic when your are ready. (Note: This feature only works on Windows XP SP2 or later, where auto-run from a removable drive was introduced.)

Transferring Data

RootsMagic To-Go will transfer your data files to the removable drive and to your home computer. Click the "Transfer data" button to bring up the transfer screen.

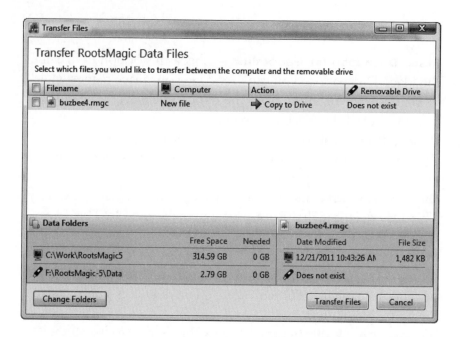

RootsMagic To-Go will display a list of files that are available to transfer between your computer and the flash drive. There may be files on your computer that need to be transferred to your flash drive, and there may be files on your flash drive that need to be transferred back to your computer.

RootsMagic To-Go keeps track of which files have changed and tells you which way you need to copy each file. Each file in the list will tell you which direction the file needs to be copied. It will also tell you whether a file exists on both the computer and flash drive, or just on one of them.

> ### 💣 Warning
>
> When you transfer files, don't modify both the desktop copy and flash drive copy of the file without syncing your data in between. If you do happen to modify both copies of the data file, RootsMagic To-Go doesn't know which one to keep and tells you there is a conflict. Then you have to tell RootsMagic which copy to keep.

Just mark the checkbox in front of any of the files you want to transfer, then click the "Transfer Files" button.

RootsMagic To-Go will show all the databases in whatever folder you've told RootsMagic to store your data files in. If you didn't specify a folder in RootsMagic, the Documents or My Documents folder will be used by default. If the folder is not the one you want to transfer from, click the "Change Folders" button and you can set the sync folder for both the computer and flash drive.

> **Note**
>
> RootsMagic To-Go does not transfer your multimedia files to the removable drive. RootsMagic doesn't change the media pathnames in your file though, so when you transfer the file back to your desktop computer the media will remain linked.

Merging Duplicate Records

Two heads are not better than one.

Sometime you may find that you have the same person entered more than once in the same database. This is especially common after importing a GEDCOM file into an existing database.

RootsMagic helps you clean up these duplicate records by providing a "merge" capability. Merging lets you combine two records for a person into a single record.

RootsMagic allows you to manually merge duplicate records (one at a time), or it can search for duplicates for you. In addition, it also provides a number of different automatic merge options.

> **Warning**
>
> You should always make a backup before a session of merging, so that if you accidentally merge the wrong records, you can restore your database from a backup.

Manual Merge

 To merge duplicate records one at a time, highlight one of the duplicate records on the main screen, then select **"Tools > Merge > Manual merge"** from the main menu, or click the right mouse button and choose "Manual merge" from the popup menu. RootsMagic will open the manual merge dialog.

Before you can merge records, you must select the records you want to merge. The merge screen will display the two records side by side, including names, sex, facts, and all immediate family members. The person who was highlighted on the main screen will already be selected on the left side of the dialog (the "primary" record).

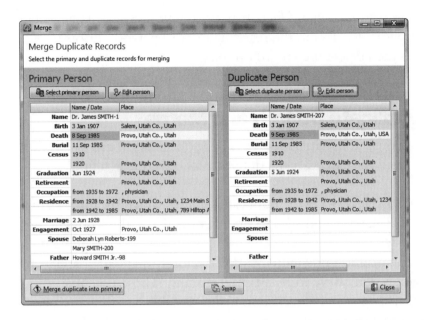

Click the **"Select duplicate person"** button and RootsMagic will bring up the search screen for you to select the duplicate record. This search screen is exactly the same as the one described in the chapter titled "Searching for Information" (page 75). Select the person, and his or her data will be displayed on the right half of the merge screen.

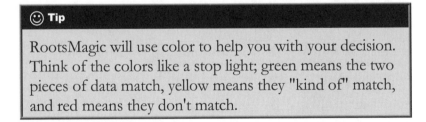

☺ **Tip**

RootsMagic will use color to help you with your decision. Think of the colors like a stop light; green means the two pieces of data match, yellow means they "kind of" match, and red means they don't match.

If you want to switch the position of the two records, simply click the **" Swap"** button before performing the merge.

When you are sure you want to merge the two records together, click the **"Merge duplicate into primary"** button. RootsMagic will copy all of the information (including family links, facts, notes, and sources) from the record on the right to the record on the left. If both records contain facts that are identical, RootsMagic will not duplicate the fact in the resulting merged person. RootsMagic will then delete the record on the right.

Duplicate Search and Merge

Although the manual merge is handy at times, it can also be tedious to search for the duplicate records one at a time.

RootsMagic can do a "duplicate search", which means it analyzes your database, and tries to find records that it thinks might be duplicates. It compares the names of the individuals in your database and finds individuals with closely matching names (the names don't have to be an exact match). These potential matches are then checked to make sure they are the same sex, and to check other information that you choose.

To do a duplicate search and merge, choose "Tools > Merge > Duplicate search merge" from the main menu.

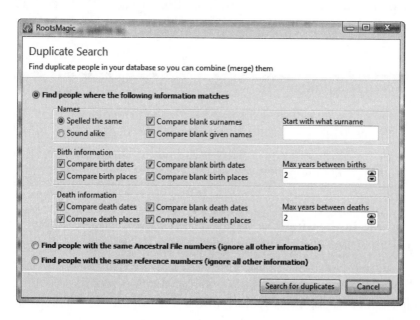

RootsMagic offers three different kinds of duplicate searches.

Find people where the following information matches lets you set options to have RootsMagic compare people using.

➢ **Names** lets you tell RootsMagic how people's names must match to be considered duplicates. You can specify whether matching names have to match exactly, or if they just need to sound alike. You can also choose whether blank names (both given and surnames) will be considered as matches with non blank names. Checking these boxes often leads to many false duplicates.

➢ **Start with what surname** lets you tell RootsMagic where in the database to start the duplicate search. If you leave this blank, then RootsMagic will search the entire database for duplicates. If you enter "D", then RootsMagic will start with surnames beginning with the letter "D". If you enter "Jones", then RootsMagic will start with people with the last name "Jones".

➢ **Birth information** tells RootsMagic whether to compare birth information of people when checking for duplicates. You can choose to compare birth dates and / or birth places. You can also enter a maximum number of years between birth dates. If you set this value to 0, RootsMagic will only consider two individuals duplicates if they were born the exact same year. A value of 5 means that two individual's birth dates can be 5 years apart and still be considered duplicates. The smaller this number, the fewer duplicates RootsMagic will find. You can also tell RootsMagic whether you want to consider individuals without birth dates or birth places as possible duplicates. If you don't check these boxes, RootsMagic will not consider any individuals whose birth date (or place) is blank, even if they match in other ways.

➢ **Death information** works the same as the birth options (except with death data of course).

Find people with the same Ancestral File Numbers finds individuals with matching Ancestral File numbers. All other criteria are ignored.

Find people with the same reference numbers finds individuals with matching Reference numbers (REFN). All other criteria are ignored.

After you have made your choices and clicked the OK button, RootsMagic will search through your database for records that might be duplicates and displays them in a list.

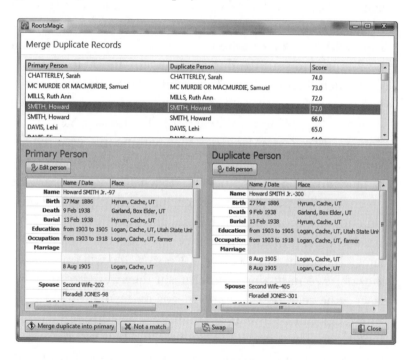

The list is sorted so that the most likely matches are at the top of the list. As you scroll down through the list of possible duplicates, the lower half of the dialog will display the full information about the two highlighted records.

If the two records on the row are duplicates, click the "Merge duplicate into primary" button and RootsMagic will merge the two records.

If the two records on the row are NOT matches, you can click the "Not a match" button and RootsMagic will remove the pair from the merge list, and will not display them as matches in any future duplicate search merges. You can select "Tools > Merge > View 'not duplicates' list" from the menu to see a list of all pairs you have marked as not duplicates, and you can remove pairs from that list.

RootsMagic also provides buttons on the merge list to edit both the primary and duplicate records.

> ☺ Tip
>
> When you merge duplicate records, you may find that the resulting record has two spouses, which happen to be the same person. This is because the spouse records are also duplicated. When you merge the duplicate spouse records, this situation will correct itself. **Don't** just delete the extra spouse, or you will end up with two families, one with an "unknown" spouse.

Automatic Merges

RootsMagic offers several automatic merge options when you select **"Tools, Merge, Automatic merges"** from the main menu. The following dialog box will appear where you can select any or all of the merges offered.

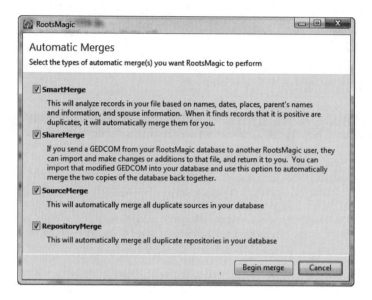

SmartMerge

SmartMerge will search for duplicates, and will assign a "score" to each pair of potential matching records based on: names, birth, christening, death, and burial, parent data, and marriage data. If the matching records "score" high enough, SmartMerge will automatically merge the records for you. Any conflicting data in any of the above fields will disqualify the records from being SmartMerged.

This is very useful as a first pass in doing a merge, then you can run the duplicate search and merge to pick up the duplicate records that automatic SmartMerge missed.

SmartMerge may reject records that appear to be exact duplicates, but this is usually because there is not enough information for SmartMerge to base its score on. In these cases, SmartMerge errs on the side of safety.

ShareMerge

This is one of the most useful merge options available if you intend to share data with family members who are also using RootsMagic. This option is explained in more detail in the following section "Collaborating With Family Members".

SourceMerge

This option will automatically merge all sources which are exact duplicates. If you select this option, you should also select the following option to merge duplicate repositories as well, since RootsMagic won't merge sources which are identical except for pointing to different repositories (even if the repositories are identical).

RepositoryMerge

There may be times when you find duplicate repositories in your database. Unfortunately, you can't just delete the duplicates because it will leave sources without their repository. This option will automatically merge all exactly duplicate repositories.

Collaborating With Family Members

One of the biggest problems facing families doing genealogy, is how to share their data back and forth without having to resort to long merge sessions.

Even when multiple family members start with the same original database, they may each enter different people, or make modifications to the same person. Then when you try to consolidate that information, you must either sit through a long merge session, or evaluate each database, picking and choosing which data is different and which is the same. RootsMagic offers several features that greatly simplify this process.

Globally Unique ID – Any time you create a new person in RootsMagic, that person will be assigned a "hidden" ID number, which is unique to that person. This number is unique to that person… no other person (in any database) will ever receive that same unique ID number. If you export your database to a GEDCOM file, that unique ID number will travel with that person. And when you import that GEDCOM file into a RootsMagic database, that unique ID will come in with the person.

So what does this mean to me? Let's say you have a "master" database that you would like to share with family members. Simply create a GEDCOM file of your data and send it to them. When they import that GEDCOM file into their copy of RootsMagic, each person will have the same "unique ID" as the corresponding person in your master database.

You can now add, edit, or make other changes to people in your database, and they can do the same in their database. It is not necessary to keep the two databases "in sync".

I can already hear you asking *"how will we ever get those two databases combined into a single complete database"*?

Simple, just have your family member send you a GEDCOM file of their database, and import it into your database (remember… only do this if you are *both* using RootsMagic). At this point you will have a large number of duplicates, some of which are identical, and others that may differ a little bit. But RootsMagic knows which people are *really* the same, since their "unique ID" traveled with them.

So... select **"Tools > Merge > Automatic merges"** from the main menu, and leave all four options selected. RootsMagic will automatically merge the duplicate repositories and sources that exist. Then it will automatically merge everybody in the database who has the same unique ID. If there is conflicting information in the two people's data, RootsMagic will keep both copies of that data. For example, if the birth date of a person was changed in one of the databases, RootsMagic will keep both birth facts for the person.

Research Aids

Research is the process of going up alleys to see if they are blind. - Marston Bates

Although RootsMagic is designed to store information you have already collected, it can also assist you in your research. RootsMagic provides both To-Do lists and Research Logs to help you keep track of what you need to do, as well as the research you have already completed.

So what is the difference between a to-do list and a research log?

A to-do list is simply a place to keep track of tasks you need to do. This can be a research task, but can also be a task like answering a letter, cleaning up data, making a phone call, or sending out a Shareable CD to the family.

A research log is where you keep track of research you have done towards a specific objective. You can create research logs for people, families, events, or places. Then any time you check a source for information about that objective, you can add it to the research log. And by including research that didn't turn up anything useful, you can make sure you don't keep repeating that search over and over.

To Do List

The to-do list provides a place to save all those tasks you need to accomplish. It lets you enter an unlimited number of "tasks" for each person or family. You can even enter general to-do tasks which are not specific to a single person.

You can access a person's to do list from the main screen by highlighting that person, then clicking the "todo" button on the toolbar, then selecting "Person". You can also access the to-do list from a person's edit screen by clicking the **"To Do"** button.

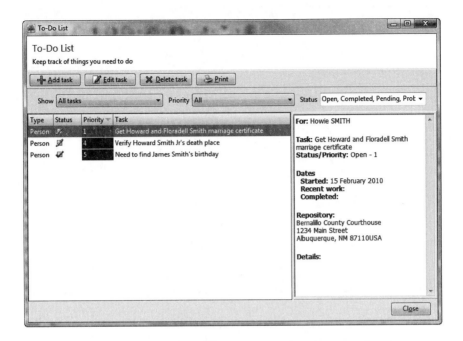

You can filter the To-Do list in several different ways:

- **Show** lets you filter based on whether the to-do items are person, family, or general to-do items
- **Priority** lets you filter based on the priority assigned to each to-do item
- **Status** lets you filter based on whether each to-do item is open, completed, pending, or a problem

And finally, you can sort the to-do list on any of the columns displayed (type, status, priority, or task name) by simply clicking on the column header you want to sort by.

Add task lets you add a new task to the list. If you are in a person's edit screen RootsMagic will ask you whether the to-do item is for the person or one of his families. The following dialog will appear where you can enter the task information.

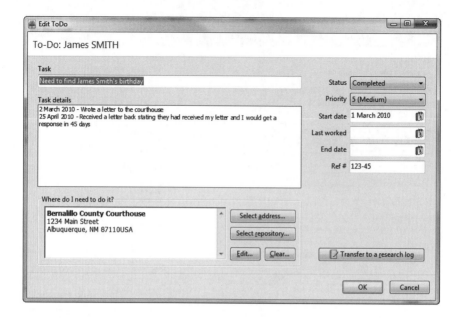

- ➢ **Task** is a one-line description of the task.
- ➢ **Task details** allows you to enter full details on the task, what needs to be accomplished, and what the results were.
- ➢ **"Where do I need to do it?"** lets you enter the place where you need to do this task. You can select either a repository or an address, as well as edit the location or clear it.
- ➢ **Status** lets you specify whether the task is still open or whether it has been completed. You can also denote if there is a problem with the task.
- ➢ **Priority** lets you specify how urgent this task is from 1 (highest priority) through 9 (lowest)
- ➢ **Start date** lets you enter the date you created this task.
- ➢ **Last worked** lets you enter the most recent date you worked on this task.
- ➢ **End date** lets you enter the date you finished this task. Although many people will just delete a task they have finished, others want to keep a record of the tasks.
- ➢ **Personal file number** lets you enter a number or text to tie this todo item to your paper records.

Edit task lets you modify the highlighted task in the list. You can also double click a task in the list to edit the task. **Delete task** will delete the highlighted task from the list. This is useful when you have completed the task and no longer need it.

Print will let you print the "to do" list for the current person.

RootsMagic also has a "master todo list" which lets you view all the todo items in the database, and allows you to enter "general" todo tasks which aren't tied to a specific person or family. To access the master todo list, do "Lists > Todo list" from the main menu. You can add, edit, delete or print tasks from here.

If your to-do item is a completed research task, you can click "Transfer to a research log" to copy the information into any existing research log.

Research Manager

The Research Manager lets you keep track of research you have done. You can create research logs for people, families, events, or places. You can also create general research logs for other research goals as well.

You can access the Research Logs list by selecting Lists > Research Manager from the main menu, or by clicking the Research Log button on the Edit Person screen. When you open the list from the main menu, RootsMagic will display all the research logs for the entire database, while opening the list from the Edit Person screen will only display research logs for that person.

You can filter the list of research logs displayed by typing text into the "Search" field and clicking the magnifying glass button (or pressing Enter). RootsMagic will display only those research logs which contain the words you entered. This is useful when trying to find research logs referring to a specific name, place, or source.

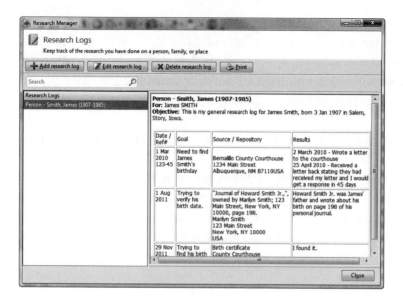

You can add, edit, delete or print research logs directly from the Research Manager.

Adding a Research Log

Each Research Log you create includes a name and objective, and then as many research items as you wish to add to it. Click the "Add research log" button to create a new research log.

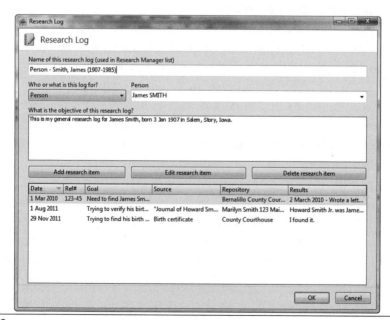

Generally you will create a research log for a person you are researching, or a research goal you are trying to solve. You can then keep track of every source (document, website, etc) that you check towards that goal. You can add, edit or delete research items from the Research Log screen.

To add a new item to your research log, click the Add research item button.

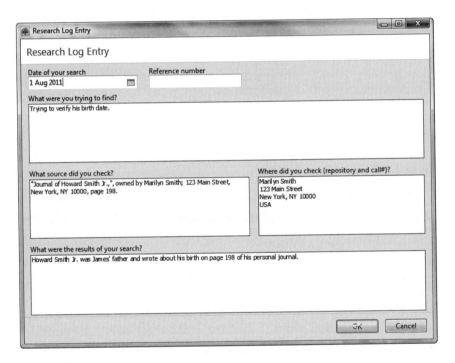

You can then enter the date and source you checked, what you were trying to find in that source, and what the result of that search was.

GenSmarts Integration

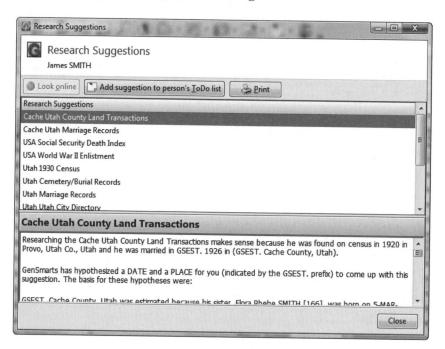

GenSmarts is an add-on program which can make research suggestions for individuals in your database. Although GenSmarts is normally run as a standalone program, RootsMagic has integrated direct support for it.

If you have GenSmarts installed, all you have to do is highlight a person on the main RootsMagic screen and select "**Tools > GenSmarts suggestions**" from the menu. You can also customize the toolbar to add a GenSmarts button which can be clicked (customizing the toolbar is described on page 27).

RootsMagic will automatically request research suggestions from GenSmarts and will display this dialog.

As you highlight each research suggestion, details about that suggestion will be shown in the bottom half of the dialog.

If the highlighted record type is available online, you can click the "Look online" button and RootsMagic will do an online search for the person in that record.

You can click the "Add suggestion to person's ToDo list" button to (what else?) add the suggestion to the person's todo list. This lets you keep track of any progress you have made on that suggestion.

And finally, you can print the list of suggestions (along with all the details for each suggestion).

> **Note**
>
> If you don't own GenSmarts, you can order it directly from RootsMagic at www.rootsmagic.com. You can also download a free trial version as well.

Correspondence List

The Correspondence List is designed to help you keep track of all your genealogy related correspondence. The list does not provide the capability to write the letter itself. That is for your word processor or good old pen and pencil.

What it does do is provide a location to enter information about letters and packages you send (and receive), so that you can easily see whether you ever wrote that letter you meant to send.

It is also useful for keeping track of exchanged emails while collaborating with family and other researchers.

To access the correspondence list, select "Lists > Correspondence list" from the main menu.

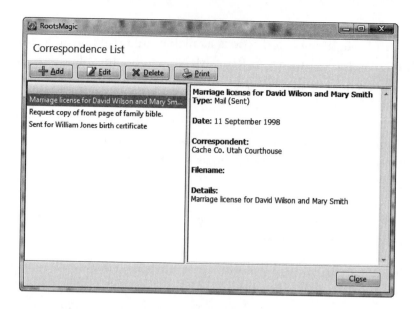

To add an item to the correspondence list, click the **"Add"** button and RootsMagic will display the following dialog.

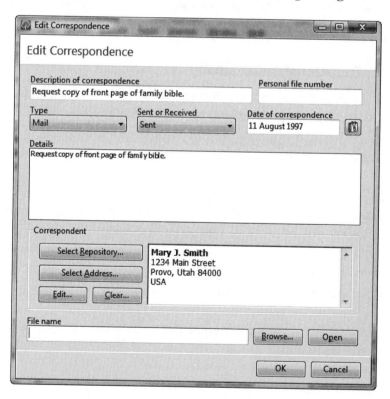

> **Description of correspondence** – A brief description of the correspondence that is displayed in the correspondence list.

> **Personal file number** – Allows you to enter a number which ties this entry to your hard copies.

> **Type** – Lets you specify the type of correspondence: mail, email, telephone, fax, or other.

> **Sent or received** – Lets you specify whether you sent the correspondence or received it from someone else.

> **Date of correspondence** – Enter the date you mailed or received your letter or package.

> **Details** – Enter details about why you wrote, or what the received correspondence was about.

> **Correspondent** – Lets you enter the person or organization you corresponded with. You can select either a repository or an address. You can also edit the correspondent information or clear it altogether.

> **File name** – Lets you enter a file name for the correspondence. This is useful if you wrote a letter in your word processor and want to be able to access it from RootsMagic. You can click the "Browse" button to select the file with the file dialog. If you click the "Open" button, RootsMagic will open the file using whatever program it is associated with in Windows.

To edit an item in the correspondence list, highlight the item in the list, and click the "Edit" button. RootsMagic will display the same dialog used when you added the item. Make any desired changes and click the OK button.

To delete an item in the correspondence list, highlight the item in the list, and click the "Delete" button. RootsMagic will ask if you are sure you want to delete the item.

To print the correspondence list, click the "Print" button. RootsMagic will allow you to print the correspondence as described on page 152.

Named Groups

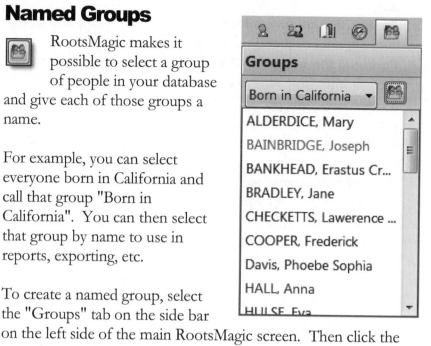

RootsMagic makes it possible to select a group of people in your database and give each of those groups a name.

For example, you can select everyone born in California and call that group "Born in California". You can then select that group by name to use in reports, exporting, etc.

To create a named group, select the "Groups" tab on the side bar on the left side of the main RootsMagic screen. Then click the named groups button.

On the Named Groups screen you can add, edit or delete named groups which can be used on the Groups panel or elsewhere in the program.

To create a new named group click the "New" button. RootsMagic will open the Select People screen described on page 210. Select the people you want in your group, then click the OK button. You can then enter the name for this group. RootsMagic will add that group to the Named Groups list.

To edit a named group highlight the group in the list and click the "Edit" button. RootsMagic will open the Select People screen again and you can change or re-select the people for the group.

To just change the name of the group highlight the group name in the list and click the "Rename" button.

To delete a named group highlight the group in the list and click the "Delete" button.

After you close the Named Groups screen RootsMagic will let you display any groups you have created on the side list. When you select a group from the drop list, RootsMagic will display the members of that group in the list.

But you aren't limited to accessing the groups from that screen. You can also select named groups when exporting or printing many reports where you have the option to select people. Normally in those situations you can choose "Everyone" or "Select from a list". But when you have named groups, those groups are also included to choose from.

Sending Books to Family Members

One of the best ways to collect information from family members is to send them a book of your family and ask them to provide any missing information. Simply include a letter with a copy of the book specifying what information you want for each person.

As an alternative (albeit a labor intensive one), you can add facts to people and enter a sequence of underline characters where unknown dates or places would go. When you print a book with underlines like this, the sentences will read like:

He was born _____ in _____.

and your relatives can simply fill in the blanks. Make sure you offer to send a copy of the completed book if they reply with additional information.

☺ **Tip**

Here is a hint once told me by a user. He found that he could get a 100% return of his books from a woman if he intentionally made her birth date about 3 years too early in the book.

Other Printouts

RootsMagic also provides several other printouts that can be helpful in your research. Most of these printouts can be found under the "Lists" section of the Reports dialog.

The **Fact list** allows you to generate lists of any facts you are missing or have duplicated. For example, you can print out a list of every person who is missing a birth fact, or any person you have multiple death facts for. In addition, it is also useful for determining what information you have entered into RootsMagic that you do not have any documentation for.

The **Individual list** will help you track down those end-of-line individuals that you need to research to take your family line back further.

The **Problem list** will point out potential data errors, such as people being born after their mother died. To create the problem list, do "Tools > Problem Search" from the main menu, then generate the problem list. You can print the resulting list from that screen. While many of these are data entry errors, some of them may be erroneous data that you typed in correctly. This list is described in more detail on page 261

The **Missing Information list** lets you print a list of people who are missing any fact or facts. You can even find people who are just missing a date or place for a fact. RootsMagic will leave a blank on the list so you can use the list as a worksheet to find the information.

The **Surname Statistics list** will create a list of all surnames in your database, how many times each surname occurs, and the earliest and most recent year the surname occurs.

The **LDS Ordinance list** is useful if you are a member of the LDS Church and need to know which people have not had their ordinances completed.

Creating a Family Website

One of the best ways to find out more about your family is to get in contact with other people who are researching the same information. In the past, this required writing a lot of letters and making a lot of phone calls. With the advent of the Internet and the World Wide Web, it is becoming easier to make contact with other researchers, if you can let them know of your research interests.

RootsMagic can help you with this by helping you create a website with your genealogical information, and links where other researchers can email you if they have any common information. You can learn how to create a family website by reading the chapter titled, "Putting Your Family on the Web" (page 276).

Keeping a Research Database

When doing your research, you will sometimes come across individuals who might be a part of your family line, but you aren't sure and can't prove anything yet.

One way to keep track of these individuals is to create a new database called RESEARCH. When you come across unproven ancestors, enter them in the research database the same way you enter your family into your main database.

Entering your unproven ancestors into RootsMagic allows you to maintain unproven family lines, facts, and documentation on each of these people, but by keeping these individuals in a separate database, you eliminate the problem of removing them if they turn out to be unrelated.

Then, when you prove that these folks really are part of your family, you can drag and drop them into your main database.

Tools

If the only tool you have is a hammer, you tend to see every problem as a nail. - Abraham Maslow

RootsMagic provides a large number of tools that make managing your data easier.

Problem Search

When entering information into any program there is the possibility of making a mistake. RootsMagic's problem search is designed to help you find these mistakes.

To search for potential problems, do **"Tools, Problem search, Problem list"** from the menu, tell RootsMagic which problems you want it to search for, and it will generate a list of any person who has one of the selected problems.

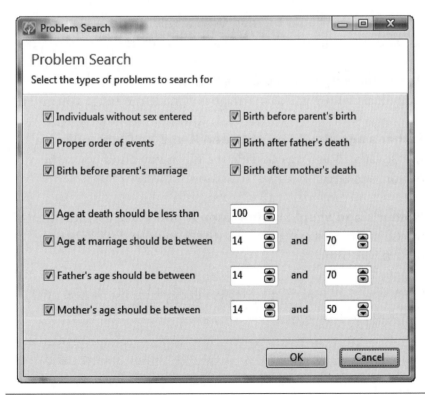

Individuals without sex entered will find individuals who have "Unknown" entered for their sex.

Proper order of events will catch problems like a person getting married before their birth or after their death.

Birth before parent's marriage will list individuals whose birth date falls before their parent's marriage date.

Birth before parent's birth will list individuals whose birth date is earlier than their mother's or father's birth date.

Birth after father's death will list individuals whose birth date is after their father's death date.

Birth after mother's death will list individuals whose birth date is after their mother's death date.

Age at death should be less than X will list individuals whose age at death is greater than the value you enter.

Age at marriage should be between X and Y will list individuals whose age at marriage is outside the range you enter.

Father's age should be between X and Y will list individuals whose father's age was outside the range you enter when the person was born.

Mother's age should be between X and Y will list individuals whose mother's age was outside the range you enter when the person was born.

Once you click OK, RootsMagic will display a list of potential problems which looks like this.

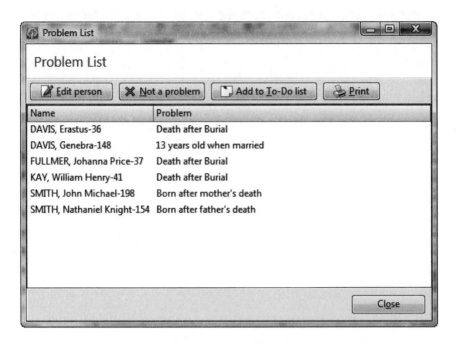

RootsMagic allows you to edit the person by highlighting the problem and clicking **"Edit person"**.

If a problem in the list isn't really a problem (for example if Aunt Mary really was 102 years old), you can highlight the non-problem and click the **"Not a problem"** button. RootsMagic will remove the item from the list and will not display it as a problem the next time you run the problem search. If you ever want to see what "problems" RootsMagic is ignoring, you can do "Tools, Problem search, View 'not a problem' list". You can remove items from that list so that the problem search will detect them once again.

Sometimes you may not be able to (or have time to) fix a problem right away, so you can highlight the problem and click the "Add to To-Do list" to add the problem to the person's to-do list.

If you want to print the problem list, simply click the "Print" button on the dialog.

Setting the Living Flag

When you import a GEDCOM file you may often have individuals with no birth or death dates, or other means for RootsMagic to know how to apply the "Living" flag for the person.

The "Set Living" function lets you set (or clear) the living flag for any group of people in your database. Select **"Tools > Set living"** from the main menu and RootsMagic will bring up a dialog asking if you want to set the living flag to true or false for a group of people. Choose the desired setting and click OK. RootsMagic will then bring up the selection screen (page 210) for you to choose the individuals whose living flag you want to change.

Setting Relationships to a Person

RootsMagic can display relationships of the highlighted person in the status line at the bottom of the screen. You can choose which person to base these relationships on. Select **"Tools > Set relationships"** from the menu and RootsMagic will bring up the following dialog.

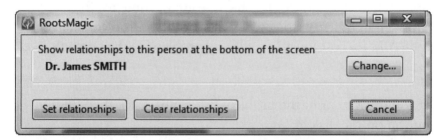

RootsMagic will default to the currently highlighted person, but you can click "Change" to select a different person. Click "Set relationships" to set the relationships to that person.

From that point on (until you change it), RootsMagic will display the relationship of the highlighted person on the main screen to that person. For example, if you set relationships for yourself, then when your 3rd great grandfather is highlighted, the status line will display "third great grandfather".

Color Coding People

Have you ever wanted to be able to quickly tell whether a person in your database is part of a particular group? RootsMagic makes this easy by letting you color code any group of people. Selecting **"Tools > Color code people"** from the main menu and RootsMagic will bring up the following dialog.

You can set or clear the display color for any group of people.

> **Set color** – Lets you choose the color to set for a group of people. You can select from 15 different color code groups (including black).
> **Clear color** – Lets you clear the color for any group of people.
> **Clear all colors** – Lets you clear (reset) the color for the entire database.

You can perform these operations for:

➤ Ancestors of the current person.
➤ Descendants of the current person. You can also choose whether to include the spouses of descendants.
➤ People selected from a list. If you choose this option, RootsMagic will bring up the selection screen (page 210) for you to choose the individuals whose color you want to set or clear.
➤ The current highlighted person on the screen.

When you set the color for a group of people, it sets the color for people matching those characteristics at that instant. If you later add or edit people you may need to re-run the color coding.

The Date Calculator and Calendar

The date calculator lets you calculate dates and the amount of time between dates. Selecting **"Tools > Date calculator"** from the main menu will bring up the date calculator. The date calculator can also be brought up when you are entering dates for facts (like birth, death, etc.).

 Tip

The date calculator is the perfect tool for determining an approximate birth date from a tombstone inscription like **"Died 12 March 1942 at the age of 82 Years, 10 Months, and 2 Days".**

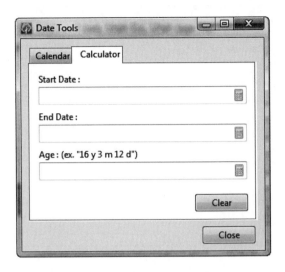

The calculator depends on which fields you have filled out.

If you fill out...	Calculate will determine...
Start date and Age	End date
End date and Age	Start date
Start date and End date	Age

When you are using the date calculator while entering facts for a person, it contains 2 additional buttons labeled **"Select Start"** and **"Select end"**. Clicking on these buttons will copy either the start date or the end date into the fact's date field, and will then close the date calculator. Clicking the **"Clear"** button simply erases all the fields in the date calculator so you can do another calculation.

The calendar tab shows a calendar where you can look up dates to see what day of the week they fell on. You can click the arrows to move back and forth by months or years. The longer you hold the arrow down the faster RootsMagic cycles through the months or years.

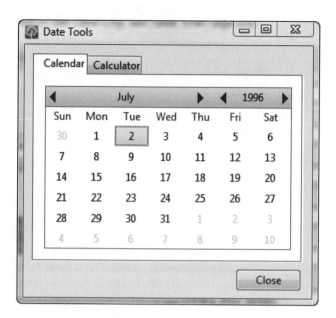

The Relationship Calculator

If you have ever wondered how you are related to another person in your database, the relationship calculator is the quickest way to find out. Simply do **"Tools > Relationship calculator"** from the main menu.

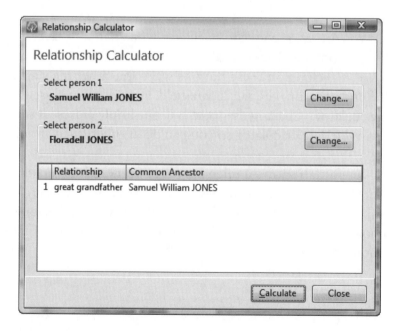

You must first select the 2 individuals whose relationship you want to know. Person 1 will already contain the name of the person who was highlighted on the main screen. Click on the "Change" button for person 2 and select the other individual. Finally, click the "Calculate" button and RootsMagic will tell you how the two people are related, and who the common ancestors are.

 Tip

If you want a chart that shows the relationship between two people, check out the Relationship Chart described on page 182. RootsMagic also provides a supercharged version of the Relationship Calculator called the Kinship List. The Kinship List will print out every relative of a person and list their relationship to that person.

The Soundex Calculator

The Soundex calculator simply calculates the Soundex code for any name you type into it.

To access the Soundex calculator, select "Tools > Soundex calculator" from the main menu. There are no buttons to click; it calculates the code as you type it in. You can backspace and type in other names to find their Soundex code as well. When you are done, simply click the Close button.

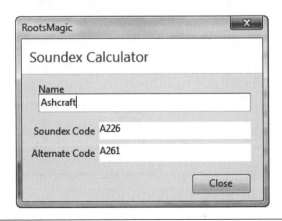

Many census and other types of records use the Soundex method to group similar sounding names together. For example, "Smith" and "Smythe" both have the same Soundex code "S530", so grouping by Soundex would keep all the Smiths and Smythes together.

Note

Some genealogical records (most notably census records) use a slightly modified algorithm when calculating the Soundex code. Although only a few names actually end up with different codes, RootsMagic supports both algorithms. If RootsMagic calculates two different Soundex codes, make sure you check under both codes.

Spell Checking

RootsMagic provides a built-in spell checker, and includes the ability to add your own words to its dictionary (which is especially important for family names).

To spell check the text in a single note, click the spell check button on the note editor toolbar, or click the right mouse button in the note editor and select Spell Check from the menu, or press F7 while the cursor is in the note field. RootsMagic will begin spell checking the note text.

☺ Tip

Note fields also provide a feature called "live" spell checking. If you've been wondering why some words in your note had a squiggly red line under them, that is the spell checker telling you it doesn't know the word. You can right-click the word and RootsMagic will display a list of suggestions without you having to open the full spell check screen described below. If you want to turn this feature off, go to Tools > Program options to disable it.

To spell check all the notes in your database at once, select "Tools > Spell check" from the main menu. RootsMagic will display the following dialog and allow you to check individual notes, family notes, and fact notes (in any combination). Select the types of notes you want to spell check, then click OK. RootsMagic will begin checking the notes in your database.

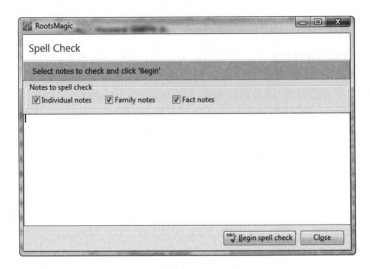

When an unknown word is found, RootsMagic will display the Spell Check dialog with the unknown word. You can type in the correct spelling, or you can select one of the suggested replacements from the Suggestions list.

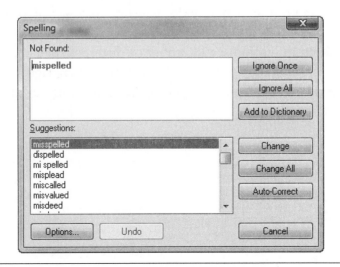

- ➢ **Ignore Once** – Causes this occurrence of the misspelled word to be skipped. If the same misspelled word appears later, it will be reported.
- ➢ **Ignore All** – Causes this and all further occurrences of the misspelled word to be skipped. You might use this button if the word reported as a misspelling is actually spelled correctly. If the word is one you use frequently, you may wish to ignore it permanently by selecting the Add button.
- ➢ **Add to Dictionary** – Causes the reported word to be added to the dictionary. Use the Add button if a correctly spelled word you use often is reported as a misspelling (e.g., your family name). If the word is not used frequently, you may want to select the Ignore or Ignore All buttons instead.
- ➢ **Change** – Causes the reported word to be replaced with the highlighted word in the Suggestions list. Only this occurrence of the reported word is replaced. If you want this and all following occurrences of the word replaced, select the Change All button. If the Change To box is empty, the Change button changes to Delete.
- ➢ **Change All** – Causes this and all following occurrences of the reported word to be replaced with the highlighted word in the Suggestions list. If you want only this occurrence of the word to be replaced, use the Change button.
- ➢ **Auto-Correct** - Causes this misspelled word to be auto corrected to the highlighted suggestion as you type from now on.
- ➢ **Options** - Lets you set a number of different spell check options, including choosing the dictionary language.
- ➢ **Cancel** – Exits from the spell check dialog without making any more changes.

Search and Replace

Probably the most powerful data manipulation feature in RootsMagic (and possibly the most dangerous to your data if used improperly) is global search and replace. **To do a global search and replace**, select **"Search, Search and replace"** from the main menu. RootsMagic will display the following dialog.

RootsMagic doesn't simply search and replace any and every piece of data. You must tell it what type of data you want to search and replace by selecting from the **"Search in"** drop list. You can search and replace in:

Names – Given	Multimedia filenames
Names – Surnames	Notes – General
Names – Nicknames	Notes – Family
Names – Prefix	Notes – Facts
Names – Suffix	
Places	

Then just type in the text you want to search for, and the text you want to replace it with, and click **OK**. RootsMagic will bring up each item to replace one at a time for you to confirm. You can **"Replace"** or **"Skip"** the item and go onto the next item, or you can **"Replace all"** items without confirmation.

> ☺ **Tip**
>
> Keep in mind that if you want to search for every instance of Stafford in place names and wanted to change them to Staffordshire, the replace all option would also change Stafford, Stafford, England to Staffordshire, Staffordshire, England. So you want to take account of all punctuation and spaces. So to replace Stafford correctly, you would search for Stafford, England and replace it with Staffordshire, England.

Search and replace can also be used as "Search and Delete" by just leaving the **"Replace with"** field blank. RootsMagic will then search for each occurrence of the text you enter, and replace it with nothing (thus deleting it). Be careful with this new knowledge.

> ☺ **Tip**
>
> Although search and replace can be used to update broken media links, it is easier to open the Media Gallery (**Lists > Media Gallery**) and select **"Tools > Fix broken media links"** to have RootsMagic fix them automatically.

Count Trees In Database

The "Count trees" command simply counts the number of trees in your database. This is especially useful if you have imported GEDCOM files into your database. Often those GEDCOM files may contain multiple unlinked trees that you are unaware of.

To generate a list of the trees in your database, select "Tools >
Count trees" from the main menu. RootsMagic will count the
number of trees and display them in a list.

The list will list each tree in your database, along with the name
and record number of one person in each tree to help you find
the tree in your database.

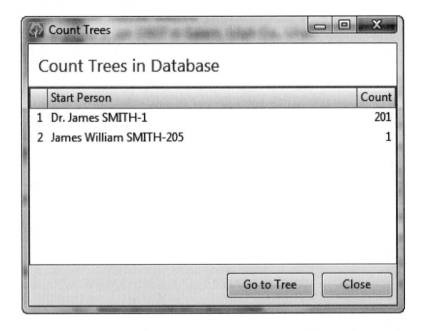

You can bring a tree up on the main screen by highlighting the
tree in the list and clicking the "Go to tree" button.

Putting Your Family on the Web

Oh what a tangled web we weave...

Creating a Family Website

With the explosive growth of the internet it is becoming easier to make contact with family members and other researchers. RootsMagic provides an automatic website creator built right into the program.

RootsMagic will create all the files necessary for your website, and will place those files together in a directory on your hard drive. Your website can include: notes, sources, photographs, email link, surname index, and a bibliography.

To create a website from your RootsMagic data, select "Internet, Create a web site" from the main menu. The RootsMagic WebWizard will appear.

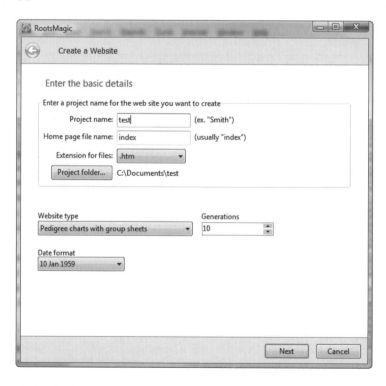

The first screen of the wizard asks you for basic information for your website.

- ➢ **Project name** is the name of your "project". RootsMagic will use this name to create a subdirectory in your project folder to hold all the project files.
- ➢ **Home page file name** lets you select the "starting" file for your web site. Usually you should set this to "index".
- ➢ **Extension for files** lets you specify whether you want the file extensions for your files to be .htm or .html. Usually you will just pick .htm, but some internet servers require the use of .html.
- ➢ **Project folder** lets you select where you want RootsMagic to create the project folder for your website.
- ➢ **Website type** lets you select the general format for your web site. RootsMagic offers a wide variety of formats, including family group sheet, pedigree chart, pedigree chart with group sheet combo, ancestor book, descendant book and alphabetical book. The book formats print your data in a narrative (sentence) structure, while the pedigree chart and family group sheet formats are more graphical. The Ancestor Book, Descendant Book, and Pedigree Chart formats start with the person who was originally highlighted on the main screen.
- ➢ **Generations** lets you specify the number of generations you want to include. Not all formats need the number of generations.
- ➢ **Date format** lets you choose what format you want dates to be displayed on the website.

When you have finished filling in the first page, click the **"Next"** button to continue designing the home page of your site.

- ➢ **Title of website** lets you specify the text that is displayed at the top of your home page.
- ➢ **Introduction** is a brief paragraph or two where you can tell visitors about your family, research, surnames, or any other information. This provides an opportunity for you to enter a few lines explaining your purpose for creating the website, or a few details about the starting person for this website. For example, you might write something like "This site contains the descendants of Jeremiah Johnson. Jeremiah was one of the original settlers of Johnson County back in 1823".
- ➢ **Don't include a photo on the home page** tells RootsMagic not to put any photograph on the home page.
- ➢ **Use photo of starting person** tells RootsMagic to include a photo of the person who was originally highlighted. Not all website types have a starting person, so sometimes this option isn't available.
- ➢ **Use file** lets you select any photo whether it is being used by RootsMagic or not. Click the **Browse** button to select a photo off your hard drive.

➢ **Contact information** allows you to enter a physical address and email address where visitors to your site can contact you. RootsMagic will place these addresses on your home page, and will even turn your email address into a link that visitors can click on to send you email.

When you are happy with your choices, click the **"Next"** button to continue. You can also click the left arrow button in the upper left corner of the wizard to move back to the previous screen in case you need to change something there.

The next screen asks you to select the visual appearance of the website. You can select the various colors or background textures for the site, as well as choosing whether you want a "navigation bar".

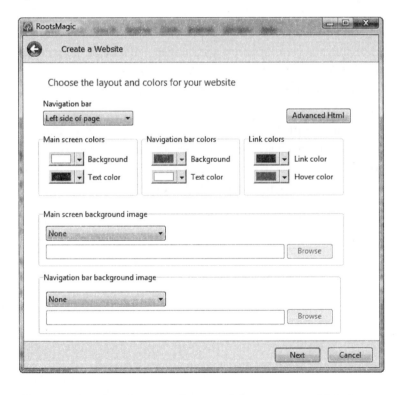

The Navigation bar is a small part of the screen which has navigation links to the various pages in your site. You can have the navigation bar on the left side of the screen (which is the default), or on the screen top, or bottom, or top and bottom. You can even choose not to have a navigation bar at all.

The Advanced HTML button lets you enter pure HTML code that will be placed at the top and bottom of each page that RootsMagic generates. Be careful with this feature. While it is powerful, you can make a mess of your web pages if you don't know exactly what you are doing. But if you do mess up, just run the WebWizard again and remove anything you entered here and all will work again.

Colors lets you select the color for both the main screen and the navigation bar, as well as the text color in each. You can also choose the color of links, including the color when the user's cursor hovers over the link.

Background textures lets you choose background images for both the main screen and navigation bar. You can select any image off your hard drive. RootsMagic also provides several nice textures which are fairly easy to read text on.

When you are happy with your choices, click the **"Next"** button to continue. You can also click the left arrow button in the upper left corner of the wizard to move back to the previous screen in case you need to change something there.

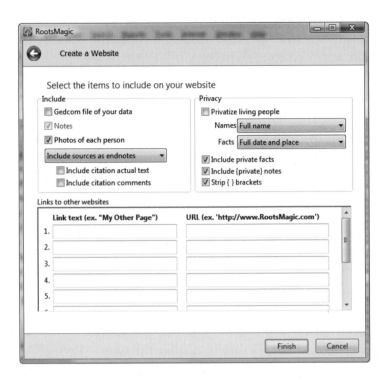

GEDCOM file of your data lets you tell RootsMagic to create a GEDCOM file of the people in your database. If you check this box, a GEDCOM file will be created and a link will be created on your home page where a person can click and download the GEDCOM file.

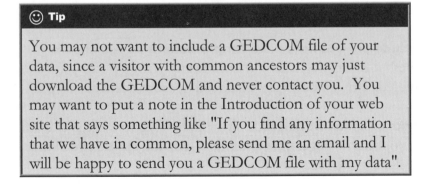

😊 **Tip**

You may not want to include a GEDCOM file of your data, since a visitor with common ancestors may just download the GEDCOM and never contact you. You may want to put a note in the Introduction of your web site that says something like "If you find any information that we have in common, please send me an email and I will be happy to send you a GEDCOM file with my data".

Notes will include any notes you have entered for the person.

Photos of each person lets you include the photos of each person on your website. RootsMagic will use the primary photo you have attached to each person.

Sources - Lets you tell RootsMagic how to export sources for the website (if at all). You can include sources as endnotes (where each fact will link to its sources) or a bibliography, which is just an alphabetical list of the sources. You can also choose whether to include actual text or comments with the citations.

Privacy options lets you "privatize" your website. If you don't check the "privatize living people" box, people's information will be included whether they are living or not. If you do check this box, RootsMagic will use the two drop lists to determine exactly how to do the filtering.

➢ Names – Lets you choose whether to display the full name of living people, or whether to display the word "Living".
➢ Facts – Lets you select whether to display the full date and place for each fact, or to not display the fact at all. You can also choose from several other filtering options, like date only, year only, place only, and year and place.

Include private facts lets you choose whether RootsMagic should include any facts (birth, marriage, death, etc.) that you have marked as "private".

Include private notes and **Strip brackets** let you choose whether RootsMagic should include any private notes you have entered. Private notes are described in more detail on page 85.

Links to other websites lets you include up to 10 web site links on your home page. Just enter the URL and the text you want to display for the link.

When you are ready to generate your website, click the **"Finish"** button and RootsMagic will create the web site files and then display the following screen.

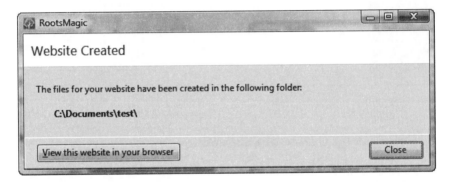

View this website in browser will bring up the website you just generated. This preview is just looking at the HTML files on your hard drive. They are not actually on the Internet until you upload them.

Here is an example of what a RootsMagic generated pedigree chart page looks like:

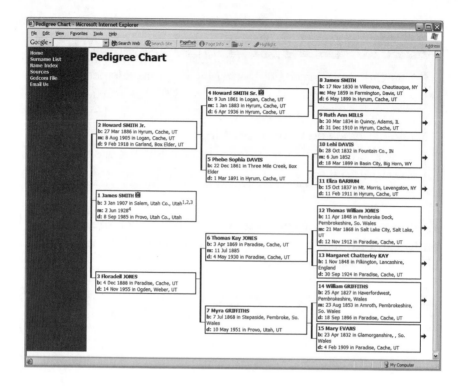

Uploading Your Website

Once RootsMagic has created the files for your family web site, you need to upload them to the Internet.

You can upload it to a server owned by your Internet provider. Most Internet providers offer free server space with your Internet account. If you aren't sure if your provider offers free server space, call or send them an email. They can also provide you with the necessary software and information on uploading to their server. You can also get free server space for your website by visiting www.rootsweb.com.

To upload the website that RootsMagic creates, you will probably need an FTP program, which is software that copies files from your computer to the internet (and vice versa). There are a number of FTP programs available, but two of the more popular are CuteFTP (www.cuteftp.com) and WS_FTP (www.ipswitch.com).

Tip

After you have uploaded your family website, you will want to register your website with the many search engines on the internet, such as Google. This will help others find your website when they use one of these search engines.

The Internet Menu

The Internet item on RootsMagic's main menu provides a number of capabilities which require Internet access.

- ➢ **Create a website** - Creates a website (HTML) from the information in your database, and allows you to upload it to your home page (page 276)
- ➢ **RootsMagic News** - Read the latest news and updates about RootsMagic
- ➢ **RootsMagic Website** – Opens the browser to RootsMagic.com
- ➢ **Technical support** – Opens the browser to the RootsMagic technical support page
- ➢ **Message Boards** - Internet message boards for RootsMagic products
- ➢ **FAQ** – Opens the browser to the RootsMagic Frequently Asked Questions page
- ➢ **Learning Center** – Tutorials, online classes and more to help you get more out of your software
- ➢ **Family reunion planner** - Hundreds of ideas, tips, and resources for planning the perfect family reunion

Other Internet Resources

There are a number of resources on the Internet to assist you when learning and using RootsMagic.

http://www.RootsMagic.com

This website provides information about RootsMagic, including:

➢ Online classes (webinars)
➢ Message boards
➢ A list of RootsMagic user groups
➢ Support site with knowledge base
➢ Program updates
➢ And more

ROOTSMAGIC-USERS mail list

This is an Internet mail list where you can get in contact with other RootsMagic users. To join the RootsMagic Users mail list, send email with the word subscribe in the body to:

ROOTSMAGIC-USERS-L-request@rootsweb.com

If you want to receive the mail list in "digest" format, send email with the word subscribe in the body to:

ROOTSMAGIC-USERS-D-request@rootsweb.com

Facebook
http://www.facebook.com/rootsmagic

Twitter
http://www.twitter.com/rootsmagic

New FamilySearch

FamilySearch is the largest genealogy organization in the world. Millions of people use FamilySearch records, resources, and services to learn more about their family history. For over 100 years, FamilySearch has been actively gathering, preserving, and sharing genealogical records worldwide. Patrons may freely access their resources and service online at FamilySearch.org, or through over 4,500 family history centers in 70 countries, including the renowned Family History Library in Salt Lake City, Utah.

One of their many projects is the FamilySearch Family Tree or "New FamilySearch". It is an online system that allows users to search for ancestors, contribute new persons and information, and retrieve missing information from a single, central database.

> **⚙ Note**
>
> Currently, New FamilySearch is not completely open to the general public. No official date has been announced for access to the general public yet.

Activating New FamilySearch Features

The New FamilySearch features are not enabled by default and must be activated by the user. To enable the New FamilySearch features select **Tools > File Options** from the menu, open the FamilySearch section and check "Enable FamilySearch Support".

Once FamilySearch support is enabled, you will see an icon next to each person's name on the pedigree, family, and descendant views on the main screen.

When the icon is gray it means your RootsMagic person hasn't been matched to FamilySearch yet. Clicking the gray icon will tell RootsMagic to see if it can find any matches on FamilySearch.

A blue icon means that the person has been matched up with a corresponding person on FamilySearch. Clicking the blue icon will tell RootsMagic to display your person side by side with the matching FamilySearch person, and let you copy data back and forth between RootsMagic and FamilySearch.

FamilySearch Person Tools

The FamilySearch Person Tools screen lets you 1) Find matches on FamilySearch, 2) Share data with FamilySearch, 3) Engage in discussions about people on FamilySearch, and 4) View and reserve ordinances on FamilySearch.

Find Matches on FamilySearch

In order to work with New FamilySearch, people in your RootsMagic file need to be matched with records on New FamilySearch.

Why would you want to match people in your file to someone on FamilySearch? Here are a few reasons:

1. Monitor the person on New FamilySearch for changes
2. Update the person on New FamilySearch with information from your copy of the person
3. Retrieve information about the person on New FamilySearch and add it to your own
4. If you are LDS, reserve and complete ordinances on behalf of the person

If FamilySearch support is enabled, you will see an icon next to each persons' name on the pedigree, family, and descendant views on the main screen. If you see a gray icon next to a person's name, it means that the person is not matched to New

FamilySearch. Clicking on the gray icon will bring up the FamilySearch Matches screen:

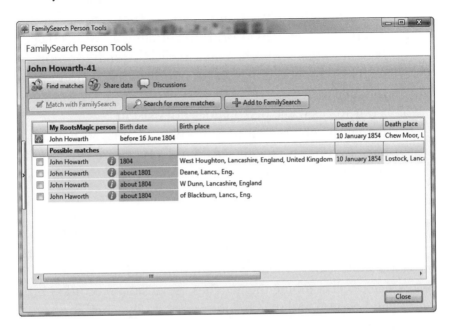

Your person in RootsMagic will appear at the top of the list. Next, the FamilySearch person that you are currently matched to, if any, will appear. And lastly, possible matches to your person that are found on New FamilySearch.

There are columns for name, birth date, birth place, death date, death place, father, mother, and spouse. Colors are used to visually describe how well the information matches your own. The colors make it easy to spot good and poor matches without having to actually read the text of the records.

Green indicates an identical or near-identical match.
Yellow indicates a close match.
Red indicates a poor match.

To view more information about any of the matches, click on the information icon next to the name (the letter "i" in a circle).

If no matches were found, there are three possibilities:

1. The person you are searching for is living. New FamilySearch will not return matches for living persons.
2. There is not enough information about your RootsMagic person to find a match. You can click "Search for more matches" for additional search options to find more possible matches.
3. Your RootsMagic person does not exist in New FamilySearch. If your person isn't on FamilySearch already you can click the "Add to FamilySearch" button to add the person and his information to FamilySearch.

Check the boxes next to the name of each match to your RootsMagic person. When you are done, click "Match with FamilySearch". RootsMagic will link your person to the match(es) in New FamilySearch. If you checked more than one name, RootsMagic will combine the matches into a single record in New FamilySearch and match your person to the combined person.

RootsMagic will then search for any additional matches. When you are finished searching for matches, press Close to return to the main screen. If you matched your RootsMagic person to a New FamilySearch person, the icon next to the person's name will now be blue.

If you are unable to find a match for your RootsMagic person in New FamilySearch, press the "Search" button for additional search options. You will see this screen:

You may search by names and events, Person ID, or Ancestral File Number (AFN). RootsMagic will enter whatever information it knows about the person into the search fields. You can make your own changes or adjustments to the search, then click Search. Any records matching the search criteria will appear in the list of matches.

Sharing Data with FamilySearch

Once a RootsMagic person has been matched to New FamilySearch, you may wish to compare the two and exchange information between RootsMagic and New FamilySearch. You can just click on the blue FamilySearch icon next to the person's name.

The FamilySearch Person Tools screen will come up with the "Share data" tab selected.

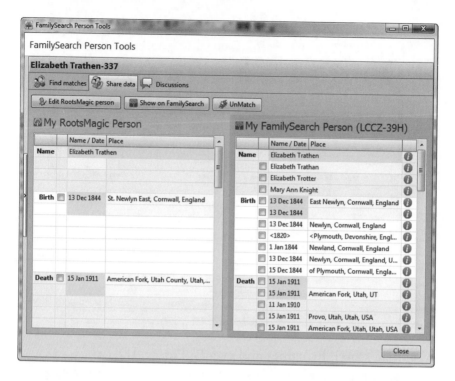

Your RootsMagic person will appear on the left, and the matching FamilySearch will appear on the right. RootsMagic will line up matching names, facts, events, and relationships between the two records. As mentioned before, color coding is used to visually describe how well the information matches your own. The colors make it easy to spot good and poor matches without having to actually read the text of the records.

Green indicates an identical or near-identical match.
Yellow indicates a close match.

To view more information about any of the facts, click on the information icon to the right of the fact.

You can copy a fact by clicking on the checkbox next to the fact. RootsMagic will pop up a menu of options available for that fact. You can copy facts or people from RootsMagic to FamilySearch, or from FamilySearch into your RootsMagic file. Just select the desired action and click OK.

Discussions

Discussions are a feature of New FamilySearch that allow you to collaborate with others to discuss what information is correct or incorrect for a person. RootsMagic has full support for discussions by clicking the "Discussions" tab on the FamilySearch Person Tools.

RootsMagic will display a list of all the discussions for a person on the left. Just click a discussion and RootsMagic will display the discussion and any comments about that discussion.

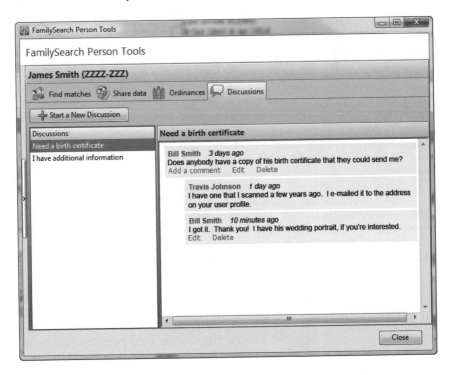

Keep in mind that not every person in FamilySearch can have discussions (living individuals for example). If a person on FamilySearch is not allowed to have discussions, RootsMagic will indicate that and the "Start a New Discussion" button will be disabled.

Working with Multiple People

While RootsMagic makes it easy to work with individuals in New FamilySearch with the FamilySearch Person Tools, it also allows you to work with groups of people just as easily.

On the left side of the FamilySearch Person Tools screen is a tall thin button (look close... it can be hard to see). If you click that button, RootsMagic will display a list of everyone in your file.

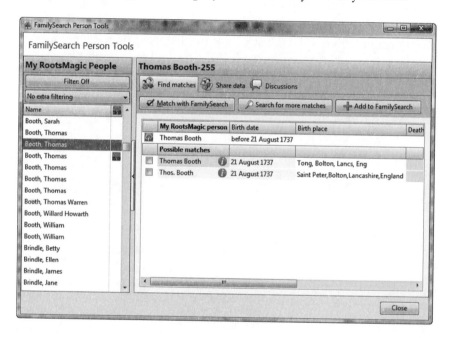

The "My RootsMagic People" list shows all persons in your RootsMagic database. Next to each name is the temple status icon and the FamilySearch link icon. When you click on a name in the list RootsMagic will fill the "Find matches", "Share data", and "Discussions" screens on the right with that person.

You may limit this list to smaller groups by using the two filters at the top of the list.

The first filter lets you select the ancestors of a person, or any group of people using named groups (named groups are described on page 256).

The second filter provides special filtering based on FamilySearch settings. This filter is in addition to the first filter (both filters work together). You may choose from:

- No extra filtering
- People matched to FamilySearch
- People not matched to FamilySearch
- People changed on FamilySearch
- People ready for temple work
- People with temple work complete
- People not ready for temple work
- People with reserved ordinances

FamilySearch Central

 FamilySearch Central is a feature which brings together all of RootsMagic's powerful FamilySearch tools into one convenient screen. To open FamilySearch Central select **"File, FamilySearch Central"** from the Main Menu or click the FamilySearch button on the toolbar.

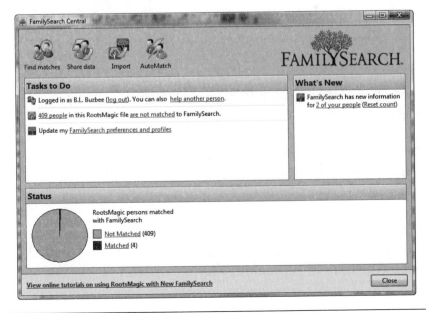

FamilySearch Central is divided up into three sections – "Tasks to Do", "What's New", and "Status". Each section has blue underlined hyperlinks. Clicking on any of the hyperlinks will take you to the screen to accomplish the task or view the suggested information.

The "Tasks to Do" section presents a list of things that the user should do including helping other people, matching individuals to new FamilySearch, and updating your preferences and profile on FamilySearch.

The "What's New" section shows the how many of the matched persons have been updated on FamilySearch since the last time you viewed that person.

The "Status" section presents graphs to summarize the number of people in the user's file that have been matched and/or updated.

FamilySearch Central also includes buttons at the top of the screen – "Find matches", "Share data", "Ordinances", "Temple Work", "Import", and "Automatch". If you do not have LDS support turned on, the "Ordinances" and "Temple Work" buttons won't be visible.

The **Find matches, Share data** and **Ordinances** buttons simply open up the FamilySearch Person Tools with the appropriate tab selected.

The Temple Work button lets you prepare names for the temple. This feature is described in the section titled LDS Features.

The Import button lets you import information from FamilySearch into RootsMagic. Just select the starting person and the number of generations of ancestors and descendants you want and RootsMagic will begin importing. You will probably want to keep the number of generations fairly low (probably no more than 4 or 5 generations of descendants at a time) because you can end up with tens of thousands of names being imported which can take forever.

The AutoMatch button is a great timesaver which will go through each unmatched person in your database and see if there is a match on FamilySearch. If there is an undeniable match, RootsMagic will match the RootsMagic person up with FamilySearch. Again, for a large database this can take a very long time, but is still much faster than manually matching one person at a time.

Helping other people with FamilySearch

When you are logged in, FamilySearch Central will display a link for you to "Help another person". Clicking that link will let you enter the name, birth date, and "helper id" of the person you want to help. You will need to get the helper id directly from the person you are trying to help. If the other person has registered with FamilySearch they can log into the website under their own name and change that helper id at any time.

Once you have logged in as a helper for a person, all RootsMagic FamilySearch screens will have a yellow banner at the top saying that you are in helper mode and will show the name of the person you are helping. This is important because anything you do on FamilySearch while in helper mode will have that person's name listed as the contributor.

More Help with New FamilySearch

For more help with using RootsMagic with New FamilySearch you may want to watch the free online class at:

http://www.rootsmagic.com/FamilySearch/Tutorials

LDS Support

Members of the LDS church have additional requirements which RootsMagic provides support for. These features are optional, and can be enabled or disabled by checking the **"LDS Support"** checkbox in the database options dialog (see page 314).

Entering Information

Although it is possible to enter LDS ordinances the same way as births, deaths, and other facts, RootsMagic provides an LDS ordinance template for each person in your database.

To bring up the LDS ordinance template, highlight the person on the main screen and select **"Edit > LDS ordinances"** from the main menu, or click the BEPS button in the info section, or press **Ctrl+L**.

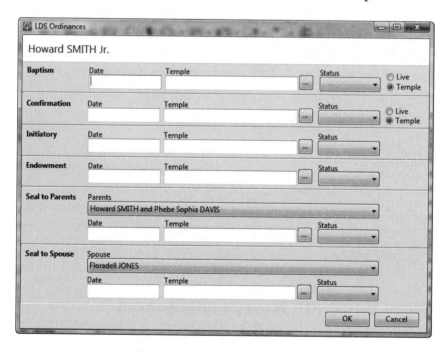

Simply fill in the blanks with the dates and temples for the baptism, confirmation, initiatory, endowment, sealing to parents, and sealing to spouse. If the person has more than one spouse or set of parents entered, the drop lists in those sections can be used to switch between the other spouses or parents.

The baptism field has a checkbox which allows you to specify whether the baptism was done while the person was living (or whether it was done by proxy). Switching between live and proxy causes the place field and place list to switch between temples and places.

In addition to date and temple fields, each ordinance also has a status field, which support special LDS statuses. If you have a date and a temple for an ordinance, you should just leave the **"Status"** field blank (don't even use **Completed**, since that status means the work has been done but you don't know when or where). Below is the list of statuses which are available (some are only available in certain types of ordinances).

Status	What it means
Completed	The ordinance is finished but you don't know when or where.
Submitted	The ordinance is submitted and waiting for completion.
Child	Died before 8 years old
Stillborn	Stillborn (ordinances not required)
Pre-1970	Ordinance probably done before 1970
BIC	Born in the covenant (only used for sealing to parents)
Do not seal	Do not seal
Canceled	Ordinance canceled and considered invalid (seal to spouse only)
DNS/CAN	Do not seal / Canceled
Excluded	Patron excluded this ordinance from being cleared in this submission
Uncleared	Data for clearing ordinance request was insufficient

Printing Information

The LDS ordinance lists will print LDS ordinance information for the people in your database.

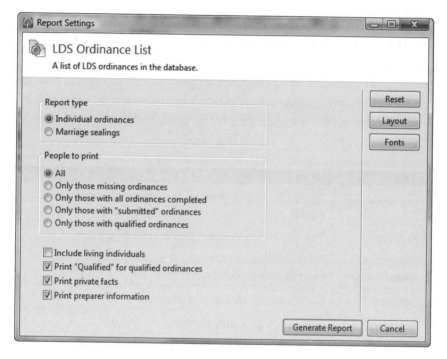

To print the LDS ordinance lists, click the Print button on the toolbar, or select **"File > Print"** from the main menu. Then select the list called "LDS Ordinance List". RootsMagic will display the following dialog.

"Report type" lets you select which unfinished ordinance list to print.

➤ **Individual ordinances** - lists individuals and the dates for LDS baptism, endowment, and sealing to parents.
➤ **Marriage sealings** - lists families and the marriage date and sealing to spouse date.

"People to print" lets you select which individuals to include in the selected list.

- ➢ **All** – Everyone in the database
- ➢ **Only those missing ordinances** - prints only individuals who are missing at least one ordinance
- ➢ **Only those with all ordinances completed** - prints only individuals who are not missing any ordinances
- ➢ **Only those with "submitted" ordinances** - prints only individuals who have at least one ordinance with a status of "Submitted".
- ➢ **Only those with "qualified" ordinances** - prints only individuals who have at least one ordinance which is qualified for temple work.

Include living individuals gives you the option to ignore living individuals (since you can't do temple work for them anyway).

Print 'qualified' for qualified ordinances will cause RootsMagic to print the word "qualified" for any ordinance that is qualified for temple work.

Print private facts lets you choose whether RootsMagic should include any facts that you have marked as "private".

FamilySearch

One goal of the LDS genealogist is to submit names for temple ordinances. For members of The Church of Jesus Christ of Latter-day Saints, New FamilySearch is the system through which temple ordinances are checked and reserved.

Ordinance Status

When LDS Support is enabled, you have the option to display the LDS ordinance status next to each name in the pedigree, family, and descendant views. The status is indicated by an icon

to the right of each name. These icons, and their meanings, are
listed below:

Icon	Status	Description
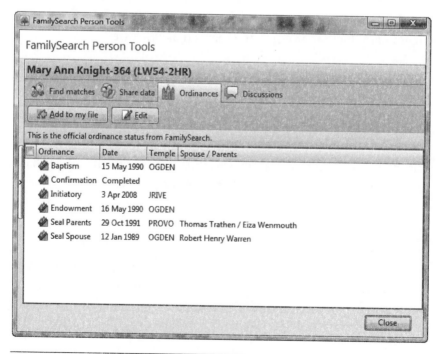	Ready	This person appears to have temple ordinances that are ready to be done. You'll have to check for duplicate matches in New FamilySearch before reserving the missing ordinances.
	Need More Information or Reserved	More information is required or already-reserved ordinances must be completed before you may reserve missing ordinances.
	Complete	All ordinances for this person are either done or not needed.

By clicking on the temple status icon, RootsMagic brings up the
FamilySearch Person Tools with the "Ordinances" tab selected.
The information presented on that screen will either be "official"
or "unofficial" depending on whether the person has been
matched with FamilySearch yet.

Unofficial Ordinance Status

If a person has not been matched with New FamilySearch, RootsMagic will present an "unofficial" ordinance status. The unofficial status is calculated by RootsMagic based on information in your personal database. While it is often a good indicator of what ordinances have and have not been completed, you will not be able to reserve any ordinances with New FamilySearch until a match has been made on the system and the official ordinance status can be determined.

Official Ordinance Status

Once a person has been matched with New FamilySearch, RootsMagic is able to get that person's "official" ordinance status. The official status is determined by FamilySearch based on data on that system rather than data in your personal database.

When viewing the official ordinance status, you may click on "Add to my file" to copy ordinances which you are missing into your own personal file.

Reserving Ordinances

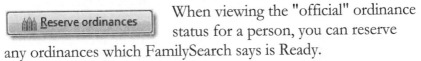 When viewing the "official" ordinance status for a person, you can reserve any ordinances which FamilySearch says is Ready.

RootsMagic will display a list of the person's ordinances with a checkbox next to any available ordinances. Mark the ordinances you want to reserve and click "Reserve Selected Ordinances".

RootsMagic will display a confirmation screen where you can choose whether you want to do the ordinance work yourself, or submit it to the temple file. You will also need to agree to certain policies before you will be allowed to reserve the ordinances for the person.

If you want to see a list of all the people in your database who have ordinances which can be reserved, open the FamilySearch

Central screen and click the link that tells you how many people in your database are ready for temple ordinances.

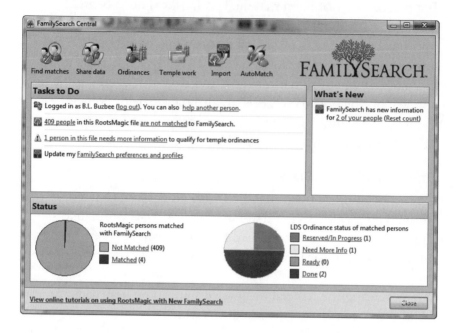

When you click on the link to see people who are ready to have temple ordinances reserved, RootsMagic will display a list of those people. When you highlight one of those people RootsMagic will display the person's ordinances with a checkbox next to any available ordinances. Mark the ordinances you want to reserve and click "Reserve Selected Ordinances".

RootsMagic will display a confirmation screen where you can choose whether you want to do the ordinance work yourself, or submit it to the temple file. You will also need to agree to certain policies before you will be allowed to reserve the ordinances for the person.

Preparing Names for the Temple

Once you have reserved names for temple work you can begin preparing those names for temple work. On the FamilySearch Central screen you can click the "Temple Work" button to prepare some or all of the names you have reserved to take to the temple.

This screen has 3 tabs: 1) Reservations, 2) Requests, and 3) Cards.

Reservations

These are ordinances which you have reserved. RootsMagic will display all names / ordinances you have reserved. It gets this information directly from FamilySearch so this list will even include ordinances you have reserved directly from the FamilySearch site itself.

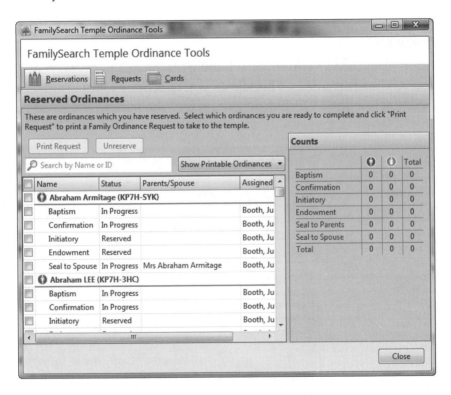

You can select which ordinances you are ready to complete and then print a Family Ordinance Request to take to the temple. Just put a check next to the ordinances you want to print cards for and click the "Print Request" button. Keep in mind that as you check ordinances, RootsMagic may check other ordinances for that person or other people in the list if those other ordinances are prerequisites to the one you selected.

When you click "Print Request" you will have 3 options: print the request, save it to a file so you can print it later, or email it to another family member so that they can print it and take it to a temple near them.

This form (which has a bar code on it) will be taken to the temple where they will print the ordinance cards from it. Once these ordinances are completed, FamilySearch Central will update the official ordinance status for the person in RootsMagic automatically.

Requests

RootsMagic allows you to view Family Ordinance Requests that you've already printed. This allows you to reprint a request in case you lose the FOR before getting it to the temple.

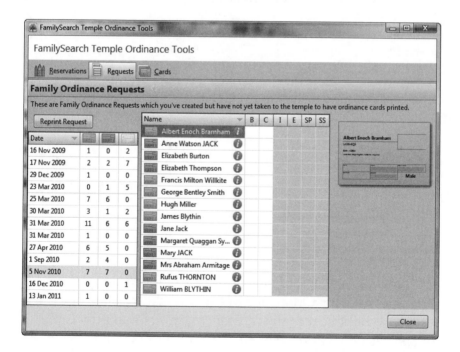

Cards

RootsMagic helps you track the temple ordinance cards which have been printed by the temple. If you give cards to other people to help out, you may track which helpers you have given the cards to as well as the progress of each ordinance. RootsMagic will display a list of cards which you have printed. When you give cards to another person, simply check those cards and click "Give to Helper" to keep track of that card.

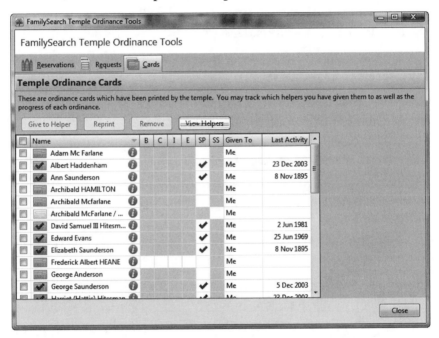

At any time you can click "View Helpers" to get a list of the people you have given cards to along with the progress on the cards you have given them. As you can see, the helper doesn't have to be an individual. It can also be a group like High Priests, Young Men, etc.

RootsMagic will not automatically remove cards from your list so that you can continue to track the results. When you are ready to remove a completed card from the list, just check the card and click the "Remove" button. You will be asked to confirm your choice.

RootsMagic Options

The more alternatives, the more difficult the choice. - Abbe' D'Allanival

RootsMagic offers a number of options that you can use to personalize the way the program and your databases operate. To bring up the Options dialog, select **"Tools > Program Options"** or **"Tools > File Options"** from the main menu. You can then choose which category of options you want to change by clicking on an item on the left side of the Options dialog.

Program Options

Program options are those options that affect the program as a whole and are not specific to any one database.

General Program Options

The "General" program options lets you choose settings which apply to the program and not to a specific file.

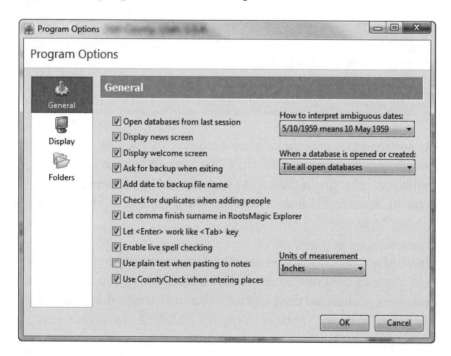

Open databases from last session lets you tell RootsMagic whether to open up the databases that were open the last time you used the program.

Display news screen tells RootsMagic whether to display the RootsMagic News each time the program starts.

Display welcome screen tells RootsMagic whether to display the welcome screen whenever no databases are open.

Ask for backup when exiting specifies whether RootsMagic will ask you if you want to make a backup when you exit the program.

Add date to backup file name lets you choose whether the current date will be added to the file name when you create a backup. This helps prevent you from overwriting the previous backup with each new one.

Check for duplicates when adding people determines whether RootsMagic checks each time you add a new person to see if you may have already added them.

Let comma finish surnames in RootsMagic Explorer enables or disables the feature in RootsMagic search screens where a comma can be typed to finish typing a surname during incremental searches.

Let Enter key work like Tab key makes the Enter key move from field to field instead of closing the dialog.

Enable live spell checking tells RootsMagic whether to underline misspelled words in notes with squiggly red underlines.

Use plain text when pasting to notes tells RootsMagic to strip out formatting when pasting text into notes.

Use CountyCheck when entering places tells RootsMagic whether to check whether a place existed at the time of the event.

How to interpret ambiguous dates determines whether RootsMagic interprets dates entered like 1/2/1997 as January 2, 1997 (US) or Febrary 1, 1997 (pretty much everywhere else).

When a database is opened or created tells RootsMagic whether to tile all windows, cascade all windows, or maximize the new window when opening or creating a database.

Units of measurement tells RootsMagic whether to use inches or centimeters in report and other settings.

Display Options

RootsMagic allows you to change the font and colors used on the main screen with the "Main screen" item in the Options dialog.

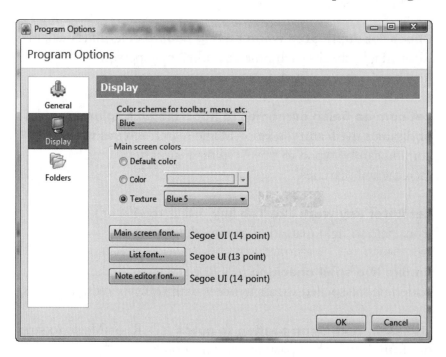

Color scheme for toolbar, menu, etc. lets you select the colors used for the toolbar buttons and other parts of the screen. You can select from Windows default, Blue, Silver, or Green.

Main screen color lets you select the color for the main navigation views. You can select any color, or choose from several textures offered by RootsMagic.

Main screen font lets you select the font to be used on the main screen. RootsMagic will display the standard Windows font dialog, where you can select both the font typeface and size. If you select a font size that is too large to fit on the screen, RootsMagic will reduce the font size to fit.

List font lets you select the font used in the edit screen list, Explorer list, and side list on the main screen. This lets you have a different font than used on the main views.

Note editor font lets you select the font used on a person's note editing page. This allows you to choose a larger font while editing, but does not change the font used when printing the note (the font for printing notes is chosen from the reports dialog).

Folders

The Folders option allows you to enter default folders where RootsMagic will look for certain types of files. You can just type in the full folder name, or click the button with the ellipses (...) to bring up a dialog to select the folder.

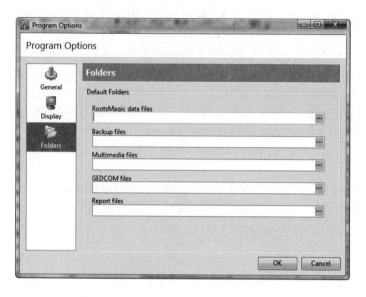

File Options

File options are those options that pertain to the current database. You can choose from General, Preparer, or FamilySearch categories. Since file options apply to the currently seleected file, it will not be available if you don't have any files currently open.

General Options

The "General" file option lets you choose settings for the currently selected database, including formats and how you want RootsMagic to treat the database when it is opened.

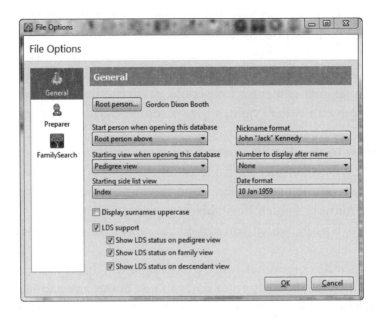

Root person lets you select the "root" person. The root person is the person that RootsMagic uses as the starting person on the main screen when you open a database. When you click "Root person", RootsMagic will display the search screen, where you can select the new root person. **If you ever get lost in your database**, you can use the **"Search > Go to root person"** command (or just press **Ctrl+Home**) to bring the root person back to the main screen.

Start person when opening this database lets you choose whether to start with the root person when opening the database, or whether to start with the person who was highlighted the last time you used the database.

Starting view when opening this database lets you specify whether RootsMagic will start up in the Pedigree, Family, Descendants, People, or WebSearch view. You can also just have RootsMagic open to the view from the last time you used the database.

Starting side list view lets you choose which of the side list tabs should open by default; index, family, bookmarks, history, or groups. You can also have RootsMagic open to the tab from the last time you used the database.

Nickname format determines how RootsMagic will display nicknames that you enter for people. You can have nicknames displayed with either "quotes" or (parentheses) around them.

Number to display after name on main screen lets you choose which number to display after the person's name in the info view on the main screen. You can choose between the record number (which RootsMagic assigns), the reference number (REFN, which you can add as a fact), or no number.

Date format determines how RootsMagic will display dates you enter. You can actually enter dates in just about any format and RootsMagic will automatically convert them to the format you select here.

Display surnames uppercase lets you tell RootsMagic whether you want it to display and print surnames (last names) in all uppercase.

LDS support enables or disables the printing of LDS (Mormon) information on printouts. It also determines whether LDS information is displayed for the highlighted person on the main screen. If this box is checked, the letters B, E, P, and S may appear in the status area to the left of the name of the highlighted person, where B = baptism, E = endowment, P = sealing to parents, and S = sealing to spouse. A temple icon will also appear next to the name of every person on the pedigree, family, and descendant view if you mark those options.

Preparer

The "Preparer" item in the options dialog allows you to enter the preparer (or submitter) name and address. This is the name and address that RootsMagic will print at the bottom of printouts if requested. Each database can have a different preparer.

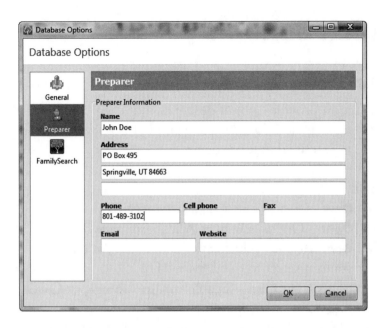

FamilySearch Options

The "FamilySearch" section has two checkbox options: 1) turn New FamilySearch support on or off, and 2) whether to check for duplication when reserving ordinances. These features are described on page 287.

Quick Summary

Main Menu Commands

This section provides a brief description of each command in the main menu. In addition, the page number is provided where the feature is described in more detail.

❖ **File**
 ➢ **New** - Creates a new database (page 29)
 ➢ **Open** - Opens an existing database (page 31)
 ➢ **Open Recent** – Displays the most recent databases which you can select to open (page 31)
 ➢ **Search for Files** – Search for RootsMagic or GEDCOM files on your computer (page 31)
 ➢ **Close** - Closes the currently selected database (page 33)
 ➢ **Rename** - Renames the current database (page 38)
 ➢ **Delete** - Deletes the current database from the hard drive (page 38)
 ➢ **Copy** – Creates a copy of the current database (page 38)
 ➢ **Database tools** – Tools for cleaning up and testing the integrity of the database (page 38)
 ➢ **Print a report** - Brings up the Print Dialog where you can select and print a chart, form, book, etc. (page 124)
 ➢ **Printer setup** - Lets you select the printer and page orientation (portrait or landscape)
 ➢ **Import** - Imports GEDCOM, Family Tree Maker, PAF, Legacy, or Family Origins files into the current database (page 222)
 ➢ **Export** - Exports all or some of the data from the current database to a GEDCOM file (page 225)
 ➢ **FamilySearch Central** – Allows direct interaction with New FamilySearch (page 301)
 ➢ **Backup** - Makes a back up copy of the current database (page 35)
 ➢ **Restore** - Restores a backed up database (page 38)

- ➢ **Properties** - Displays the number of records in the database (page 38)
- ➢ **Exit** - Exits from RootsMagic
- ❖ **Edit**
  - ➢ **Person** - Brings up the edit screen for the currently highlighted person (page 50)
  - ➢ **Delete**
    - ▪ **Person** - Removes the highlighted individual from the database (page 47)
    - ▪ **Family** - Removes the highlighted family from the database (page 47)
  - ➢ **Unlink**
    - ▪ **from Spouse** - Unlinks the highlighted person from his/her currently displayed spouse (page 48)
    - ▪ **from Parents** - Unlinks the highlighted person from his/her currently displayed parents (page 48)
  - ➢ **Rearrange**
    - ▪ **Children** - Lets you rearrange the children in the current family (page 47)
    - ▪ **Spouses** - Lets you rearrange the spouses of the current person (page 47)
  - ➢ **Swap husband and wife** - Switches the husband and wife in a family (page 49)
  - ➢ **LDS Ordinances** – Brings up the LDS ordinance template for the currently highlighted person (page 298)
- ❖ **Lists**
  - ➢ **Source list** - Brings up a list of all sources, and allows you to edit them (page 96)
  - ➢ **To-Do list** – Brings up a list of all todo tasks in your database and allows you to edit them (page 246)
  - ➢ **Research manager** – Brings up a list of research logs you have created (page 249)
  - ➢ **Media Gallery** - Brings up a gallery with all media items in the database.
  - ➢ **Address list** – Brings up a list of all addresses in your database and allows you to edit them (page 61)

➢ **Repository list** - Brings up a list of all repositories, and allows you to edit them (page 113)

➢ **Correspondence Log** – Brings up the correspondence log (page 253)

➢ **Place list** - Brings up a list of all places in your database, and allows you to edit them (page 67)

➢ **Fact type list** - Brings up a list of fact types, and allows you to add to or edit them (page 69)

➢ **Source Templates** - Brings up a list of all the source types in the database (page 99)

❖ **Add**

➢ **Individual** - Adds an unlinked individual to the database (page 39)

➢ **Spouse** - Adds a spouse/partner to the highlighted person (page 39)

➢ **Parents** - Adds parents to the highlighted person (page 39)

➢ **Child** - Adds a child to the highlighted person (page 39)

❖ **View**

➢ **Pedigree view** - Switches the main screen to the "Pedigree" view (page 12)

➢ **Family view** - Switches the main screen to the "Family" view (page 13)

➢ **Descendants view** – Switches the main screen to the "Descendants" view (page 15)

➢ **People view** - Switches the main screen to the "People" view (page 16)

➢ **Web search** - Switches the main screen to the "WebSearch" view (page 19)

➢ **Timeline view** – Switches the main screen to the "Timeline" view (page 21)

➢ **Immediate family** - Displays all the immediate relatives of the highlighted person (page 79)

➢ **Sidebar** - Displays or hides the sidebar (page 27)

❖ **Search**

➢ **Person list** – Brings up the person list (RootsMagic Explorer) (page 75)

- ➢ **Family list** – Brings up the family list (page 80)
- ➢ **Go to root person** – Brings the "root" person back to the main screen (page 313)
- ➢ **Move to primary person** – Moves the currently highlighted person to the primary position
- ➢ **Search and replace** – Allows you to perform a search and replace in many fields of your database (page 273)
- ➢ **Bookmarks** - Lets you mark the current person so you can quickly return to him or her (page 81)
- ➢ **History** – Brings up a list of the most recently visited people in your database (page 81)
- ➢ **Back** – Moves to the most recently visited person on the main screen (page 81)
- ➢ **Forward** – Moves forward to the most recently visited person on the main screen (page 81)
- ❖ **Reports**
  - ➢ **Print a report** - Opens the Report Selection screen (page 124)
  - ➢ **Publisher** – Print a book made up of multiple report types (page 215)
  - ➢ **Pedigree chart** - Prints a pedigree chart for the highlighted person (page 134)
  - ➢ **Family group sheet** - Prints a family group sheet for the highlighted family (page 136)
  - ➢ **Narrative reports** - Prints a book starting with the highlighted person (page 140)
  - ➢ **Charts**
    - ▪ **Wall charts** – Prints large ancestor, descendant, and hourglass wall charts (page 187)
    - ▪ **Timeline charts** – Prints graphical timelines with bars representing the life span of people (page 187)
    - ▪ **Box charts** – Prints ancestor and descendant box charts which can be included in printed reports (page 144)
    - ▪ **Relationship Chart** - Prints a box chart that shows you exactly how the two people are related (page 182)

- **Photo tree** - Prints a photo pedigree ancestor tree (page 185)
- ➤ **Lists** - Lets you select a list type and print it (page 148)
- ➤ **Individual summary** - Prints a summary for the highlighted person (page 181)
- ➤ **Custom reports** - Lets you design and print a custom report (page 203)
- ➤ **Calendar** - Prints a calendar with birthdays and / or anniversaries (page 179)
- ➤ **Scrapbooks** – Prints a scrapbook for a person, family, source or place (page 184)
- ➤ **PrintMyChart.com** – Takes you to an online discount wall chart printing service (page 202)
- ❖ **Tools**
  - ➤ **Merge**
    - **Automatic merges** - Automatically merges as many duplicate records as it can (page 241)
    - **Duplicate search merge** – Finds potential duplicate records and allows you to merge them if desired (page 236)
    - **Manual merge** - Merges two duplicate records together (page 236)
    - **View "not duplicates" list** – Opens the list of records which you have marked as not duplicates (page 236)
  - ➤ **Problem Search**
    - **Problem list** – Creates a list of potential problems in your database (page 261)
    - **View "not a problem" list** – Displays a list of items you have marked as "not a problem" (page 261)
  - ➤ **Count trees** – Counts the total number of distinct trees in your database (page 274)
  - ➤ **Spell check** – Spell checks the notes in your database (page 270)
  - ➤ **Gazetteer** - Helps you find cities around the world (page 104)

- ➤ **Mapping** - Displays online maps of the places and people in your file (page 110)
- ➤ **Color code people** – Lets you set a color on the main screen for any group of people (page 265)
- ➤ **Set living** – Lets you set or clear the Living flag for any group of people (page 264)
- ➤ **Set relationships** – Sets the relationship of everyone in the database to the current person (page 264)
- ➤ **Date calculator** - Allows you to do date calculations (page 266)
- ➤ **Relationship calculator** - Calculates the relationship between any two people (page 268)
- ➤ **Soundex calculator** - Calculates the Soundex code for a surname (page 269)
- ➤ **Calendar** - Displays a perpetual calendar (page 266)
- ➤ **GenSmarts suggestions** – Runs GenSmarts (if installed) to provide research suggestions for current person (page 252)
- ➤ **Create a Shareable CD** – Lets you create and burn a CD of your data to share with others (page 219)
- ➤ **File Options** - Lets you change options for the current file (page 312)
- ➤ **Program Options**- Lets you change the program settings (page 308)
- ❖ **Internet**
  - ➤ **Create a website** - Creates a website (HTML) from the information in your database, and allows you to upload it to your home page (page 276)
  - ➤ **RootsMagic News** - Read the latest news and updates about RootsMagic
  - ➤ **RootsMagic Website** – Opens the browser to RootsMagic.com
  - ➤ **Technical support** – Opens the browser to the RootsMagic technical support page
  - ➤ **Message Boards** - Internet message boards
  - ➤ **FAQ** – Opens the browser to the RootsMagic Frequently Asked Questions page

- ➢ **Learning Center** – Online classes, tutorials, and more
- ➢ **Family reunion planner** - Hundreds of ideas, tips, and resources for planning the perfect family reunion (requires Internet access)

❖ **Window**

- ➢ **Tile vertically** - Arranges your open databases side by side
- ➢ **Tile horizontally** - Arranges your open databases above each other
- ➢ **Cascade** - Arranges your open databases in a cascading arrangement
- ➢ **Close all** - Closes all currently open databases

❖ **Help**

- ➢ **Contents** - Brings up the RootsMagic help system
- ➢ **Check for updates** – Check if there are any updates to the version of RootsMagic you are using
- ➢ **Learning Center** – Online classes, tutorials, and more
- ➢ **Technical support** – Opens the browser to the RootsMagic technical support page
- ➢ **Register RootsMagic** – Register your program with us in case you lose your unlock key
- ➢ **About RootsMagic** - Display the full version number you are using

Built-in Fact Types

Fact Type	Description
Adoption	Pertaining to creation of a child-parent relationship that does not exist biologically.
Alternate name	Another name by which a person is known.
Ancestral file number	A unique permanent record file number of an individual record stored in Ancestral File.
Annulment	Declaring a marriage void from the beginning (never existed).
Baptism	The event of baptism (not LDS), performed in infancy or later.
Baptism (LDS)	The event of baptism performed at age eight or later by priesthood authority of the LDS Church.
Bar Mitzvah	The ceremonial event held when a Jewish boy reaches age 13.
Bas Mitzvah	The ceremonial event held when a Jewish girl reaches age 13, also known as "Bat Mitzvah."
Birth	The event of entering into life.
Blessing	A religious event of bestowing divine care or intercession. Sometimes given in connection with a naming ceremony.
Burial	The event of the proper disposing of the mortal remains of a deceased person.
Caste	A name assigned to a particular group that this person was associated with, such as a particular racial group, religious group, or a group with an inherited status.
Census	The event of the periodic count of the population for a designated locality, such as a national or state Census.
Christening	The religious event (not LDS) of baptizing and/or naming a child.
Christening (adult)	The religious event (not LDS) of baptizing and/or naming an adult person.

Confirmation	The religious event (not LDS) of conferring the gift of the Holy Ghost and, among Protestants, full church membership.
Cremation	Disposal of the remains of a person's body by fire.
Death	The event when mortal life terminates.
Degree	A degree earned by a person (see also Graduation).
Description	The physical characteristics of a person, place, or thing.
Divorce	An event of dissolving a marriage through civil action.
Divorce filed	An event of filing for a divorce by a spouse.
DNA	Results of a DNA test
Education	Indicator of a level of education attained.
Election	An event where a person is elected to some office.
Emigration	An event of leaving one's homeland with the intent of residing elsewhere.
Endowment (LDS)	A religious event where an endowment ordinance for an individual was performed by priesthood authority in an LDS temple.
Engagement	An event of recording or announcing an agreement between two people to become married.
Excommunication	An event where a person is expelled from the communion of a church and deprived of its rights, privileges, and advantages.
First Communion	A religious rite, the first act of sharing in the Lord's supper as part of church worship.
Graduation	An event of awarding educational diplomas or degrees to individuals.
Illness	The state or condition of being sick.
Immigration	An event of entering into a new locality with the intent of residing there.
Living	The state of being alive at a particular time.
Marriage	A legal, common-law, or customary event of

	creating a family unit of a man and a woman as husband and wife.
Marriage Bann	An event of an official public notice given that two people intend to marry.
Marriage contract	An event of recording a formal agreement of marriage, including the prenuptial agreement in which marriage partners reach agreement about the property rights of one or both, securing property to their children.
Marriage license	An event of obtaining a legal license to marry.
Marriage settlement	An event of creating an agreement between two people contemplating marriage, at which time they agree to release or modify property rights that would otherwise arise from the marriage.
Military	The state of being in the military service, whether during peacetime or war.
Miscellaneous	An event which is so general that it doesn't fit in any category.
Mission	The state of being sent to an area to spread religion or carry on educational or charitable activities.
Namesake	An individual who a person is named after.
Nationality	The national heritage of an individual.
Naturalization	The event of obtaining citizenship.
Occupation	The type of work or profession of an individual.
Ordination	A religious event of receiving authority to act in religious matters.
Probate	An event of judicial determination of the validity of a will. May indicate several related court activities over several dates.
Property	Pertaining to possessions such as real estate or other property of interest.
Reference number	A description or number used to identify an item for filing, storage, or other reference purposes.
Religion	A religious denomination to which a person is affiliated or for which a record applies.
Residence	The act of dwelling at an address for a period of time.

Retirement	An event of exiting an occupational relationship with an employer after a qualifying time period.
Sealing to parents (LDS)	A religious event pertaining to the sealing of a child to his or her parents in an LDS temple ceremony.
Sealing to spouse (LDS)	A religious event pertaining to the sealing of a husband and wife in an LDS temple ceremony.
Separation	An event where the conjugal cohabitation of a husband and wife ceases.
Social security number	A number assigned by the United States Social Security Administration. Used for tax identification purposes.
Stillborn	The event where an infant is dead at birth.
Will	A legal document treated as an event, by which a person disposes of his or her estate, to take effect after death. The event date is the date the will was signed while the person was alive.

Keyboard Shortcut Keys

There are shortcut keys on most RootsMagic screens. The shortcut key for a button will be underlined. Pressing the Alt key and then the underlined letter will trigger the command. If the underline isn't showing up until after you press Alt, there is a Windows setting you need to change to allow the underline to always show.

Here are a few shortcut keys on some of the main screens you will use in RootsMagic.

Main Screen Shortcut Keys	
Ctrl+N	Create a new file
Ctrl+O	Open a file
Ctrl+P	Print a report
<Enter>	Edit the highlighted person
<Del>	Delete the highlighted person
Ctrl+<Del>	Delete the highlighted family
Ctrl+L	Edit LDS ordinances
I	Add a new individual
S	Add a spouse to the highlighted person
P	Add parents to the highlighted person
C	Add children to the highlighted person
Ctrl+F	Find (open RootsMagic Explorer)
Ctrl+Shift+F	Open family list
Ctrl+Home	Go to root person
Ctrl+H	Search and replace
Ctrl+B	Bookmark current person
Ctrl+<Left>	Move back to previous person
Ctrl+<Right>	Move to next person in history list
<F7>	Spell check
Ctrl+W	Create a website

<F1>	Open help screens
Ctrl+C	Color coding
Ctrl+V	View family tab in side bar
Ctrl+<F4>	Close current file
Ctrl+<F6>	Cycle through open files

Edit Screen Shortcut Keys	
Alt+A	Add a new fact
Alt+D	Delete the highlighted fact
Alt+P	View options menu
<Up>, <Down>	Move up and down the list of facts
<Tab>	Begin editing the highlighted fact
Alt+V	Save a modified fact
<Cancel>	Cancel modifications to a fact
Alt+N	Edit the note for the highlighted fact
Alt+S	Edit the source citations for the highlighted fact
Alt+M	Edit the media album for the highlighted fact
Alt+H	Share the highlighted fact
Alt+R	Edit address for the highlighted person or family
Alt+T	Edit to-dos for the highlighted person or family
Alt+O	Close the edit screen

Note Editor Shortcut Keys	
Ctrl+X	Cut highlighted text to clipboard
Ctrl+C	Copy highlighted text to clipboard
Ctrl+V	Paste clipboard text at cursor position
Ctrl+Z	Undo last edit
Ctrl+B	Turn on **BOLD**

Ctrl+I	Turn on *ITALICS*
Ctrl+U	Turn on <u>UNDERLINE</u>
Ctrl+F	Find text in the note
Ctrl+R	Search and replace text in the note
<F7>	Spell check note
Shift+<F7>	Thesaurus
Ctrl+T	Character map
Ctrl+O	Open a text file
Ctrl+S	Save to a text file

RootsMagic Explorer Shortcut Keys	
<Up>, <Down>	Move up and down the list of people
Alt+F	Find a person by criteria
Alt+M	Find a person by maiden or nicknames
Alt+I	Find previous matching person
Alt+X	Find next matching person
Alt+R	Find a person by their record number
Alt+E	Edit the highlighted person
Alt+L	Edit LDS info for highlighted person
Alt+G	Go to highlighted family member
Alt+S	Select the highlighted person

Template Language Reference

Sentence templates allow you to tell RootsMagic how to write a sentence for a given fact or source citation. You simply write a sentence with "fields" and "switches" to show where things like names, dates, and places fit. Square brackets [ ] indicate the name of a field to be displayed, while angle brackets < > indicate a switch, or conditional statement, that will determine what, if any, data is displayed.

There are two types of templates: Fact Sentence Templates and Source Templates. Fact Sentence Templates are used when a particular fact is written in a narrative report or website. Source Templates are used when a source citation is written in a report or a website. While each type of template has its own unique features, they both share the same basic usage and rules.

Fields

Fields are pieces of a template that are replaced with meaningful text at the time the sentence is written. They are written using square brackets with the name of the field inside. Field names are not case sensitive, so for example, [Date], [date], [daTe], [DATE] are all equivalent field names. Throughout this topic, most have the first letter Capitalized so they stand out, especially when several words are used together like PlaceDetails.

Fields in a fact sentence template may look like this:

[Person] was born< [Date]>< [PlaceDetails]>< [Place]>.

In this example, when RootsMagic encounters a person's birth when writing a narrative report, it takes this template and replaces [Person] with the person's name, [Date] with the date of the birth, [PlaceDetails] with the details (hospital or address) within the place where the birth occurred, and [Place] with the place (city, county, state, country) of birth.

Fields in a source template for the full (first) footnote may look like:

[Author], <i>[Title]</i> ([PubPlace]: [Publisher], [PubDate]).

while the fields in a source template for the bibliography might look like:

[Author:Reverse]. <i>[Title]</i>. [PubPlace]: [Publisher], [PubDate:Year].

In this example, when RootsMagic encounters a book source, it replaces the source fields [Author] with the author of the book, [Title] with the title of the book, [PubPlace] with the place of publication, [Publisher] with the name of the publisher, and [PubDate] with the date of publications (usually a year).

RootsMagic also allows modifers which change the look or content of the fields. Notice the **<i>** and **</i>** formatting codes which tell RootsMagic to format the text in italics font, **:Reverse** tells RootsMagic to show the surname first, and **:year** tells RootsMagic to show only the year part of the date.

Fact Sentence Fields

Fact sentence templates are created using a combination of pre-defined fields referring to a person or persons, pre-defined fields referring to fact details, as well as plain text and punctuation.

Formatting codes can be used in Fact sentence templates, if desired, but are more commonly used in the Notes field to emphasize a portion of the note text. The field names and field options in templates are not case sensitive – they can be all lower case, all upper case, or first letter of each word capitalized, etc. First letter capitalization is used here, particularly where multiple words are involved, to make it easier for people to read.

The pre-defined fields for use in fact sentence templates are:

Field	Field Type	Description
Fields referring to a person or persons:		
[Person]	1 person	The principal person of the event
[Spouse]	1 person	The spouse of the principal person
[Couple]	1 or 2 people	Both the principal person and spouse, if entered
[Husband]	1 person	The husband in the principal person's marriage
[Wife]	1 person	The wife in the principal person's marriage
[ThisPerson]	1 person	The main witness that the witness sentence is about. Witness fact sentences only.
[OtherPersons]	1 or more person	All witnesses to the event, regardless of role. In witness fact sentences, this excludes the main witness.
[Role]	1 or more person	All witnesses to the event with the specified role. The name of the role is typed in square brackets, e.g. [Witness], [Doctor], [Minister]
[Field(#)]	1 person	In the case of fields that refer to more than one person, you can refer to a specific person by number by writing the number in parentheses after the field name. For example, to get the 3rd bridesmaid, type [Bridesmaid(3)].
[Field 1,Field 2,...]	1 or more person	Any number of person fields may be combined into a single group by writing all the field names within square brackets, separated by commas. For example, to get all the groomsmen and bridesmaids, type

		[Groomsman,Bridesmaid].
Fields referring to fact details:		
[Date]	Date	The date of the event
[Place]	Place	The place where the event happened
[PlaceDetails]	Place	Details about the place where the event happened (for example, the name of the church or cemetery, or the street address)
[Desc]	Description	The description of the fact

Source Fields

Source fields are not predefined by RootsMagic, but are defined for each source template. To use those fields in a template, type its name in square brackets, or you can drag the field from the field list into the respective template (full footnote, short footnote or bibliography). A source template is made up of source fields, plain text and punctuation, as well as formatting codes when required.

Field Options

You can set options for every field that control both what is written and how it is written. You type the options within the field's square brackets. You can add as many options as necessary to a field, each option separated by a colon, but no extra spaces. For example:

[Person:Given:Surname]
[PublishDate:Year]
[Place:Reverse:Proper]

Most of these options can be used both in sentence templates and in source templates.

Option	Field Types	Description
Capitalization Options		
:NoCaps	Any	Default. Makes no changes in capitalization.
:Upper	Any	Changes to upper case, e.g. "JOHN DOE"
:Lower	Any	Changes to lower case, e.g. "john doe"
:Caps	Any	Capitalizes the first letter and makes no changes to subsequent letters, e.g. "John doe"
:Proper	Any	Forces "proper" capitalization, e.g. "John Doe"
Abbreviation Options		
:NoAbbrev	Source Template	Default. Look for a "||" and process the information that precedes it, e.g. Post Office Box 1010||PO Box 1010 = Post Office Box 1010
:Abbrev	Source Template	Look for a "||" and process the information that follows it, e.g. Post Office Box 1010||PO Box 1010 = PO Box 1010
Name Part Options (May include one or more)		
:Full	Name & Witness names	Dr. John Robert "Johnny" Doe Jr.
:Reverse	Name & Witness names	Doe, Dr. John Robert "Johnny" Jr. (reverses first name in a group only)

Option	Field Types	Description
:Given	Name & Witness names	John Robert
:First	Name & Witness names	John
:Surname	Name & Witness names	Doe
:Prefix	Name	Dr.
:Suffix	Name	Jr.
:Nickname	Name	Johnny
:Casual	Name & Witness names	Nickname, if known, otherwise first name
Age Options		
:Plain	Age	No prefix.
:At	Age	"at the age of Age". Default for fact/role sentence ages
:Commas	Age	", age Age,"
Fact Place Options		
:Original	Place in Fact/Role Sentences	Original version of place (default), e.g. "Brownsville, Utah Territory"
:Short	Place in Fact/Role Sentences	Abbreviated version of place, e.g. "Ogden, Utah"
Place Options		
:Full	Place or Place Details in source template or fact/role sentence	Ames, Story, Iowa, United States

Option	Field Types	Description
:Reverse	Place or Place Details in source template or fact/role sentence	United States. Iowa. Story. Ames
:ReverseComma	Place or Place Details in source template or fact/role sentence	United States, Iowa, Story, Ames
:First	Place or Place Details in source template or fact/role sentence	Ames
:Last	Place or Place Details in source template or fact/role sentence	United States
Place & Description Prefix Options		
:Plain	Place, Place Details, or Description	No prefix. Default for source templates and description fields
:In	Place, Place Details, or Description	"In Text". Default for fact/role sentence places
:At	Place, Place Details, or Description	"At Text". Default for fact/role sentence place details
:A	Place, Place Details, or Description	"A Text" or "An Other text"
Date Options		
:Plain	Date	Full date, e.g. "6 Apr 1830", no "in" or "on" prefix. (Default for source templates)
:InOn	Date	"on 6 Apr 1830" or "in Apr 1830". (Default for fact/role sentences.)

Option	Field Types	Description
:Year	Date	Year only, e.g. "1830"
:DayOfWeek	Date	Show the day of week with the date, e.g. "Tuesday 6 Apr 1830"
:NoDayOfWeek	Date	Removes the day of week from the date (default)
:Commas	Date	Adds commas to the date, e.g. "6 Apr, 1830" or "Tuesday, 6 Apr, 1830"
:NoCommas	Date	Removes commas from the date (default)
Person Options		
:Name	Fact Sentence People	Default. The names of the people in roles
:Poss	Fact Sentence People	Possessive form of names, e.g. John's. To get the full name possessive, i.e. "John Doe's", you would enter [Person:Full:Poss]
:HeShe	Fact Sentence People	He/She/They
:HisHer	Fact Sentence People	His/Her/Their
:HimHer	Fact Sentence People	Him/Her/Them
:Age	Fact Sentence People	Age of person at time of event
:Role	Fact Sentence People	Role of witness
:Count	Fact Sentence People	# of people in the group, i.e. [role1,role2,role3:count], e.g.

Option	Field Types	Description
		[child:count] or [son,daughter:count]
Person Name Cycling Options		
:Cycle	Fact Sentence People	Prints the full name first and then cycles between He/She and the casual name in subsequent uses. Default for "Person" and "Couple" in regular fact sentences and default for "ThisPerson" in witness fact sentences.
:NoCycle	Fact Sentence People	Print the name as specified without cycling

Formatting Codes

Formatting codes allow you to tell RootsMagic how you want the font to look in the report. Formatting codes are contained inside of a left angle bracket "<" and right angle bracket ">". They are used in pairs - the first tells RootsMagic to turn on the formatting, and the second, with a "/" after the left angle bracket (</ >) to turn off the formatting. For example:

<i>[Title]</i>

The <i> and </i> formatting codes tell RootsMagic to display the title in italics font.

Code	Used in	Description
Formatting Codes		
<i> ... </i>	Fact sentence and Source templates, fields, and notes	Displays the text in italics
<b> ... </b>	Fact sentence and Source templates, fields, and notes	Displays the text in bold
<u> ... </u>	Fact sentence and Source templates, fields, and notes	Displays the text in underline
<sc> ... </sc>	Fact sentence and Source templates, fields, and notes	Displays the text in small caps (upper case letters remain unchanged, lower case letters are changed to upper case, but in a smaller font)
^{...}	Fact sentence and Source templates, fields, and notes	Displays the text in superscript
_{...}	Fact sentence and Source templates, fields, and notes	Displays the text in subscript

Formatting codes can be nested within other formatting codes or switches, but cannot be included within the square brackets indicating a field.

Switches

A switch allows you to write different information, depending on the information that is available. Switches are contained inside of a less-than and greater-than sign (< >). Inside of the switch are any number of pieces, separated by a "|". For example:
<First Piece|Second Piece|Third Piece|Fourth Piece>
You can set the kind of switch by using a special character after the first less-than sign. There are five special switch characters, ? for the Value switch, % for the Gender switch, @ for the Living switch, # for the Plural switch, and ! for the Private switch. For example:

<%actor|actress>

In a switch that depends on information about a person or a group of people, such as value switches, gender switches, living switches, and plural switches, you can specify which person or group of people the switch applies to by writing the field names of the people either immediately after the special character (living, plural) or enclosed in square brackets ([value], [gender]) and then followed by the special character again.

<#Doctors#doctor|doctors>

Two of the switches, Gender (%) and Living (@), will refer directly to the focus subject if a field name is not entered. For example:

<@He is living|He is not living>.

The Private switch (!) is used in source templates to privatize things such as a street address data that you want to record, but not make public. The trigger that activates the Private switch is a checkbox in the Sources, Options tab in the Report Settings dialog.

Simple Switches

A simple switch requires no special character and can have any number of pieces.

<First Piece|Second Piece|Third Piece|Fourth Piece>

RootsMagic will look at each piece, beginning with the first. If the piece has a field with a value, or has no fields, it is written and all the remaining pieces are skipped. For example, lets look at the basic birth sentence with conditional brackets added:

[Person] was born< [Date]>< [PlaceDetails]>< [Place]>.

The angle brackets < > indicate that if there is no value entered, neither the field nor the space before it will be shown. This applies to the [date], [placedetails] and [place] fields.
In the following source templates examples:

<privately held by [LastKnownOwner], >

would only write something if "[LastKnownOwner]" has a value, or in this example:

<[Format],|digital image,>

would write "database and digital images," if that's what you entered into the [Format] field, or it would write "digital image," if you didn't enter anything into the [Format] field.

Value Switches

A value switch is similar to a simple switch except that it allows you to check for a value without actually writing that value. It is indicated by a "?".

```
<?[Expression]| Show this if True.>
<?[Expression]| Show this if True. | Show this if False.>
<?[Expression]|| Show this if False.>
```

For example:

```
<?[Nurse]|He had a nurse.>
<?[Nurse]|He had a nurse.|He didn't have a nurse.>
<?[Nurse]||He didn't have a nurse.>
```

would check to see if the role of [Nurse] had a value. If it did, it would write "He had a nurse." If it did not have a value, it would write "He didn't have a nurse."

Note that what comes after the "?" is different from the gender and living switches. The gender and living switches need the role of a person or group of people followed by their special character. The value switch takes any expression including fields in brackets and other switches.

Gender Switches

A gender switch checks the gender of a person or group of people and writes the appropriate text. It is indicated by a "%". It is of the form:

```
<% Males & Unknowns > or
<% Males & Unknowns | Females > or
<% Males | Females |Unknowns > or
<% Male | Female | Unknown | Multiples > or
<% Male | Female | Unknown | Male & Mixed Multiples | Female Multiples > or
<% Male | Female | Unknown | Male Multiples | Female Multiples | Mixed Multiples >
```

or it can take the form to process a list of one or more roles

```
<%roles%| Male | Female | Unknown | Male Multiples | Female Multiples | Mixed Multiples >
```

In this first example, the switch looks at the default [person]:

```
<%He was an actor.|She was an actress.>
```

In this second example, the switch looks at the role name [child]:

```
<%Child%[child] was a son.|[child] was a daughter.|[child] was a child.|[child] were
sons.|[child] were daughters.|[child] were children.>
```

In the first example, the "person" is the focus person to which
the sentence applies. In the second example, [child] refers to a
role assigned to someone in a shared event. The role [child] could
be assigned to one or more people.

Roles which are added as "Just type name of witness" menu, or
"This person is NOT in the file" in Edit Share Event, do not
have a gender, and may affect results of this switch.

Living Switches

A living switch checks if a person or group of people is living and
writes the appropriate text. It is indicated by a "@". It is of the
form:

```
<@ Living > or
<@ Living | Not Living >
<@roles@ Show this if all Living | Show this if one or more Not Living >
```

For example:

```
<@He has brown hair.|He had brown hair.> (This assumes that his hair never turned gray.)
<@Doctors,Nurses@They are doctors and nurses.|They were doctors and nurses.>
```

Plural Switches

A plural switch looks at the number of people in a group and
writes the appropriate text. It is indicated by a "#". It is of the
form:

```
<#roles# Single > or
<#roles# Single | Plural > or
<#roles# Single | Plural | None >
```

For example:

```
<#Doctors#His doctor was|His doctors were> [Doctor].
They had <#Children#a child|<Children:count> children|no children>.
```

There <#Heir1,Heir2#was one heir|was more than one heir|were no heirs>.

Private Switches

A private switch is used for fact sentence templates and source templates. For sources, this allows you to write different text depending on whether you have or have not checked the "Hide private data in the endnotes, footnotes, and bibliography" option in the Sources, Options tab, telling RootsMagic whether to display the private or the not private information for this switch. It is of the form:

<! Private | Not Private >

For example:

<!<[Address]>|(The address is private.)>.

If the checkbox is checked, "(The address is private.)" would print. If the checkbox was unchecked, the address data that was entered in the [Address] field would print, if one was entered, otherwise nothing would print.

Escape Characters

If you ever want to write an actual <, >, /, [, or] in your sentence, you must precede it by a "/". This tells RootsMagic to print the following character and to not treat it as a switch or a field. For example:

[Person] /[This is in brackets/]. would print:

John Doe [This is in brackets].

and [person] is a /[person/] would print

John Doe is a [person].

thus allowing the keyword "person" to be enclosed within square brackets without being interpreted as a field.

Tip: To include a field value within square brackets, such as [John Doe], you can enclose the field within a switch with the square brackets outside the switch, i.e. [<[person]>].

Switches Within Switches

RootsMagic allows you to put switches within other switches, also known as nesting. This allows you to create very powerful and flexible sentence templates.

Internet · 285